D1147188

THE PRINCIPLES OF
EXERCISE THERAPY

THE PRINCIPLES
OF
EXERCISE THERAPY

M. DENA GARDINER, B.A., F.C.S.P.

Diploma of Bedford Physical Training College
Teacher of the Chartered Society of
Physiotherapy (T.M.M.G. and T.E.T.)
formerly Deputy Principal of the London Hospital School of Physiotherapy

FOURTH EDITION

Revised by the Teachers of Physiotherapy, The London Hospital

BELL & HYMAN

Published by
BELL & HYMAN LIMITED
Denmark House
37-39 Queen Elizabeth Street
London SE1 2QB

Fourth edition, 1981
Reprinted 1983, 1985
© The executors of the late
M. Dena Gardiner 1980

ISBN 0 7135 1246 6

Printed and bound in Great Britain at
The Camelot Press Ltd, Southampton

FOREWORD TO THE FOURTH EDITION

by

I. H. M. CURWEN, M.B., Ch.B., D.Phys. Med.

Consultant in Rheumatology and Rehabilitation,
Queen Mary's Hospital, Roehampton

IT is always a pleasure to be asked to write a foreword to a book when you admire the author and approve its contents. Exercise therapy together with passive movement, mobilisation and manipulation today form a major part of the work of the practising physiotherapist. The principles on which these therapies are based remain, but practice and experience together with advances in physiological knowledge alter with time the techniques employed.

Dena Gardiner was a great teacher, an innovator and a person with a quick and receptive brain, always willing herself to learn and to modify her approach and teaching in the light of experience. There could be no more fitting memorial to her than the publication of a new edition of her book ably edited and revised by teachers from her own school.

Over the years I have been lucky enough to have had working with me a number of distinguished teachers of physiotherapy and I think it is important for their profession to retain the name of the original author of a valuable textbook. I hope that this text will continue for many years to stimulate students in learning and start them enquiring and questioning along the lines it lays down.

FOREWORD TO THE FIRST EDITION

by

WILLIAM TEGNER, F.R.C.P.

Physician in Charge, Department of Physical Medicine,
The London Hospital

PHYSIOTHERAPY is no static art. Methods of treatment constantly change and many that were once prominent and popular have lost popularity. In this way many treatments involving the use of electrical currents have gone out of fashion, massage itself is looked at with a cold scientific eye and does not emerge unscathed from the appraisal, and passive treatments of inert patients making no effort to help themselves are regarded as possibly prolonging rather than cutting short invalidism. Yet in spite of all this more patients are referred for physiotherapy than ever before. The gospel of activity has been widely preached and the prescription of activity and movement has taken the place of the passive treatments so widely advocated before the second world war. There seems little doubt that this phase of activity is a notable advance and that patients are reaping the benefit of it.

No one could be better qualified than Miss Dena Gardiner to write on the Principles of Exercise Therapy, for she holds both a Diploma in Physical Education and the double teacher's qualification of the Chartered Society of Physiotherapy. She has a deservedly high reputation as a teacher and demonstrator and, as this book will show, she has succeeded admirably in setting out the principles that govern the therapeutic value of activity.

PREFACE TO THE FIRST EDITION

THIS book has been written for all those who are interested in the use of exercise to promote physical rehabilitation. It is, however, primarily designed to provide students training in physiotherapy with a simple theoretical background for the practical instruction they receive in the performance and use of movement and exercises for therapeutic purposes.

I have attempted to collect and integrate the various techniques now in common use and to arrange them according to the purpose for which they are designed. To do this I have drawn freely upon the ideas and experience of others as well as my own but, except in the case of forced passive movements which have only rarely been ordered by any doctor for whom I have worked, I have included only those procedures which I have tried out and found to be of value in the treatment of patients at one time or another.

New and widely varying techniques are constantly being developed and no one of these can claim to be suitable for all patients or all physiotherapists. A sound knowledge of basic principles, an open mind and a spirit of enquiry are essential to progress and the discovery of the methods most suitable to achieve results.

> I keep six honest serving men,
> (They taught me all I knew)
> Their names are What and Why and When
> And How and Where and Who.
>
> KIPLING'S *The Elephant Child*

Although there are a considerable number of male physiotherapists to facilitate description throughout the text I have referred to the physiotherapist as 'her' and to the patient as 'him'.

I would like to express my gratitude to all who have helped me in the preparation of this book. In particular my thanks are due to Dr. W. S. Tegner, B.M., B.Ch., F.R.C.P., who not only read my manuscript and gave me valuable advice but has kindly written the foreword.

I am deeply indebted also to Dr. L. A. W. Kemp, B.Sc., F.Inst.P., physicist to the London Hospital, for his interest and patience in helping me to prepare the chapter on Mechanical Principles and to Dr. M. Partington, M.B., of the Physiology Department, for many helpful suggestions.

Miss Y. Moyse, M.A., who was at the time Public Relations Officer for the Ling Physical Education Association, encouraged me to undertake the task of writing this book, and she has at all times advised and helped me in the preparation of the manuscript. I would like to take this opportunity of expressing my appreciation and thanks for the time and energy she has given to help me.

My colleagues in the Chartered Society of Physiotherapy have always been ready to discuss controversial matters and to give me advice whenever I asked for it, and I am most grateful to them and to Miss Chatwin, M.C.S.P., who lent me a typewriter for as long as I needed it.

M. D. G.

PREFACE TO THE FOURTH EDITION

DENA GARDINER dedicated this book to the students of the London Hospital School of Physiotherapy where she taught from 1943 to 1960. Many generations of students at the London Hospital and elsewhere have benefited from this text, first published in 1953, which Miss Gardiner revised in 1957 and 1963. Shortly before her death in September 1978, her publishers asked Miss Gardiner if she wished to make any further revisions before reprinting. She expressed reticence and soon became too ill. Subsequently, the teaching staff at the London Hospital decided to undertake the considerable task as a meaningful and continuing tribute to a much-respected colleague.

Our guiding principle has been to maintain as much of the original text as is compatible with modern practice. It contains a wealth of basic knowledge and the bibliography points the student to the sources of more advanced knowledge. We have been fortunate to gain ready agreement from her closest family and friends and from Bell and Hyman Ltd to include large sections from Miss Gardiner's *PocketBook of Exercise Therapy* published in 1975. Miss Gardiner considered it to be her best work.

We acknowledge willing help from colleagues in our endeavours and the patience of the publishers as we wrestled with the task of revision. Certainly our admiration for Dena Gardiner has continued to grow as we have sought to emulate her expositional skill with the written language.

THE TEACHING STAFF,
Physiotherapy School,
The London Hospital

This book
is dedicated to

THE STUDENTS OF THE LONDON HOSPITAL SCHOOL
OF PHYSIOTHERAPY

whom it has been my privilege to teach, and to the memory of
Cicely Read and Helen Heardman, both of Bedford Physical
Training College, who never failed to give help and
encouragement to all who were willing to learn

CONTENTS

PART I

I

MECHANICAL PRINCIPLES

THE mechanical principles utilised in Exercise Therapy are defined here to ensure that they are understood and applied correctly.

FORCE

Force is that which alters the state of rest of a body or its uniform motion in a straight line.

Composition of Forces

The application of a force to a body is specified by—

(*i*) the direction of the force; this may be represented by the direction of an arrow,

(*ii*) the magnitude of the force; this may be represented by the length of the arrow.

The tail of the arrow drawn to represent a force can be taken as the point of application of that force.

FIG. 1

A single force applied to a body, which is free to move, causes movement in the direction of the force (Fig. 1).

a. Two forces acting in the same direction and at a common point

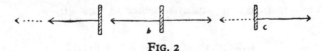

FIG. 2

are equivalent to a single force acting in that direction, whose magnitude is equal to the sum of the magnitudes of the individual forces.

b. Two equal forces acting at a common point, and in opposite directions, will result in a state of equilibrium.

c. Two unequal forces acting at a common point and in opposite directions will result in movement in the direction of the greater force, the magnitude of the force producing this movement being equal to the difference between the magnitudes of the two unequal forces which oppose each other.   Much of the physiotherapist's work involves the application of forces to oppose, equal or augment the forces of muscle action and of gravity acting upon the human body.

d. Sometimes it is inconvenient to apply force in a particular direction and in these circumstances two forces acting at an angle to each other may be compounded to produce the desired effect.

If two forces represented by the lines AB and AC act at A, then the

FIG. 3*b*.

FIG. 3.*a*. The Parallelogram of Forces

diagonal AX of the parallelogram ABXC represents the force to which they are equivalent.   One example of this occurs when the Deltoid Muscle contracts during shoulder abduction, the action of the anterior and posterior fibres of the muscles being compounded to work with the middle fibres and so vastly increasing their power (Fig. 3a).

The principle of compounding forces is also employed in some arrangements for balanced traction.

e. Two unequal forces acting at different points and in opposite directions produce rotation of the body (Fig. 3b).   One example of this occurs when the Trapezius Muscle and Serratus Anterior Muscle contract to rotate the Scapula.

TENSION

Tension is defined as a system of forces tending to separate parts of a body combined with equal and opposite forces which hold the parts together.   It is measured in Newtons.

In physiology the terms *tension* and *force* are used synonymously, e.g. intra-muscular tension is the force of muscle contraction.   The *strength* of a muscle is its ability to generate tension.

MECHANICS OF POSITION

GRAVITY

Gravity is the force by which all bodies are attracted to the earth. Newton concluded from experiments and observations that a force of attraction existed between all material objects, and that the magnitude of this attraction was directly proportional to the mass of each body and inversely proportional to the square of the distance between them.

The gravitational attraction of the earth for every other body is directed towards the earth's centre.

The force of gravity acts continuously upon the human body, and if unopposed the latter will fall to the ground. The effects of gravity can be counterbalanced when a force equal and opposite to it is employed, such as the support of a plinth, the buoyancy of water, or an isometric muscular contraction. If, however, gravity is opposed by a force which is greater, movement will occur in the direction of that force.

For example:

a. From the standing position the heels can be raised from the ground by the contraction of the calf muscles, working in opposition to the resistance of gravity, provided the force of their contraction exceeds the force of gravity.

b. The heels will remain raised as long as the force of contraction of the muscles is equal to that of gravity.

c. The heels will be lowered to the ground by the action of gravity if the muscles relax.

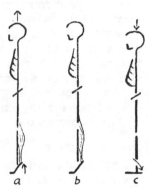

FIG. 4

Movement of joints may occur as the result of gravity or of muscular action, and each may control the effect of the other. In the erect position balance is maintained by the integrated contraction of many muscles, called the anti-gravity muscles, while true relaxation can only occur under conditions in which the muscles are no longer required to work against the effects of gravity.

THE CENTRE OF GRAVITY

The centre of gravity of a rigid body is the point through which the earth's attraction effectively acts whatever the position of the body, i.e. the point through which the line of action of the weight acts. A rigid body will balance when it is supported only at its centre of gravity.

a. A uniform rod will balance at a point exactly half-way along its length (Fig. 5a).

b. The centre of gravity of an irregular piece of cardboard can be discovered by suspending it consecutively from at least two points at

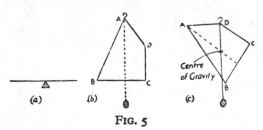

FIG. 5

its margin, and marking on it the line taken by a plumb line when the latter is attached at the point of suspension in each position. The point of intersection of the two lines will be the centre of gravity (Figs. 5*b* & *c*), which need not necessarily lie within the body, as in the case of a ring or a boomerang.

The centre of gravity of the human body in the anatomical position is reputed to be in the vicinity of the body of the second sacral vertebra. Its position must vary, however, according to the anatomical structure of the individual, being higher in men and children than in the average woman, because of the greater amount of weight they carry in the upper half of the body. Direct support at the centre of gravity of the human body is obviously impossible and its exact position is merely of interest in assessing the distance between it and the point of support.

The location of the centre of gravity will vary with each of the many and varied postures the body assumes.

LINE OF GRAVITY

The line of gravity is a vertical line through the centre of gravity.

When the human body is in the fundamental standing position the line of gravity through the body of the second sacral vertebra passes through the vertex and a point between the feet, level with the transverse tarsal joints. The relationship of body structures to this line is subject to considerable variation in accordance with individual differences in posture and anatomical structure. It is estimated that on an average when posture is good the line passes through the mid-cervical and mid-lumbar vertebrae and in front of the thoracic vertebrae. The external ear and the point of the shoulder are in the same frontal plane and lie lateral to the line, and the central axis of the knee joint and the ankle joints are postero-lateral.

BASE

The base, as applied to a rigid body, is the area by which it is supported. In the case of a cube the face on which it rests is the base, whereas the effective base of a chair may be considered as the area bounded by the lines joining the legs (Fig. 6*a*).

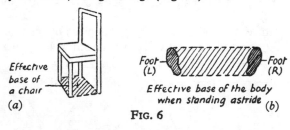

Effective base of a chair *(a)*

Foot (L)   Foot (R)

Effective base of the body when standing astride *(b)*

FIG. 6

In the lying position the posterior aspect of the whole body forms the base, and in stride standing it is an area as wide as the feet and as long as the distance between their outer borders (Fig. 6b).

EQUILIBRIUM

Equilibrium results when the forces acting upon a body are perfectly balanced and the body remains at rest.

Stable Equilibrium. If the forces acting upon a body at rest tend to restore it to its original position after it has been displaced, the body is said to be in stable equilibrium. The condition of equilibrium is most stable when the centre of gravity is as low as possible and the line of gravity falls near the centre of an extensive base. It becomes progressively less stable as the centre of gravity is raised and the line of gravity falls nearer to the margin of the base.

Unstable Equilibrium. If a body is given an initial displacement and the forces acting upon it increase this initial displacement, however small the latter may be, the body is said to be in unstable equilibrium. A centre of gravity which is as high as possible and a small base result in *relatively* unstable equilibrium, because even very small displacements cause the line of gravity to fall outside the base, and the body will fall to the ground, e.g. Toe st.

Neutral Equilibrium. If, in spite of displacement of a body, the height and position of its centre of gravity remain the same in relation to the base, the body is said to be in neutral equilibrium, as, for example, when a ball moves on a plane surface.

The stability of the human body is greatest in the lying position. It becomes progressively less stable as the centre of gravity is raised and the base is reduced, as in the sitting and standing positions.

FIXATION AND STABILISATION

Fixation describes a state of immobility and stabilisation that of relative immobility. Active fixation of joints is usually obtained by a co-contraction of muscles and passive fixation by means of manual pressure, straps or sandbags. Fixation is a means of preventing movement in joints, e.g. in maintaining postures or for localising movement to specific joints. It is used to improve the efficiency of muscles by fixing their origin or to localise movement in the performance of passive movements.

A suitable background for activity is achieved by stabilisation of areas which are not required to take part in the movement; some adjustments of the position of these areas may need to be made during the progress of the movement to increase its efficiency or to maintain balance.

Fractures, joint injuries and disease necessitating long-term immobility of joints usually require fixation by mechanical means such as splintage, balanced traction or operative measures, e.g. bone grafting or plating.

MECHANICS OF MOVEMENT

AXES AND PLANES

An axis is a line *about* which movement takes place and a plane is the surface which lies at right angles to it and *in* which the movement takes place. The terms are used to facilitate the description of movement or direction, and as far as axes and planes of joint movement are concerned, they are described with the body in the anatomical position.

a. A *sagittal axis* lies parallel to the sagittal suture of the skull, i.e. in an antero-posterior direction, as an arrow might have pierced a yeoman in attack or in flight. Movement about this axis is in a *frontal plane*.

b. A *frontal, or transverse, axis* lies parallel to the transverse suture of the skull. It is also horizontal and at right angles to the sagittal axis. Movement about a frontal axis is *in a sagittal plane*.

c. A *vertical axis* lies parallel to the line of gravity and movement about it is in *a horizontal plane*.

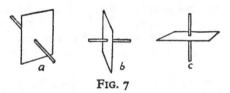

FIG. 7

The hands of a watch moving about the central pin and over the watch face, or a pencil thrust through a sheet of paper and turned to represent the three axes, are convenient examples to demonstrate axes and planes.

Movements of the body occur at joints, therefore axes pass through joints and the part moved is in the plane which lies at right angles to the axis of the movement.

Abduction and adduction (except of the thumb) and side flexion movements are said to take place about a sagittal axis and in a frontal plane, flexion and extension (except of the thumb) about a frontal axis and in a sagittal plane, and rotation occurs about a vertical axis and in a horizontal plane.

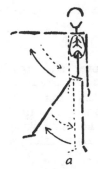  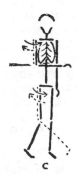

FIG. 8

(a) Movement about a Sagittal Axis and in a Frontal Plane

(b) Movement about a Frontal Axis and in a Sagittal Plane

(c) Movement about a Vertical Axis and in a Horizontal Plane

The Plane of Movement and Gravity

Although it is conventional and often convenient to indicate the type and direction of movements of the body with reference to these axes and planes, normal functional movements are by no means so simple.

The anatomical structure of the joints and the directions of the muscles acting upon them dictate the active movements. In many instances there is more than one axis and therefore more than one plane about these axes, and it can be said that movements take place in planes at right angles to their axes during any part of the movements.

Movement in the Horizontal Plane. Movement in the horizontal plane is not affected by gravity and is therefore stated to be 'gravity free'. Weak muscles which are unable to produce movement against gravity can often succeed in doing so when the part moved is supported horizontally, when the only external resistance which opposes them is the frictional resistance of the supporting factor.

Movement in the Inclined Plane. Movement.in this case can be up the incline or downwards. When muscles work to produce movement up the incline, the resistance offered to them by the force of gravity is modified and reduced by the reaction of the plane. The latter is greatest when the incline is nearly horizontal, therefore the resistance to the muscles is least when the incline is nearly horizontal and increases as it approaches the vertical. Movement downwards is produced by the force of gravity, the magnitude of its force increasing as the inclination approaches the vertical and the reaction of the plane decreases.

Movement in the Vertical Plane. Upward movement is produced by a force such as that of muscular contraction which exceeds the force of gravity. Downward movement is produced by the force of gravity and occurs at a specific speed which can be modified and controlled by muscular action.

SPEED

Speed is merely the rate at which a body moves, and takes no account of the direction, i.e. a car has a speed of sixty kilometres an hour. Speed is uniform if the car travels the same distance during every second that it moves, but if it slows down at a turning and then increases speed along a straight road to make up for lost time, its speed is variable, but the average speed for a given time can be calculated.

Speed of Relaxed Passive Movements

The speed at which a passive movement is performed must be slow and uniform so that relaxation can be maintained.

Speed of Active Exercises

Natural Speed. There is a natural speed for every exercise which varies to some extent for each individual and, in general, this is the speed at which exercises should be done. The effect of many exercises can be modified, however, by an alteration in the speed of their performance.

Reduced Speed. Exercises done more slowly require greater muscular effort and more control. Decrease in the speed of repetitive movements ensures time for full-range movement.

Increased Speed. Rapid movement also requires strong muscular effort but momentum is gained and this may help to increase the range of joint movement provided the direction is not reversed before the free limit is reached. Exercises performed rapidly are stimulating but frequently lead to inaccurate or 'trick movements' and full-range movement is rarely achieved.

VELOCITY

The notion of velocity incorporates not only the rate of motion but also the *direction*, e.g. an aeroplane travels at 1000 kilometres an hour *in an easterly direction*. A change in either speed or direction is said to alter the velocity.

WORK

Work is defined as the product of *force* and the *distance* through which the force acts. It is measured in joules or ergs.

ENERGY

Energy is the *capacity* of a body for doing work. *Potential Energy* is the capacity for doing work by virtue of position and a body's capacity for doing work because of its velocity is called *Kinetic Energy*.

POWER

Power is the *rate* of doing work or the rate of energy expenditure. It is measured in joules per second or ergs per second.

ACCELERATION

Acceleration is the rate of change of velocity. A positive acceleration causes an increase and a deceleration, or retardation, a decrease in velocity.

Movement under Gravity. Galileo dropped heavy bodies from the leaning tower of Pisa and established the fact that all bodies, irrespective of their weight, are subject to the same uniform acceleration as they fall freely under gravity.

MOMENTUM

The momentum of a body is the quantity of motion it possesses, and it is represented by the product of mass and velocity. The force responsible for the momentum will generate movement slowly in a relatively heavy body and more rapidly in a lighter body.

INERTIA

Inertia is the resistance of a body to any change in its state of rest or motion. A body at rest tends to remain at rest indefinitely, while a moving body tends to continue moving at a constant speed and in a straight line unless acted upon by a force. Inertia may be defined as the *reversed effective force* of a body.

A railway truck in a goods yard requires considerable force to start it moving, but once it gets going it continues until another force, such as collision with the buffers of another truck, impedes it. If there was

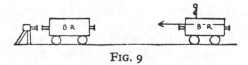

FIG. 9

a man standing in the first truck he would be thrown forward at the moment of collision, as his body would continue moving, owing to inertia.

Once the inertia of the body is overcome and movement is initiated, it is more economical to continue moving, as in a well co-ordinated swimming stroke or running action, to avoid the additional expenditure of force which would be required to overcome the inertia on stopping, starting or altering speed. Weak muscles may be unable to exert sufficient force to overcome inertia, yet may be able to produce movement or control with assistance at the right moment.

FRICTION

Friction is the force which opposes motion when one surface slides upon another. It may be sufficient to prevent movement altogether, e.g. as in the case of rough surfaces or substances, such as rubber, when they are in contact with one another. The frictional resistance obtaining during movement (dynamic friction) is slightly less than the so-called limiting friction, i.e. the friction obtaining just as sliding is about to set in. Dynamic friction may be further reduced during movements of a limb, while the latter remains supported by a plane surface, by the use of a polished surface such as a table or plinth on which the limb will slide. The use of talcum powder or oil on the supporting surface will further reduce friction and make the movement easier, whereas suspension of the part to be moved virtually eliminates all frictional resistance. The increase of friction plays an important part in safety measures such as non-slip floors in gymnasia, slopes, stairs, non-slip footwear, rubber ferrules on walking aids, etc.

SIMPLE MACHINES, PENDULUMS AND ELASTICITY

A machine is a contrivance which enables an applied force to overcome a given resistance. The use of a machine usually makes it possible for the magnitude of the applied force to be less than that of the resistance which it overcomes, or when this is not so, it enables the force to be applied more conveniently.

Levers and pulleys are examples of simple machines in common use in everyday life and their principles are also ultilised for the production of movement in the human body.

LEVERS

A lever is a rigid bar which is capable of movement about a fixed point called a *fulcrum* (F). Work is done when a force or *effort* (E), applied at one point on the lever, acts upon another force or *weight* (W), acting at a second point on the lever. The perpendicular distance from the fulcrum to the effort (E) may be called the *effort's arm* and that from the fulcrum to the weight (W) as the *weight's arm*.

In the body a lever is represented by a bone, which is capable of movement about a fulcrum formed at the articulating surfaces of a joint; the effort which works the lever is supplied by the force of muscular contraction, applied at the point of insertion to the bone, while the weight may be either at the centre of gravity of the part moved, or of the object to be lifted.

There are three Orders or Classes of levers, each of which is characterised by the relative positions of the fulcrum, effort and weight.

1st Order. The fulcrum is between the effort and the weight; it may be situated centrally, or towards either the effort or the weight, consequently the effort's and the weight's arms may be equal, or one may exceed the other in length.

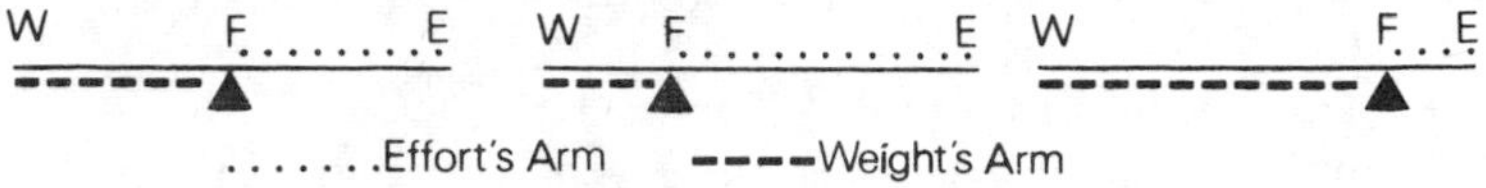

.... Effort's Arm   ----Weight's Arm

FIG. 10.   1st Order of Levers

2nd Order. The weight is between the fulcrum and the effort, and the effort's arm must therefore always exceed the weight's arm.

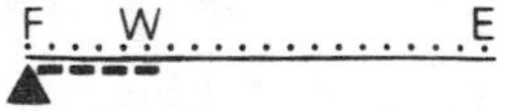

FIG. 11.   2nd Order of Levers 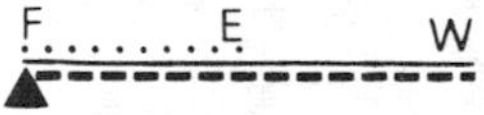   FIG. 12.   3rd Order of Levers

3rd Order. The effort is between the fulcrum and the weight, and the weight's arm must therefore exceed the effort's arm.

Mechanical Advantage. The efficacy of a force in relation to a lever is dependent upon two factors, i.e. the force exerted (W) or (E), 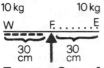 and its perpendicular distance from the fulcrum (weight's arm or effort's arm). The product of these two factors is known as the Moment of Force (or torque). When the weight's and effort's arms are of equal length an effort of a magnitude equal to that of the weight will be required to lift it. No advantage

FIG. 13.   State of Equilibrium

is gained but the machine is useful for measuring weights as, for example, in the common balance.

If, however, the length of the effort's arm exceeds that of the weight's arm, less effort will be required to achieve a similar result and an advantage will be gained by the use of the lever. This is known as a Mechanical Advantage, and it is obtained in levers of the 1st Order when the fulcrum is nearer to the weight than to the effort, and in all levers of the 2nd Order. It is never obtained in levers of the 3rd Order.

Mechanical Advantage is the ratio of the weight to the effort, expressed thus:

$$M.A. = \frac{W}{E}$$

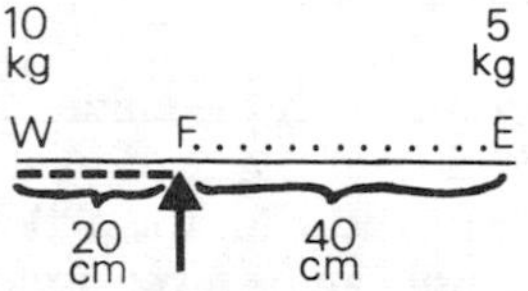

FIG. 14.   Mechanical Advantage

Moment of Force 10 × 20 = 200 cm kg.   40 × 5 = 200 cm kg.

$$M.A. = \frac{10}{5} = 2$$

Conversely, in cases in which the weight's arm exceeds the effort's arm, a condition of Mechanical Disadvantage occurs, as in levers of the 1st Order, when the fulcrum is nearer to the effort than to the weight and in all levers of the 3rd Order.

Levers of the Body

Examples of all three Orders of levers are found in the human body, but those of the 3rd Order are most numerous.

1st Order. The feature of this Order is stability, and a state of equilibrium can be achieved either with or without mechanical advantage. One example of this type of lever is demonstrated during nodding movements of the head; the skull represents the lever, the

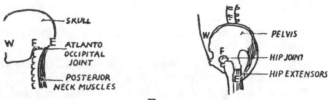

Fig. 15

atlanto-occipital joints the fulcrum, the weight is situated anteriorly in the face, and the effort is supplied by the contraction of the posterior Neck Muscles, applied at their attachment to the occipital bone. Another example is tilting movements of the pelvis on the femoral heads.

2nd Order. This is the lever of power as there must always be a mechanical advantage. An example in the lower limb is demonstrated when the heels are raised to stand on the toes. The tarsal and metatarsal bones are stabilised by muscular action to form the lever, the fulcrum is at the metatarsophalangeal joint, and the weight of the body is

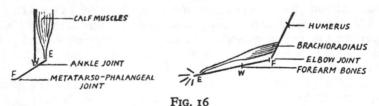

Fig. 16

transmitted through the ankle joint to the talus. The effort is applied at the insertion of the tendo-calcaneum by the contraction of the Calf Muscles. In the arm, the action of Brachioradialis Muscle in flexing the elbow joint can be taken as another example of a type of lever which is relatively uncommon in the body.

3rd Order. In the human body there are more examples of the 3rd Order of levers than of any other type. This type of lever, in which there is always a mechanical disadvantage, is the lever of velocity, the loss of mechanical advantage being outweighed by the advantage gained by speed and range of movement. Both in the days of primitive man and in modern times, speed and range of movement have often proved to be a greater asset than power.

When the lever is the forearm, the fulcrum is the elbow joint, and when the effort is supplied by the contraction of the Brachialis Muscle applied at its insertion, and the weight is some object held in the hand,

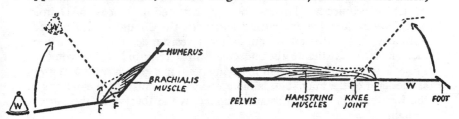

FIG. 17

it can be seen that a small amount of muscular contraction will be translated into a much more extensive and rapid movement at the hand. The action of the Hamstring Muscles in flexing the knee is another simple example.

Levers at Home and at Work

Many examples of lever are found in the use of common tools and household utensils. A seesaw, a tack lifter, and a crowbar used across a log as fulcrum are all levers of the 1st Order, while a pair of scissors are twin levers of this type with a common fulcrum. The use of a laden wheelbarrow is typical of the 2nd Order, and it is worthy of note that every door is made easier to open owing to the fact that the handle is placed as far from the hinges as possible. The 3rd Order is demonstrated by a man lifting a long ladder with its foot against a wall, or in the use of sugar-tongs or forceps, which are double levers of this Order.

Levers in Physiotherapy

A system of levers is the means by which the human body achieves movement and resilience.

A knowledge of the lever principles is also necessary for the understanding of a method of progression in strengthening muscles. As the strength of the muscle increases, the resistance or weight which is to be overcome must also be increased until such time as no further progression is possible or desirable. As the insertions of muscles constituting the effort factors are at fixed points in relation to the joints, the only factors capable of variation are the weight and its perpendicular distance from the fulcrum. Added resistance to the muscle action can therefore be applied, either by increasing the weight to be overcome or by increasing the length of the weight's arm. The latter is usually referred to as increasing the leverage.

Increasing the leverage is concerned with the situation of the point of application of a given weight. For example: Abduction of the arm at the shoulder joint with the elbow flexed reduces the leverage, and relatively weak muscles can perform the movement, whereas when the elbow is straight and the leverage is increased a more powerful contraction is required. This can be demonstrated in the case of Deltoid paresis, with the patient sitting and with the shoulder girdle fixed. Similarly, the situation of an external resistance, be it manual or mechanical, will dictate the muscular effort required to overcome it. For example: With the patient in a lying position a known resistance given at the level of the knee joint is more easily overcome by the extensors of the hip than the same resistance applied at the foot when the knee is straight.

ANGLE OF PULL

A force is most effective when it is applied at right angles to a lever.

Mechanical Efficiency of a Muscle

Mechanically, the pull is most efficient when the muscle is inserted at right angles to the bone. This efficiency is decreased as the angle of pull is reduced, because some of the force is used in pulling the bone of insertion towards the joint representing the fulcrum. This approximation of the articular surfaces has a stabilising effect upon the joint

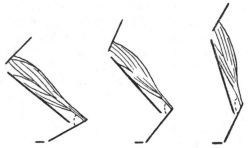

FIG. 18.   The length of the muscle is the same in each case. Which foot will gain maximum efficiency from the pull and which ankle is the most stable?

which is greatest when the direction of the pull of the muscle is longitudinal, i.e. in the long axis of the bone of attachment. The mechanical efficiency of the muscle pull is also reduced when the angle of insertion is increased from the right angle. In this case the joint becomes less stable as the angle increases.

Efficiency of a Resistance

The sustained pull of a force offering resistance will also be maximal when it is applied at right angles to a lever, and will decrease as the angle of pull becomes acute or obtuse.

A force offering resistance to movement of one of the body levers may be applied by means of a rope or through the physiotherapist's hand. The effect of this resisting force is maximal when it is applied at right angles to the moving bone. During the course of a movement,

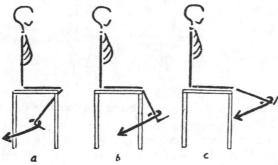

FIG. 19. The effect of the resisting force is maximal when it is applied at right angles (*b*)

when the angle of pull must vary, the right-angled pull is employed in that part of the range in which maximum resistance is required. This usually coincides with the part of the range in which the pull of the working muscles is most efficient.

PULLEYS

A pulley is a grooved wheel which is rotated about a fixed axis by a rope which passes round it. The axis is supported by a framework or block, and the whole structure may be used either as a fixed pulley or a movable pulley.

The Fixed Pulley

This is used to alter the direction of a force, and enables traction or resistance to be applied at any angle. The pulley block is fixed to some suitable support and the rope which passes round the wheel is attached to the weight at one end and the effort is applied at the other.

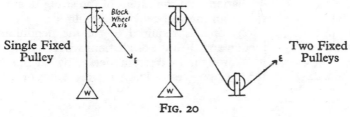

FIG. 20

Something analogous to the fixed pulley system is used in the body by some muscles to allow them to be inserted at a more advantageous angle, e.g. Digastric and Omohyoid Muscles pull round fibrous loops, and Obturator Internus Muscle turns at a right angle and glides on a ridged groove to its insertion.

The Movable Pulley

This device is used to gain a mechanical advantage when lifting heavy weights.   One simple combination is in common use for lifting

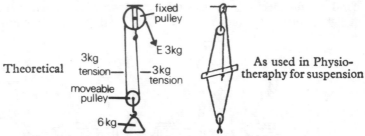

FIG. 21.   Combination of Fixed and Movable Pulleys

the trunk for Suspension exercises.   The upper pulley is fixed to an overhead support, to which one end of the rope is attached.   The rope is then wound round the movable pulley, to which the weight is attached, and round the fixed pulley, the effort being applied at the free end.

Provided the effect of friction is omitted, the tension is the same in all parts of the rope, therefore, if the weight (W) is 6 kg. the tension required in each of the two supporting ropes will be 3 kg. and the effort (E) required will be 3 kg.   This can be expressed as:

$$\text{Mechanical Advantage} = \frac{W}{E} = \frac{6 \text{ kg.}}{3 \text{ kg.}} = 2$$

If double pulleys are used the effort required can again be reduced by half.

PENDULUMS

By definition, a simple pendulum is a heavy particle, suspended by a weightless thread and free to move to and fro.

When the pendulum is at rest, the thread (or rope) is vertical, but if the particle (or weight) is drawn to one side and then released, the pendulum will swing to and fro. One complete swing in each direction is called an oscillation, and the extent of the swing to any one side from the vertical is the amplitude.

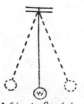

A *Simple Pendulum*

FIG. 22

A force is required to set the pendulum in motion and then the oscillations will continue until it is brought to rest, suddenly, by an opposing force, or progressively, by the resistance of the air, etc. The time taken for each oscillation is determined by the length of the pendulum and the acceleration due to gravity.

Pendular Movement

Pendular movements in the body occur chiefly at the shoulder and hip joints when the muscles are relaxed and the limb distal to the joints swings loosely to and fro. Muscular contraction may be used to initiate the movement and to maintain or increase the amplitude of the oscillations, but it is minimal compared with that required to perform the same movement at any speed greater or less than that of the pendular swing.

For example, the leg is carried forward by a pendular swing of the leg from the hip joint during slow easy walking and the same type of movement occurs to some extent at the knee. Arm-swinging exercises at natural speed can also be done in cases of marked muscular weakness without fatigue, when slow or rapid movement is impossible.

Movement in 'Axial' Suspension

A limb, supported by ropes suspended from a point vertically above the joint to be moved, is said to be in axial suspension, i.e. the point of suspension is vertically above the axis of movement. When the limb is relaxed, it will rest with the joint in the neutral position and, when movement is initiated, it will swing freely to either side of this resting position on a plane which is horizontal.

The arc of movement forms a segment of the base of a cone, the radius of which is equal to the length of the limb and the height of which is equal to the perpendicular distance between the joint and the point of suspension.

The advantage of this type of suspension is that the limb can remain fully supported throughout a wide range of movement. This support, which renders the limb gravity free and therefore weightless, aids relaxation during passive movement and relieves the physiotherapist from the

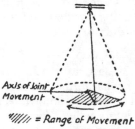

Axis of Joint
Movement

///// = Range of Movement

FIG. 23

necessity of supporting what may be a heavy part of the body, thus freeing her hands for a more accurate performance of the movement. Rhythmical active movement in suspension at a suitable speed is pendular in character and the muscle work required to maintain it is minimal, the effect being to promote reciprocal relaxation and to increase the circulation in the region of the joint which is moved.

Movement in 'Pendular' Suspension

This type of suspension represents merely a lateral or medial displacement of the point of suspension from the position which it occupies in axial suspension. In these circumstances the limb no longer rests in the neutral position of the joint, but falls to a new resting position which lies towards the vertical plane containing the new point of suspension and the joint in question. Movement on either side of this resting position causes the centre of gravity of the limb to rise, making possible pendular movement. Thus, in comparison with axial suspension, the muscle work required to produce movement away from the resting position is increased, but none is required for the return movement.

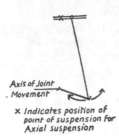

Axis of Joint
. Movement

x *Indicates position of point of suspension for Axial suspension*

FIG. 24

The effect of this type of suspension upon movement from the resting position is similar to that of an inclined re-education board, which supports the limb during movement up the incline, but differs from it in that, in pendular suspension, friction is virtually eliminated.

For demonstration purposes movement of the lower limb at the hip joint provides a convenient example. Suspension of the limb from a point vertically above the hip joint (Axial Suspension) rests it in alignment with the trunk, and movement into abduction or adduction takes place in a horizontal plane. When the point of suspension is moved medially (Pendular Suspension) the limb falls to rest in adduction, and movement into abduction requires effort and is accompanied by some flexion as the centre of gravity of the limb is raised from the resting position. If the limb is then released it will fall passively into adduction.

ELASTICITY

Elasticity is the property of a body which enables it to regain its original form after it has been distorted by the application of a force. The latter is known as a *stress* whilst the quantity (e.g. the change in length *per unit length*), which measures the extent of the change in size or shape, is called the *strain*.

Hooke's Law states that:

The strain is proportional to the stress producing it (so long as the strain is not too great, for once the so-called 'elastic limit' is passed, permanent deformation occurs).

Springs, rubber elastic and Sorbo rubber all possess the property of elasticity, and are in common use in physiotherapy.

Springs

The spiral springs used either to resist or to assist the force of muscular contraction, or to produce passive movement of joints, consist of a uniform coil of wire which is extensible.

The Extensibility of a Spring. A spring can be elongated by a force applied at one end of it in the direction of its long axis, the other end of the spring being fixed. The increase in the length of the spring is directly proportional to the magnitude of the applied force used to stretch it.

The 'Weight' of a Spring. The standard springs which are used are still graded in pounds, e.g. 50 lbs., 40 lbs., 20 lbs., etc., according to the poundage which must be applied to them to stretch them to a predetermined length. The latter is indicated by a tape inserted within the coils of the spring, the tape becoming taut when the maximum length is reached. The tape also serves to prevent the spring from being overstretched and consequently damaged.

Thus an applied force of 40 lbs. is required to stretch a 40-lb. spring to its maximum length, and any force of a magnitude less than 40 lbs. will stretch it by an amount which is proportional to the magnitude of the force.

The 'weight' of a spring is determined by the material and thickness of the wire from which it is made and the average diameter of its coils.

The Recoil of a Spring. When the applied force which stretches a spring is removed and the spring returns to its original length the potential energy stored in it during extension is released as kinetic energy, and almost all of this appears ultimately as heat in the coils of the spring.

Oscillatory Movement produced by a Spring. If a weight applied to stretch a vertical spring is raised and then released again an oscillatory movement is produced by the spring, the amplitude of which decreases progressively until the spring comes to rest in equilibrium.

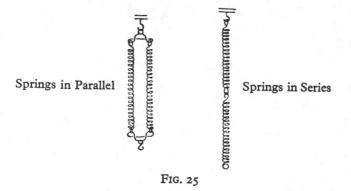

Springs in Parallel   Springs in Series

FIG. 25

Springs used in Parallel. When a spring of a specific weight is not available two equal springs of half the required weight may be used in parallel to produce the same result, e.g. two 40-lb. springs arranged in parallel are equal to a single 80-lb. spring.

Springs used in Series. The weight of two equal springs arranged in series is the same as that of a single spring, but the amount by which they must be extended in order to reach the limit of extension is double that required for a single spring. Thus when two 40-lb. springs arranged in series are extended to an amount equal to that required to stretch one of them to the limit, each of the two springs is only half extended, and the applied force needed to achieve this is therefore 20 lbs.

Rubber Elastic

Rubber elastic of different thicknesses may be used in place of springs, and in many ways it is more suitable for providing light assistance or resistance.

Sorbo Rubber

This material is both compressible and extensible and is useful for providing light resistance for gripping movements of the hand.

2

AN INTRODUCTION TO MOVEMENT

MOVEMENT is a fundamental characteristic of all animal life and the means by which the organism adapts itself to the demands made upon it by the environment in which it lives.

A system of levers provides the human body with the means of achieving a wide variety of movements and resilience in what would otherwise be a rigid bony framework.

THE BODY LEVERS

Bones form the arms, or rigid bars, of the levers and the fulcrum is at a joint where movement takes place. The structure of a joint is related to its function and determines the type of movements possible; it is interesting to note that the shape and direction of articular surfaces is such that normal functional movement is rarely unidirectional in character. No lever is functional unless some force is applied to it.

FORCES APPLIED TO THE BODY LEVERS

The forces applied to the body levers may be classified as external or internal. An *external force* is supplied from a source outside the body, e.g. the force of gravity or pressure of the physiotherapist's hands, an *internal force* is supplied by forces developed within the body, i.e. by muscular contraction. The direction of applied forces determines the direction of the movement, e.g. movement under gravity is in the direction of the earth's centre, movement resulting from muscle contraction is in the direction of the muscle's pull. The force of muscle contraction is applied at the muscle's attachment to bone and the direction of its pull is determined by the position of the muscle.

The levers of the body are rarely, if ever, subjected to the application of a single force at any one time, normally two or more are compounded or opposed. The compounding of applied forces modifies the direction of the movement and forces applied in opposition either results in movement in the direction of the greater force or, if they are equal in magnitude, a state of balance is established and no movement takes place.

TYPES OF MOVEMENT AND POSTURE

When the muscles are inactive or relatively so, movement produced by the application of an external force is known as *Passive Movement,* and that resulting from the contraction of muscles is *Active Movement*. Forces maintaining the body in specific attitudes or postures may be external or internal in character and balance or stability is achieved in both *Inactive or Active Postures* (see p. 245).

TYPES OF MUSCLE CONTRACTION

Muscle contraction may be isometric or isotonic.

Isometric (from iso- equal, and -metric, measurement) contraction involves the development of force by an increase in intra-muscular tension without any change in the length of the muscle.

Isotonic contraction constitutes an increase in intra-muscular tension accompanied by a change in the length of the muscle. The change in length may either shorten or lengthen the muscle.

TYPES OF MUSCLE WORK

Work is defined as the product of force and the distance through which the force acts (see p. 8). The types of muscle work used in controlling and moving the body levers are static, concentric and excentric.

Static Muscle Work. The muscles contract isometrically to counterbalance opposing forces and maintain stability but as there is no movement *no* work is done. Nevertheless, this type of muscle activity is usually, if inaccurately, called static muscle work to distinguish it from concentric and excentric muscle work.

Concentric Muscle Work. The muscles contract isotonically in shortening to produce movement. The attachments of the muscle are drawn closer together (*concentric- towards* the centre) and movement is in the direction of the muscle pull.

Excentric (or Eccentric) Muscle Work. The muscles contract isotonically in lengthening. The muscle attachments are drawn apart (*excentric—from* the centre) as it works to oppose the action of a force which is greater than that of its own contraction. Movement is therefore in the direction of the opposing force, i.e. in a direction opposite to that of the muscle pull.

RANGE OF MUSCLE WORK

The excursion of muscles, i.e. the amount of shortening or lengthening possible during contraction, is estimated to be about 50 per cent. of the muscle's maximum extended length. The maximum excursion possible is called the full range of muscle work and any excursion which falls short of this is called inner, outer or middle range to specify the particular part of the range in which movement takes place. The *inner range* is the part nearest to the point at which the muscle is in its shortest position, the *outer range* the part which is nearest to the point at which the muscle is most fully extended. *Middle range* indicates that the muscle is neither fully shortened nor fully extended as it works (see p. 171–2).

THE STRENGTH OF MUSCLE CONTRACTION

The strength of muscle contraction is the muscle's ability to generate tension (intra-muscular tension) (see p. 2, Tension). The strength of muscle contraction varies in proportion to the tension exerted by the forces which oppose its action. Variation in the strength of a muscle's contraction is made possible by means of a system of motor units.

A Motor Unit. A motor unit consists of a single neurone and the group of muscle fibres it supplies. When the unit is activated by stimulation of its cell (Anterior Horn Cell) all its component fibres contract.

As each muscle is made up from the fibres of a considerable number of motor units the strength of the contraction of the muscle as a whole is largely dependent on the *number* of its motor units activated at any one time. The greater the number of motor units activated the stronger the contraction of the muscle as a whole, thus a weak contraction requires the activity of only relatively few motor units, but the strongest contraction the muscle can produce, i.e. a maximal contraction, is only obtained when the fibres of all available motor units are contracting.

THE GROUP ACTION OF MUSCLES

Under normal conditions a single muscle never works alone to produce movement or secure stability. Functionally muscles work together in groups although each muscle may have some specific part to play in relation to the action of the whole group, e.g. by determining the precise direction of the movement or by maintaining its progress in a particular part of the range. The integrated activity of many groups is required for the production of efficient functional movement. The function of these groups is indicated by their names, i.e. Agonists (or Prime Movers), Antagonists, *Synergists and Fixators.*

Agonists (or Prime Movers). These are the group of muscles which contract to provide the force required to produce the movement.

Antagonists. These are muscles whose action would oppose that of the agonists, therefore their activity is inhibited and they relax progressively to control and permit the movement.

Synergists. The Greek prefix *syn-* means *with*; the name therefore indicates that these groups work *with* the agonists to provide a suitable background of activity and to facilitate the movement. Synergists may be required to modify the direction of the pull of an agonist or control joints not involved in the movement as in the case of muscles which pass over two or more joints.

Fixators. These muscles work to stabilise the bones of origin of the agonists to increase their efficiency for the production of movement and to secure stability of the body as a whole.

PATTERNS OF MOVEMENT

The site and direction of a movement are described as its pattern and a wide variety of patterns are possible. Most functional movement patterns require movement in several joints, i.e. mass movement, and observation of these patterns in everyday activities is both interesting and instructive. Movements which are localised to few or a single joint are developed or 'distilled' from mass movement patterns by a conscious process of learning.

TIMING IN MOVEMENT

Timing is the sequence of muscular contraction which takes place in the production of movement. To be satisfactory the force of each contraction is timed so that it is at its maximum when a subsequent force is superimposed upon it, otherwise the peak of effort reached will be wasted. There is a waste of effort if the timing is too slow or too fast. Faulty timing frequently accounts for inefficiency of the movement for the purpose for which it was designed, some components may be omitted and others added or the sequence is too fast or too slow, e.g. as in learning to swim or play golf.

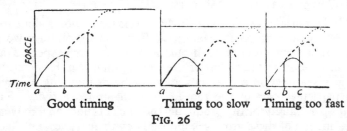

Good timing   Timing too slow   Timing too fast
FIG. 26

The timing of functional movements usually proceeds from distal to proximal as it is the distal areas which receive most of the stimuli which control the movement, i.e. the hands and feet. The smooth and orderly sequence of events which constitutes effective timing ensures the maximum efficiency of muscular contraction which is characteristic of co-ordinated movement.

RHYTHM OF MOVEMENT

The word rhythm means a regular beat or recurrence of a sequence of events.

The inspiratory muscles and the heart muscle contract rhythmically throughout life, their period of contraction alternating with a period of relaxation and inaction.

Skeletal muscles can also work for long periods of time without fatigue, provided their contraction alternates regularly with complete relaxation and consequent replenishment of the blood supply bringing oxygen to repair the effects of contraction and to remove metabolic products. The rhythm of work and rest reduces fatigue to the minimum, e.g. a hiker walking with an even stride rhythmically contracts and relaxes the Extensor Muscles of the legs, and the newcomer to industry is trained in the rhythmical sequence of the movements he is to perform at work.

Each movement has its own natural rhythm which varies to some extent in individuals. The natural rhythm varies with age, the rhythm of children's movements being relatively quick as compared with that of the adult, while that of the very elderly is slower still.

Rhythmical movements taken too quickly or too slowly usually result in faulty timing and loss of efficiency, an increase in the muscle work or a diminution of the range of movement.

THE NERVOUS CONTROL OF MOVEMENT

The motor unit is the functional unit of the Neuromuscular System which initiates and achieves movement in response to a demand for activity. The unit's muscle fibres contract in response to impulses discharged from its cell (A.H.C.) when it is stimulated. The A.H.C.s are influenced by impulses which reach them from many sources in the C.N.S. and other parts of the body. Some of these impulses are excitory and others inhibitory, and it is the predominance of one or the other type at any one time which determines the effect they have on the A.H.C.s.

The pattern of movement is planned in the initiating areas which also discharge the impulses suitable to bring it to effect.

Voluntary Movement is initiated in response to a conscious effort to perform the movement.

Reflex Movement is initiated in response to a demand made by sensory stimulation.

3

AN INTRODUCTION TO
EXERCISE THERAPY

EXERCISE Therapy is a means of accelerating the patient's recovery from injuries and diseases which have altered his normal way of living. Loss or impairment of function prevents or modifies his ability to live independently, to carry on with his work and enjoy recreation. He may react to the demands of his environment either by rejecting them and remaining inactive or by meeting them to the best of his ability by altering his pattern of activity.

The process of recovery is delayed by inactivity and the muscular weakness which results from it, the repeated use of alternative patterns of activity makes it difficult to correct them when they are no longer needed, e.g. limping after leg injuries. Although these alternative patterns may serve a useful purpose temporarily they must not be allowed to become established as they are less efficient than the normal patterns, unless a return to normal function is known to be impossible.

THE AIMS OF EXERCISE THERAPY

The aims of treatment by exercise are:

1. To promote activity whenever and wherever it is possible to minimise the effects of inactivity.

2. To correct the inefficiency of specific muscles or muscle groups and regain normal range of joint movement without delay to achieve efficient functional movement.

3. To encourage the patient to use the ability he has regained in the performance of normal functional activities and so accelerate his rehabilitation.

THE TECHNIQUES OF EXERCISE THERAPY

Movement used in treatment may be classified as follows:

Active Movement

1. Voluntary
$$\begin{cases} \text{Assisted.} \\ \text{Free.} \\ \text{Assisted-Resisted.} \\ \text{Resisted.} \end{cases}$$

2. Involuntary Reflex.

Passive Movement
1. Relaxed passive movements including accessory movements.
2. Passive manual mobilisation techniques.

Posture. Movement begins and ends in posture which is classified as either active or inactive.

Active Movement and Posture is achieved by muscular contraction in response to a demand presented in a manner suitable to the patient's ability to respond.

Passive movement and Posture result from the application of external forces when the muscles are unable to contract or when they relax voluntarily to permit movement or allow support.

The techniques which are most effective for obtaining the aims of treatment are those which (*i*) demand as much activity as possible and which (*ii*) are based on patterns of movement which are the same as those used by the patient for his normal functional activities.

(*i*) Muscles are as active as possible when all their available motor units are activated, i.e. contracting maximally. As the strength of contraction is proportional to the resistance which opposes it the application of the greatest degree of resistance possible, i.e. *a maximal resistance*, elicits a maximal contraction. When some muscles are weaker than others their strength and endurance is built up by repeating their maximal contraction against a resistance which increases in proportion to their gain in strength until a balance of muscle strength is re-established. A lengthening reaction of tight or shortened muscles is obtained by strong contraction of antagonistic muscles to restore the range of movement in stiff joints.

(*ii*) *Patterns of mass movement* are used for most functional activities. The movement patterns are natural to the patient and when they are the same or very similar to those used for his everyday activities direction is given to his effort to regain function and the same muscles are used in the same way.

When activity is impossible or contra-indicated passive movement is used to maintain the extensibility of the muscles and the free range of movement in joints. In some cases forced passive movements are used to increase the free range of movement in joints.

THE APPROACH TO THE PATIENT'S PROBLEMS

The problems arising from loss of function are different for each patient therefore treatment must be planned to meet his individual needs. In this way the patient's and the physiotherapist's time are used to the best advantage and some result should be expected from *every* treatment session; if there is none the treatment is ineffective and should be altered or discontinued.   This may seem to be a council of perfection but should always be kept in mind.

ASSESSMENT OF THE PATIENT'S CONDITION

Detailed assessment of the patient's condition is made before treatment starts so that the physiotherapist is in a position to plan it in accordance with the doctor's orders and the needs of the patient. Tests, carried out to discover the patient's needs, abilities and disabilities, are recorded on charts designed for the purpose, as a guide to the selection of suitable techniques and a means of estimating progress.   The same charts and method of testing are used on subsequent occasions, preferably by the same physiotherapist.   A series of tests provide the answer to the following questions:—

1. '*What does the patient need to do?*'
The co-operation of the patient and all those who come in daily contact with him is required to discover his needs for activity; those which are most urgent are given priority in treatment.

2. '*What can the patient do?*'
The patient's abilities provide a means of correcting or compensating for his loss of function.   Strong muscles can be used to reinforce the action of weaker ones and to gain initiation of the contraction of muscles which would otherwise remain inactive.

As there is a tendency for patients to concentrate on their inabilities and to be frustrated by unsuccessful attempts to overcome them it is important that their attention is drawn to things they can do and to realise that these can be used to restore function elsewhere.

3. '*What is the patient unable to do?*'
A series of tests for muscle efficiency and joint range, with observation of movements and reactions, reveal the extent, nature and position of the deficiencies causing loss or impairment of function.

SOME METHODS OF TESTING

Every test used must be standardised as far as possible, i.e. carried out in the same way and under the same circumstances on each occasion.   Record charts are dated and kept for use each time the test is repeated.   Some of the tests in common use are as follows:—

1. *Functional Tests*
These are used to assess the patient's needs and abilities with regard to functional activities, e.g. mobility (in bed, transfers, ambulation, etc.), personal care (eating, dressing, washing, etc.), household or garden jobs (cooking, washing up, sweeping, lifting, etc.), work and

recreation. They are carried out in the patient's normal environment or in circumstances which are as nearly like it as possible. His performance is recorded as skilled, adequate, requiring assistance (stand by, minimal, maximal) or failure. The physiotherapist and occupational therapist co-operate fully in making these tests which provide a valuable means of deciding priorities in treatment and of estimating progress.

2. *Tests of Joint Range*

Measurement of the limitation of joint range presents many difficulties in practice. A suitable position is selected for the patient so that he is stable, to make sure that any structures which would limit the normal range of movement are relaxed, e.g. calf muscles must be relaxed by flexing the knee to measure full range of ankle movement. The bone proximal to the joint in which range is to be measured is fixed and movement in the joint accomplished in a particular plane. An angle measure or goniometer is used with the pivot over the joint in question and one arm in alignment with the proximal bone, the other is in line with the area which is moved. The degree of angulation is read off on the scale and recorded as $X°$ of free movement, or, it is often less confusing to record the number of degrees the joint lacks in a particular direction, e.g. knee extension lacks 30° of the normal range. As the normal range of movement varies considerably in individuals, the contralateral joint should always be measured first when possible. When an angle measure is unsuitable an inextensible tape measure may be used to measure the distance between two bony points to provide a means of assessing an increase or decrease in range of movement.

3. *Tests for Neuromuscular Efficiency*

These may be carried out electrically, manually or mechanically.

a. Electrical Tests. These may be carried out by the doctor with the use of the electro-myograph or by means of the strength-duration curve. They are particularly valuable for diagnostic purposes.

b. Manual Muscle Testing. To be accurate and efficient manual muscle testing requires a standardised technique and considerable experience. The techniques are very clearly described in *Muscle Testing*, Techniques of Manual Examination by L. Daniels and C. Worthington (3rd edition), which is widely used. The classification of the findings at examination, however, are usually recorded according to the Oxford Classification, on a scale 0–5, i.e.,

0. No contraction
1. Flicker of contraction
2. Weak. Small movement with gravity counterbalanced
3. Fair. Movement against gravity

4. Good.   Movement against gravity and some resistance
5. Normal.

c. Circumference Measurement.   This test relies on the fact that there is a relationship between the development of power and that of hypertrophy.   A tape measure made from some inextensible material is used to measure the circumference of the limb at a predetermined level.   Experiment on normal limbs indicates that this method is unreliable even in experienced hands; although it is still used.

d. Static Power Test.   The power of static or isometric contraction may be recorded by means of a spring balance capable of registering up to 50 or 100 lbs.   The extensibility of the spring within this type of balance is virtually negligible and it can be arranged in such a way that contraction of the muscle group can take place at any predetermined point within its range.   Record can be made of the maximum poundage recorded or of the average poundage recorded as the result of three efforts made at one-minute intervals.

In some instances, such as that of gripping with the hand, compression of a spring or of a rubber sphere to which a suitable pressure recording device is attached may prove convenient.

e. Dynamic Power Test.   This is a method devised by de Lorme, and Watkins as a basis for Progressive Resistance Exercise.   The maximum weight which can be lifted *once only* through a prescribed range is called the One Repetition Maximum (1 R.M.) and the maximum weight which can be lifted ten times at natural speed without rest between lifts is the Ten Repetition Maximum (10 R.M.).   Experience in estimating the approximate weight which can be lifted is essential to avoid fatigue which results from continued trial and error and which rapidly reduces the poundage which can be lifted.

f. Endurance Test.   Endurance may be calculated by recording the drop in the maximal power of the muscles when their effort of contraction is repeated at given intervals for a specific period of time.

g. Speed Tests.   The successful performance of functional activities can be timed by the use of a stop-watch, e.g. time taken to dress or walk a measured distance.

4. Tests for Co-ordination
Co-ordination of movement, or the lack of it, is observed in the patient's gait, his performance of purposeful movements or during specific movements such as bringing the finger to the tip of the nose or moving the heel up and down along the opposite shin bone.

5. Tests for Sensation
These are described fully in any neurological textbook.

6. *Measurement of Vital Capacity and Range of Respiratory Excursions*

A spirometer is used to measure vital capacity. The patient is instructed to breath in as much as possible and then breath out through the mouthpiece of the spirometer which registers the volume in cubic centimetres.

7. *Measurement of Leg Length*

True shortening of the leg is measured from the anterior superior iliac spine or the upper margin of the great trochanter to the lateral malleolus, and apparent shortening from the umbilicus or xiphisternum to the level of the knee joint or the tip of the medial malleolus. (Methods of determining the site of shortening in the hip region are described fully in *Orthopaedic Surgery* by Walter Mercer, Ch. I, p. 10.)

8. *Measurement of the Angle of Pelvic Inclination*

Antero-posterior inclination of the pelvis may be measured by means of a pelvic inclinometer (see p. 38).

PLANNING THE TREATMENT

When the physiotherapist has completed the assessment of the patient's condition and seen his medical notes suitable activities or passive means are selected for inclusion in the treatment programme. A wide knowledge of the techniques available and the ability to apply them with skill and ingenuity are needed. The suitability of any technique used is judged by the patient's response and the extent to which it is effective for achieving or accelerating his recovery.

4

STARTING POSITIONS

SHERRINGTON stated that 'Posture follows movement like a shadow: every movement begins in posture and ends in posture'. The postures from which movement is initiated are known as Starting Positions and they may be either active or passive in character. There are five basic or fundamental starting positions and all the others are derived from them, i.e. standing, kneeling, sitting, lying and hanging.

Equilibrium and stability is maintained in these positions by a balance of forces acting upon the body, and when the force of muscular contraction is used for this purpose the contraction is isometric. The strength and distribution of this contraction is normally controlled by a series of reflexes known collectively as the Postural Reflexes but, during the learning process of new patterns of posture, voluntary effort may be required.

FUNDAMENTAL POSITIONS

1. STANDING (st.)

This is the most difficult of the fundamental positions to maintain, as the whole body must be balanced and stabilised in correct alignment on a small base by the co-ordinated work of many muscle groups. The position may be described as follows:

(*i*) The heels are together and on the same line, the toes slightly apart (so that the angle between the feet does not exceed 45°).

(*ii*) The knees are together and straight.

(*iii*) The hips are extended and laterally rotated slightly.

(*iv*) The pelvis is balanced on the femoral heads (see Pelvic Tilt, p. 38).

(*v*) The spine is stretched to its maximum length.

(*vi*) The vertex is thrust upwards, the ears are level and the eyes look straight forwards.

(*vii*) The shoulders are down and back.

(*viii*) The arms hang loosely to the sides, palms facing inwards towards the body.

It is usually preferable to modify the position of the legs to that in which the heels are slightly apart and the inner borders of the feet are parallel, as this is the natural functional position of the foot when it is used as a lever to propel the body forwards.

Muscle Work. The muscle work required to maintain the position varies with the circumstances. It is reduced considerably when the body segments are in good alignment and perfectly balanced and increased by faulty alignment or by external forces which tend to disturb equilibrium. The anti-gravity muscles of the trunk and lower limbs work isometrically to hold the position. As a method of identifying these muscle groups, let it be supposed that gravity is allowed to act unopposed upon a body in the erect position when all the muscles are progressively relaxed. The result is that the body 'folds up' and falls to the ground. If the anti-gravity muscles, and those which work with them as synergists, are now brought into action the body can be built up to a standing position. The muscle groups involved are:

a. The Intrinsic Muscles of the Feet working to stabilise the feet and to prevent curling of the toes so that the Flexors of the Interphalangeal Joints can press the balls of the toes to the ground.

b. The Plantaflexors of the Ankle, working to balance the lower leg on the foot.

c. The Dorsiflexors of the Ankle, working to counterbalance the action of the Plantaflexors and to support the medial longitudinal arch of the foot.

d. The Evertors, working to counterbalance the action of the Invertors (Tibialis Anterior and Posterior), and in the case of Peroneus Longus, to press the ball of the great toe to the ground.

The interaction of *b*, *c* and *d* may be likened to that of three guy ropes which support a flag pole, the tension in all three is reciprocal, an increase in the tension of one resulting in a slackening of the others If the pole is perfectly balanced tension in all three is minimal.

e. The Extensors of the Knee may work slightly.

f. The Extensors of the Hip, working to maintain hip extension and to balance the pelvis on the femoral heads. Slight action of the Lateral Rotators of the Hip is associated with a bracing of the legs and of the arches of the foot.

g. The Extensors of the Spine, working to keep the trunk upright. Where their action over the lumbar and cervical regions would result in increased curvature and consequent shortening of the spine, they are counterbalanced by the Flexors of these regions to ensure maximum lengthening.

h. The Flexors of the Lumbar Spine (Abdominal Muscles), working to prevent over-action of the Extensors of this region. They also assist in the maintenance of the correct angle of pelvic tilt, and support the abdominal viscera.

i. The Pre-vertebral Neck Muscles, working to control excessive extension of the neck and to straighten the cervical spine.

j. The Flexors and Extensors of the Atlanto-occipital Joint, working reciprocally to balance the head.   The Elevators of the Mandible close the mouth.

k. The Retractors of the Scapulae, working to draw the scapulae backwards so that the glenoid cavity faces more or less laterally.

l. The arms are relaxed.   Sometimes, however, it is necessary to use the Lateral Rotators of the Shoulder to keep them in the correct position.

All the muscle groups mentioned above stabilise the body in the anterior-posterior direction, in addition there must also be a balanced contraction of the lateral muscles to maintain equilibrium.

The erect posture has developed during the evolution of man, and it has to be learnt and practised by every child.   It is the position of perfect balance which requires the minimum of effort, and therefore the position itself and the muscle work required to maintain it must vary considerably in accordance with the anatomical structure of the individual.

Effects and Uses.   As the base is relatively small and the centre of gravity high, the state of equilibrium of the body is relatively less stable than in the other fundamental positions; therefore the standing position is only suitable as a starting position for exercise for those who can maintain it correctly.   The muscle work is minimal when perfect balance is achieved, therefore practice in attaining and holding a satisfactory pattern of standing posture reduces fatigue and also conditions the postural reflex.   The erect position of the whole body is the position of alertness, in which the thorax is free and the abdominal viscera are well supported; it is associated with a feeling of joy and efficiency, a fact which is demonstrated and recognised in drama and the dance.

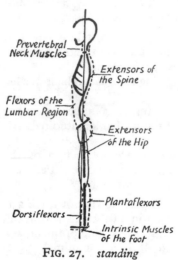

Prevertebral Neck Muscles

Extensors of the Spine

Flexors of the Lumbar Region

Extensors of the Hip

Plantaflexors

Dorsiflexors

Intrinsic Muscles of the Foot

FIG. 27.   *standing*

2. KNEELING (kn.)

The body is supported on the knees which may be together or slightly apart.   The lower leg rests on the floor with the feet plantaflexed, or, if a plinth is used, the feet may be in the mid-position over the edge.   The rest of the body is held as in standing.

Muscle Work. The lower leg is relaxed; the body must be stabilised on the knees.

a. There is interplay between the Flexors and Extensors of the Knee, to balance the femora vertically on the knees.

The muscle work of the rest of the body is as in standing, except that:

b. The Extensors of the Hip and the Flexors of the Lumbar Spine work more strongly to maintain the correct angle of pelvic tilt. A decrease in this angle and consequent increase in extension of the lumbar spine tends to occur in this position, because of the tension of the Rectus Femoris, which is stretched across the front of both the hip and knee joints.

Fig. 28.
kneeling

Effects and Uses. Although the centre of gravity of the body is relatively lower than in standing, the position is only slightly more stable and is uncomfortable for most people. It is used as a starting position for backward movement in a sagittal plane and to train control of the hip joints and lower trunk in preparation for the standing position during which the feet are pressed to the floor by the Extensors of the Knees and Dorsiflexors, so that the lower leg acts as a bracket.

3. SITTING (sitt.)

The position is taken on a chair or stool, the height and width of which allow the thighs to be fully supported and the hips and knees to be flexed to a right angle. The knees are apart sufficiently to allow the femora to be parallel and the feet rest on the floor with the heels vertically below the knees.

Muscle Work. There need be no muscle work to hold the position of the legs, as they are fully supported. The Flexors of the Hips work to maintain a right angle at these joints and to prevent the tendency to slump.

The muscle work of the rest of the body is the same as in standing.

Effects and Uses. This is a comfortable, natural and very stable position which is much used, and it is particularly suitable for those who lack the necessary strength and control to maintain a more difficult position.

Fig. 29.
sitting

Lateral and rotatory mobility of the pelvis is eliminated by the weight of the body and the position of the legs, so that lateral and rotatory movements can be localised to the spine. As none of the body weight is transmitted to the legs, many non-weight-bearing knee and foot exercises can be performed in the position, which is also suitable for training correct alignment of the upper part of the body in the habitual sitting position, which is used by the majority more than any other in everyday life.

4. LYING (ly.)

This is the easiest of the fundamental positions as the body can be completely supported in the supine position and is as stable as is possible.

FIG. 30. *lying*

Muscle Work.   This is minimal.   If the body is relaxed on a hard surface, such as the floor or the average plinth, the head rolls to one side, the lumbar spine is hollowed because of the tension of structures lying anterior to the hip joints and the latter fall into a position of lateral rotation.   On a soft resilient surface, however, such as a spring mattress, which gives way to the contours of the body and supports it completely, this does not occur.

When the lying position is used as a starting position for exercise it is usually taken on a firm surface and the following muscle groups work slightly:

a. The Head Rotators of both sides work reciprocally to stabilise the position of the head.

b. The Extensors of the Hips and Flexors of the Lumbar Spine work to combat the tendency to hollow the back.

c. The Medial Rotators of the Hips work to keep the legs in the neutral position, so that the knees and inner borders of the feet are held together.

Effects and Uses.   This is an easy position and as the trunk is relaxed and fixed by its own weight, it is a suitable position for many exercises.   As the alignment of the body is the same as in standing, static posture training can be carried out in this position.   The spine is relieved of the burden of transmitting the weight of the head and shoulders when it is in the horizontal position, therefore it tends to elongate and straighten, and this is an advantage in the treatment of spinal deformities.   Breathing is impeded slightly by pressure on the posterior aspect of the thorax and by increased pressure of the abdominal viscera on the under surface of the Diaphragm, often making the position unsuitable for those suffering from respiratory or heart conditions.   The position hinders the return of blood from the head and so may be unsuitable for the elderly, or those who suffer from high blood pressure.

5. HANGING (hg.)

The body is suspended by grasping over a horizontal bar, the forearms being pronated, the arms straight and at least shoulder width apart. The head is held high and the scapulae are drawn down and together, so that the neck appears as long as possible. The trunk and legs hang straight, with the heels together and the ankles plantaflexed.

Muscle Work

a. The Flexors of the Fingers work strongly to grasp the bar.

b. All the muscles round the wrist work strongly to reduce the strain on the joints and to act as synergists and fixators for the Flexors of the Fingers.

c. The Flexors of the Elbows work to reduce the strain on the joints.

d. The Adductors of the Shoulders work strongly to lift the body on the arms (especially Latissimus Dorsi posteriorly and Pectoralis Major anteriorly).

e. The Depressors, Retractors and Medial Rotators of the Scapulae work strongly to fix the scapulae and to brace the upper back.

f. The Pre-vertebral and Posterior Neck Muscles work reciprocally to maintain the position of the head and neck.

FIG. 31.
hanging

g. The Flexors of the Lumbar Spine and the Extensors of the Hips work to correct the tendency to arch the back as the result of the over-action of Latissimus Dorsi, working on the sacrum.

h. The Adductors of the Hips work to keep the legs together.

i. The Extensors of the Knees may work to maintain full extension.

j. The Plantaflexors work to point the toes to the floor.

Effects and Uses. As the muscle work for the arms and upper back is extensive and strong the position is only suitable for those in whom muscular strength and body weight are well balanced. As the weight of the shoulders is taken off the spine and the weight of the legs exert traction upon it, it is straightened and elongated.

The thorax is fixed in the inspiratory position and breathing is difficult, therefore the position is unsuitable for weak patients and those suffering from cardiac or respiratory conditions. The effect of stretching the body is stimulating and much enjoyed, especially by children.

For Derived Positions see Appendix, p. 280.

THE PELVIC TILT

Movement in the vertebral column and at the hip joints make it possible for the pelvis to be stabilised in a variety of positions. It may be inclined or tilted in an antero-posterior direction, laterally or rotated.

a. Antero-posterior Tilt

In erect posture the angle of the pelvic tilt can be measured in a variety of ways:

1. The angle at which an imaginary line, drawn through the symphysis pubis and the lumbo-sacral angle, lies in relation to a horizontal line can be measured. The pelvic tilt is said to be normal in the standing position when this angle measures between 50° and 60°.

2. The angle of pelvic tilt is said to be normal in the standing

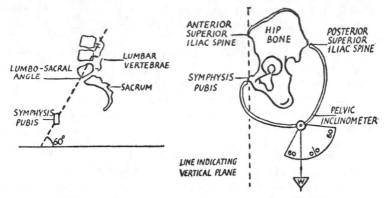

FIG. 32.   Measurement of the Angle of Pelvic Tilt
(methods 1 *left* and 2 and 3 *right*)

position when the anterior superior iliac spines and the symphysis pubis all lie in the same vertical plane.

3. The angle recorded by a pelvic inclinometer, one of the arms of which is placed over the symphysis and the other over one of the posterior superior iliac spines, is in the region of 30° in the standing position when the pelvic tilt is normal.

Maintenance of the Normal Angle of Antero-posterior Tilt of the Pelvis

The angle of the pelvic tilt in *standing* is stabilised either by the tension of the structures which lie anterior to the hip joint, which prevent the angle from being reduced, or by the action of the straight Abdominal Muscles and the Hip Extensors which prevent it from being increased.

Alteration in the Angle of Antero-posterior Tilt of the Pelvis

An increase in the angle of pelvic tilt may be called forward tilting of the pelvis, and a decrease in the angle of pelvic tilt may be called backward tilting of the pelvis.

Forward Tilting of the Pelvis. Movement of the pelvis on the

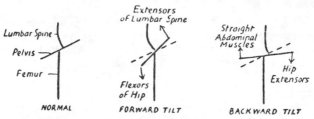

FIG. 33. Antero-posterior Tilting of Pelvis

femoral heads to produce a forward tilting is produced by the contraction of the Hip Flexor Muscles and the Extensors of the Lumbar Spine.

Backward Tilting of the Pelvis. The pelvis can be tilted backwards on the femoral heads by the contraction of the Hip Extensors and the straight Abdominal Muscles.

b. Lateral Tilting of the Pelvis

The pelvis may also be tilted laterally on one of the femoral heads. When the femur on which the pelvis is tilted is fixed as in *standing on*

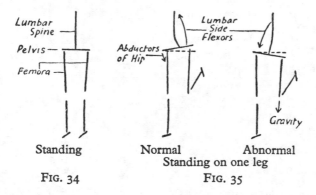

FIG. 34   FIG. 35

one leg, and the other leg is free to move, the pelvis is tilted laterally to bring the centre of gravity over the base and so maintain balance by abduction or adduction in the hip joint of the leg which is fixed. An upward inclination of the pelvis from the point of support is produced and maintained by the contraction of the Abductors of the Hip of the supporting leg.   When this occurs the Lumbar Side Flexors on the opposite side from the supporting leg work to keep the trunk erect.

When the weight of the body is transferred on to one leg and the Hip Abductors are relaxed or inefficient, the pelvis is inclined laterally and downwards towards the unsupported side by the force of gravity.

c. Rotation of the Pelvis

The pelvis can also be rotated so that the anterior superior iliac spine of one side is thrust forwards.   This rotation is associated with separation of the legs in an antero-posterior direction providing it is more than a few inches and both legs are moved.

5

ACTIVE MOVEMENT

VOLUNTARY MOVEMENT

Definition

Movement performed or controlled by the voluntary action of muscles, working in opposition to an external force.

Classification

Free Exercise. The working muscles are subject only to the forces of gravity acting upon the part moved or stabilised.

Assisted Exercise. When muscle strength or co-ordination is inadequate to perform a movement an external force is applied to compensate for the deficiency.

Assisted-resisted Exercise. Muscles may be strong enough to work against resistance in part of the range and not in others. This type of exercise ensures that the external forces applied are adapted in every part of the range to the abilities of the muscles.

Resisted Exercise. The forces of resistance offered to the action of the working muscles are artificially and systematically increased to develop the power and endurance of the muscles.

FREE EXERCISE

Free exercises are those which are performed by the patient's own muscular efforts without the assistance or resistance of any external force, other than that of gravity. They vary widely in character and effect, not only because of the nature and extent of the movement, but according to the manner in which they are performed.

This type of exercise can be used to obtain any of the effects which are produced by exercise as a whole, if and when it is used judiciously. A degree of relaxation is induced by exercises which are rhythmical or pendular in character; muscle tone is maintained and power increased according to the speed, leverage and duration of the exercise, and the relationship of the part moved to gravity; co-ordination is trained or improved as the natural pattern of group action is employed, and confidence in the ability to perform and control movement is established.

Success in achieving the required effect depends not only on the

41

selection of a suitable exercise and on the manner in which it is performed, but also on the degree of co-operation obtained from the patient and the skill of the instructor.

The great advantage of free exercises lies in the fact that once the patient has mastered the technique of their performance and is aware of their purpose, they are his own, to practise when and where he pleases. He has, in fact, been given the means to cure or to help to cure himself and need no longer rely on others for this purpose.

Whether or not he uses the exercise for home practice to help himself largely depends on his desire for rehabilitation and his confidence in the efficacy of the exercises.

The disadvantage of free exercises is that they frequently make insufficient demands on the patient's neuromuscular system to elicit the maximal response required for the rapid re-development or re-inforcement of weak muscles. When there is muscular imbalance, compensatory rather than normal patterns of movement may be used unless movements are carefully taught and supervised. Patients who have suffered brain damage or who are unable to initiate movement cannot co-operate in doing these exercises until their performance has been facilitated and voluntary control has been established.

Classification of Free Exercises

Free exercises may be classified according to the extent of the area involved; they may be:

    a. Localised
    b. General.

a. Localised exercises are designed primarily to produce some local and specific effect, for example, to mobilise a particular joint or to strengthen particular muscle groups. Movement is localised to one or more joints, either by the use of a suitable starting position, or by voluntary fixation of other areas by the patient's own muscular effort.

b. General exercises usually involve the use of many joints and muscles all over the body and the effect is widespread, for example, as in running.

The character of a particular exercise may be:

    a. Subjective
    b. Objective.

a. Exercises which are subjective are usually formal and consist of more or less anatomical movements performed in full range. The attention of the patient is deliberately focused on the form and pattern of the exercise to ensure accuracy of performance.

b. Objective exercises are those during the performance of which the patient's attention is concentrated on the achievement of a particular aim which will result from his efforts, e.g. *standing; Arm stretching upwards,* to touch a mark on the wall, or to throw a ball. The presence of a goal to be reached is stimulating to effort, like the proverbial carrot held in front of the donkey's nose, but care must be taken to see that the accuracy of the movement is not sacrificed to the achievement of the aim; e.g. in walking across a room to get a cup of tea, the quality of the walking must not be allowed to deteriorate.

The Technique of Free Exercises

1. The starting position is selected and taught with care to ensure the maximum postural efficiency as a basis for movement.

2. Instruction is given in a manner which will gain the interest and co-operation of the patient and lead him to understand both the pattern and the purpose of the exercise (see Chapter 22, 'Instructing the Patient', (p. 272).

3. The speed at which the exercise is done depends on the effect required. It is usually slow during the period of learning and later the patient is either allowed to find his own natural rhythm, or the speed required is dictated by the physiotherapist. It often helps the patient to maintain his natural rhythm at home if, during practice under supervision, he is encouraged to count aloud.

4. The duration of the exercise depends very largely on the patient's capacity. Usually three bouts of practice for each exercise, with short rest periods, or a change of activity, between, ensure sufficient practice without undue fatigue.

The Effects and Uses of Free Exercise

The effect and consequent uses of any particular free exercise depend on the nature of the exercise, its extent and the intensity and duration of its performance.

Relaxation. Rhythmical swinging movements and those which are pendular in character assist the relaxation of hypertonic muscles in the region of the joint moved. The alternating and reciprocal contraction and relaxation of the opposing muscle groups, which is required to sustain the movement, helps to restore the normal state of relaxation which follows contraction. This type of exercise is used in conjunction with other methods which induce relaxation to reduce a state of wasteful tension in muscles, which limits the range of joint movement and reduces the efficiency of neuromuscular co-ordination.

Exercises which work particular muscle groups strongly achieve reciprocal relaxation of the opposing groups, e.g. work for the Scapular

Retractors and Shoulder Extensors assists relaxation of the Pectoral Muscles.

Joint Mobility.   The normal range of joint movement is maintained by exercises performed in full range.   If and when the range of movement is limited, rhythmical swinging exercises incorporating overpressure at the limit of the free range may serve to increase it.

Muscle Power and Tone.   The power and endurance of the working muscles are maintained or increased in response to the tension created in them.   This tension is greater when the exercise is performed at any speed which is slower, or more rapid, than when the natural speed of movement is employed, and it increases with the duration of the exercise.   A high degree of tension and consequent increase in power can be developed by free exercises when the muscles work for any time against the resistance offered by the body weight, or against the mechanical disadvantage of an adverse leverage provided by a long and heavy limb.

Normally, muscle power is maintained adequately by a minimum of everyday activities, most of which are performed in the middle range.   Under abnormal conditions, however, for example during fixation of a joint, the power can only be maintained or improved by repeated static contractions, which the patient must practise throughout the day.

Neuromuscular Co-ordination.   Co-ordination is improved by the repetition of an exercise.   As the pattern of movement is established, it is simplified and becomes more efficient, and the conduction of the necessary impulses along the neuromuscular pathways is facilitated. Exercises or activities, which at one time required concentration and much effort, become with practice more or less automatic in character, and skill is developed, as for example in walking or playing the piano.

Confidence.   The achievement of co-ordinated and efficient movement assures the patient of his ability to maintain subjective control of his body, giving him confidence to attempt other and new activities, together with a feeling of exhilaration and satisfaction when they are accomplished, for example, jumping a rope, or shooting a goal. Objective exercises and activities are usually used for this purpose.

Circulatory and Respiratory Co-operation.   During vigorous or prolonged exercise it is apparent that the speed and depth of respiration is increased, that the heart beat is faster and more forceful, and that heat is produced, whereas in light exercise these changes are so slight that they are not noticed.

a. The Needs of the Active Tissues.   The active tissues involved during muscular exercise require a free supply of oxygenated blood and the removal of metabolic products to enable them to continue their activity. To meet these demands and to keep pace with them, the co-operation of the Circulatory and Respiratory Systems is enlisted.

b. Preparation for Activity. It is probable that the cerebral cortex, which initiates the muscular contraction, also prepares the body to supply the needs of the tissues concerned, by communicating with the Respiratory, Cardiac and Vaso-motor centres which form part of the Autonomic Nervous System. Sympathetic fibres from these centres convey impulses to the appropriate organs which, with the help of adrenalin, which is released into the blood stream, produce widespread results. These results include increased respiration, increased frequency of the heart beat, a rise in arterial blood pressure, and a re-distribution of blood, so that the volume of blood in the muscles is increased at the expense of that in the splanchnic area and the skin.

All these changes occur merely as the result of the anticipation of exercise as those who have taken part in competitive sports may have been aware.

c. Local Circulatory Changes in the Muscles. During active exercise the capillaries in the working muscles dilate and their permeability is increased. Many capillaries that were closed when the muscle was at rest become open and blood flows through them. In this way the capacity of the muscles to contain blood is markedly increased and the interchange of fuel and waste products between the blood and the tissue fluids is facilitated.

d. Regulation of Circulatory and Respiratory Function during Exercise. The venous return to the heart is increased during exercise and results in an increase in cardiac output. The increased venous return is caused partly by the pressure variations in the abdominal and thoracic cavities resulting from increased respiratory movements which exert a pumping action upon the large veins in the direction of the heart, and partly by the pressure of the contracting muscles on the thin walls of the peripheral veins. Valves in these veins prevent regurgitation during relaxation of the pressure.

Muscular contraction increases both the carbon dioxide content and the temperature of the blood, and both these factors stimulate the circulatory and respiratory systems to further activity. The rise in temperature of the body is kept within normal limits by dilation of the skin capillaries and stimulation of the sweat glands, thus enabling heat to be lost from the surface.

Active exercise can therefore be used to increase Respiration, to increase both the local and the general Circulation, and to provide work for the Heart Muscle.

The effect of active exercise as a whole is so widespread and varies so much in intensity according to the nature of the exercise that it has been described here only in the briefest outline.

Assisted Exercise

The Principles of Assistance

When the force exerted on one of the body levers by muscular action is insufficient for the production or control of movement, an external force may be added to augment it.   This external force must be applied in the direction of the muscle action but not necessarily at the same point, as a mechanical advantage can be gained by increasing the leverage.   The magnitude of this assisting force must be sufficient only to augment the muscular action and must not be allowed to act as a substitute for it, for if it does a passive movement results.   As

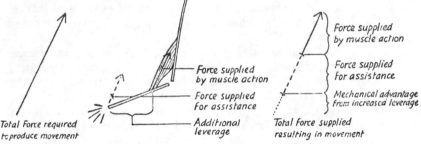

Total Force required to produce movement

Force supplied by muscle action
Force supplied for assistance
Additional leverage

Force supplied by muscle action
Force supplied for assistance
Mechanical advantage from increased leverage
Total force supplied resulting in movement

FIG. 36.   An External Force is utilised to supplement the Force of Muscular Contraction

the power of the muscle increases, the assistance given must decrease proportionally.

Technique

The general plan is to ensure that the inefficient muscles exert their maximum effort to produce movement under conditions designed to facilitate their action.   The assisting force is applied only to augment this maximum effort and not to act as a substitute for it.

1. *Starting Position.*   Stability for the body as a whole ensures that the patient's whole attention is concentrated on the pattern of movement and the effort required to perform it.

2. *Pattern of Movement.*   This must be well known and understood by the patient.   It can be taught by passive movement or in the case of limb movements by active movement of the contralateral limb.

3. *Fixation.*   Adequate fixation of the bone of origin of the prime

movers improves their efficiency. Whenever possible this fixation should be achieved by active means in order that the weak muscles may receive reinforcement from the action of those muscles with which they normally associate for the production of voluntary movement. When there is a tendency for movement to be transferred to neighbouring joints to compensate for the inefficiency of the weak muscles, movement in these joints must be controlled or 'held back' by manual pressure or other means of fixation, so that the movement is pivoted at the required joint.

4. *Support.* The part of the body moved is supported throughout to reduce the load on the weakened muscles by counterbalancing the effects of the force of gravity. This support may be provided by the physiotherapist's hands, suspension slings, a polished horizontal surface such as a re-education board, the buoyancy of water or ball-bearing skates. The advantage of manual support is that it can be effective in whichever plane is most suitable for the movement and the assistance adjusted to what is required in each successive part of the range.

5. *The Antagonistic Muscles.* Every effort must be made to reduce tension in the muscles which are antagonistic to the movement. The starting position for the movement should be chosen to ensure that tension in these muscles is minimal, e.g. a position in which the knee is flexed is suitable for assisted dorsiflexion of the foot.

6. *Traction.* Preliminary stretching of the weak muscles to elicit the myotatic (stretch) reflex provides a powerful stimulus to contraction. Other means of facilitating the activity of the muscles may also be used.

7. *The Assisting Force.* The force used to augment the action of the muscles is applied in the direction of the movement, preferably by means of the physiotherapist's hands, which should be placed in such a way that they rest on the surface of the patient's skin which is in the direction of the movement. In some cases the patient's own hands may be substituted for those of the physiotherapist, provided he thoroughly understands the procedure.

The range of movement is as full as possible, but as the power of muscles varies in different parts of their range more assistance will be necessary in some parts than in others. In general, most assistance is required to overcome the initial inertia at the beginning of movement and at the end to complete the range. The assistance provided by mechanical means varies in different parts of the range according to definite physical laws and therefore it cannot be adjusted to meet the precise requirements of the muscles, with the result that their maximum effort is rarely elicited and all too frequently the movement becomes passive in character.

8. *The Character of the Movement*.   The movement is essentially smooth as this is characteristic of efficient voluntary movement and it is performed in response to a forceful command which demands the patient's full attention.   The speed of movement depends on the muscles involved as each has its own optimum rate of contraction which varies according to its structure and the load.   Generally speaking fusiform muscles contract rapidly and multipennate ones take longer.   Very weak muscles cannot be expected to produce a sustained contraction and therefore assistance is given 'in step' with the contraction which may only be evident as a flicker in the early stages but as power increases the speed of the movement can be decreased.

9. *Repetitions*.   The number of times the movement is repeated depends on whether it is considered advisable or injurious to fatigue the muscles in question; therefore the condition which has caused the weakness must be known and understood.

10. *The co-operation of the patient* is essential during this type of exercise, the aim being for him to achieve controlled active movement without assistance.   Concentrated effort is needed to encourage the muscles to do all they can to help the movement, so praise, well earned, should not be stinted.   The ability to see results and to feel what is happening is a great help to the patient so he can be encouraged to palpate his muscles as they contract.

Effects and Uses of Assisted Exercise

(*i*) The working muscles co-operate in the production of movement which they are incapable of achieving unaided.   Provided the maximum effort of which they are capable is demanded from the weak muscles and the assisting force utilised is only complementary, these muscles will gain in strength and hypertrophy.

This type of exercise may be used in the early stages of neuromuscular re-education.

(*ii*) The memory of the pattern of co-ordinated movement is stimulated by the correct performance of a movement which the patient is unable to achieve without assistance.   By frequent repetition of the correct pattern with decreasing assistance, the patient may relearn to control the movement himself as the conduction of impulses is facilitated in the neuromuscular pathways.

Assisted exercise may therefore be helpful in training co-ordination.

(*iii*) Confidence in the ability to move is established when the patient observes the movement and the fact that his muscles co-operate in producing it.   The knowledge that the limb is supported throughout and that the movement attempted will be achieved encourages the patient to make a maximum effort.

When movement must be maintained in spite of pain in joints these exercises are very useful, e.g. in Rheumatoid Arthritis.

(*iv*) The range of effective joint movement may be increased by assisted exercise; however, as both range and control are often dependent on the efficiency of the muscles working over that joint, a technique which utilises resisted exercise for these muscles is usually preferable.

Assisted-resisted Exercise

This type of exercise constitutes a combination of assistance and resistance during a single movement and whenever it is possible it is preferable to Assisted Exercise as it meets the needs of the muscles with greater accuracy.

Resisted Exercise

The Principles of Resistance

An external force may be applied to the body levers to oppose the force of muscular contraction. Tension is increased within the muscles by the opposing force (or resistance) and the muscles respond by an increase in their power and hypertrophy. As the increase in muscular development occurs in response to the increase in intra-muscular tension it follows that the application of the maximum resistance which is consistent with the ability of the muscles to overcome it will elicit the maximum development.

The resisting force applied to an isotonic contraction must be sufficient to increase intra-muscular tension to the maximum without interfering with the ability of the muscles to produce co-ordinated movement. A maximum increase in intra-muscular tension during an isometric contraction is elicited by a resistance which equals the muscles' ability to maintain the hold.

There are five factors which contribute to the development of muscular efficiency, i.e. power, endurance, volume, speed of contraction and co-ordination. The first three are inter-related and can be built up by the use of resisted exercise.

Power develops in response to the application of the maximum resistance which is consistent with the ability of the muscles to overcome it, therefore power can be built up when they work against a progressively increasing resistance. As the essential factor in power development is the magnitude of the resistance the method used to promote it is called Progressive Resistance–Low Repetition Exercise, the number of times the movement is repeated being relatively few to allow the resistance to be as great as possible.

Endurance is a quality which develops in response to repetitive contraction, therefore as it is the number of contractions which is the essential factor, the method used in this case is called LOW RESISTANCE-HIGH REPETITION EXERCISE.

Volume, which can be observed or measured as an indication of hypertrophy, usually develops in proportion to power. It serves as a means of demonstrating progress to the patient although it is not invariably a reliable indication of successful treatment.

Skill in estimating the capacity of the muscles at every stage of treatment and in matching this with the correct amount of resistance is the keynote to success in the use of resisted exercise.

Variation of the Power of Muscles in Different Parts of their Range

Muscles which are capable of producing a considerable range of joint movement are not equally powerful in all parts of their range.

Physiologically, muscles are capable of exerting their greatest strength when they are fully extended, i.e. in outer range, and as they shorten their force diminishes. This, however, is modified in the case of some muscles by mechanical factors such as the angle of pull of the tendon of insertion, i.e. the effect of the pull on the lever is greatest when the angle of pull approaches a right angle.

For example: physiologically the Flexors of the Elbow are strongest in their outer range, but mechanically strongest at about mid-range. When both these factors are taken into account, and allowance is made for overcoming the initial inertia at the beginning of the movement, it can be roughly estimated that the muscles will be most efficient in the outer part of the middle range. This, in fact, can be proved by experiment.

It seems, however, that the relative importance of these factors varies in different muscle groups but, broadly speaking, each group is found to be most powerful in the part of the range in which it is habitually used, i.e. Shoulder Flexors in outer range, Hip Extensors in inner range. In giving manual resistance these variations in power can be felt and the resistance adjusted accordingly, but other means of providing resistance are not so accurate from this point of view.

Technique of Resisted Exercises

1. *Starting Position.* Comfort and stability for the body as a whole ensures that the patient's whole attention can be concentrated on the pattern of movement and the effort required to overcome the resistance.

2. *The Pattern of Movement.* This must be well known by the patient and can be taught as passively or a free exercise. The pattern selected should, whenever possible, be one which allows contraction of

the muscles in full range and it should be based on a natural pattern of purposeful movement.

3. *Stabilisation.* Stabilisation of the bone or bones of origin of the muscles to be resisted improves their efficiency. This stabilisation is rarely static when a natural pattern of movement is used as it is constantly being adapted to the circumstances of the movement. Provided the muscles normally responsible for the stabilisation have remained efficient they should be used for this purpose, as their action is considered to provide reinforcement for the muscles producing the movement. If, however, there is a tendency for movement to be transferred to neighbouring joints so that the pattern of movement is altered, then additional means of fixation such as manual pressure or a strap must be used to ensure movement at the required joint.

4. *Traction.* Preliminary stretching of the muscles to elicit the myotatic (stretch) reflex provides a powerful stimulus to contraction, and traction maintained throughout the range facilitates joint movement and maintains tension on the muscles and so augments the effect of the resisting force.

5. *The Resisting Force.* A variety of means may be employed to supply the force used to resist the contraction of the working muscles, e.g. manual pressure, weights, springs, etc., but in every case it should be applied in a manner which ensures that pressure is exerted on the surface of the patient's skin which is in the direction of the movement. The advantage of manual pressure is that it can be adjusted accurately to match the power of the muscles in all circumstances and in every part of the range, but it also has the disadvantage of not being easily measurable. Mechanical resistances are usually measurable and therefore provide a useful means of recording progress.

The magnitude of the resisting force, in relation to that of the muscle power, varies according to the purpose for which it is used. Maximal resistance elicits maximal effort on the part of the muscles and it is therefore used to develop power and hypertrophy. As the quality of muscular endurance is developed by repeated contraction against resistance the latter is considerably less than maximal to allow a greater number of repetitions to take place.

6. *The Character of the Movement.* The movement is essentially smooth and controlled throughout, the effort involved commanding the patient's full attention. The speed of movement is consistent with the optimum rate of contraction for the particular group of muscles in relation to the resistance which constitutes the load. The range of movement is full whenever possible, but resistance can be applied in any part of the range which is convenient or desirable and the muscles can also be resisted so that they work statically at any particular point in their range.

7. *Repetitions.* The number of times the muscles are thrown into action against a resistance varies according to the condition and the individual patient, and it is inadvisable to accept any rule of thumb procedure.

Low Resistance–High Repetition exercises appear to be more suitable for weak or elderly patients whose muscles are less resilient than those of the young and strong, and they have proved to be effective in such conditions as Osteo-arthritis. High Resistance–Low Repetition exercises on the other hand undoubtedly build up power and hypertrophy muscles suffering from disuse as the result of traumatic injury or in connection with orthopaedic surgery, e.g. meniscectomy. When there is effusion or joint changes are present, as in Rheumatoid Arthritis, static resisted contraction of the muscles passing over the joint with a high repetition figure are valuable for retaining muscular efficiency and they can be performed in any part of the range which is pain-free. The number of repetitions may also be determined by the desirability of, or the contraindication to, fatiguing the neuromuscular mechanism in the treatment of a specific condition.

8. *The Co-operation of the Patient.* The effort exerted by the patient and his interest in the treatment undoubtedly play an important part in the development of his muscles by means of resisted exercise. Interest is stimulated by precision in applying the resistance, regular measurement and recording of progress, verbal encouragement and, in suitable cases, by competition.

Resistances

A resisting force other than that provided by gravity and friction may be provided by:

1. The physiotherapist
2. The patient.
3. Weights
4. Weight and pulley circuits
5. Springs and other elastic structures
6. Substances which are malleable
7. Water

1. *Resistance by the Physiotherapist.* This is usually applied manually in the line of the movement, and the physiotherapist's hand is placed on the surface of the skin which is in the direction of the movement. To prevent waste of effort and to ensure smooth controlled pressure the physiotherapist's stance must be in the line of the movement, so that the thrusting action of the legs and the body weight are utilised. Traction or approximation may be maintained throughout the movement and the resistance varied according to the variations in power in different parts of the muscle's range.

2. *Resistance by the Patient.* The patient can resist his own movements with the sound limb, or by using his own body weight. The

latter method is probably more accurately classified as a free exercise, but is included here as the quantity of resistance is obviously much

Forward pressure   Pull & counter pressure   Downward pressure

FIG. 37. The Physiotherapist's Stance

greater when, as in this case, the muscles work with reversed origin and insertion to move the trunk on the limbs. This type of resistance is convenient, but tends to be unreliable as it cannot be measured or felt by the physiotherapist and it requires careful instruction and the co-operation and understanding of the patient.

EXAMPLES. From *high sitting* the Extensors of one Knee can be resisted by the weight and pressure of the other leg when the ankles

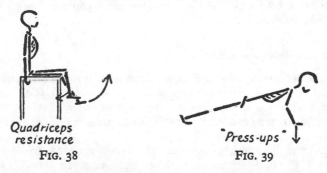

Quadriceps resistance   "Press-ups"

FIG. 38   FIG. 39

are crossed. The body can be pressed up from the floor by the arms, if their strength is sufficient.

3. *Resistance by Weights.* The direct application of weights to the body forms a simple and effective method of resisting active exercise The apparatus required is commonly sandbags, metal weights or a medicine ball, which can be applied by being held in the hand, by attachment to a shoe, or to any other part, by suitable straps. When sandbags or metal weights are used, a canvas bag may be strapped to the part and any number of units of weight can be inserted to provide the required resistance. It is essential that the means of attachment should be comfortable and efficient, but it need not be elaborate.

By this method, resistance must, of necessity, be given in the direction of gravity; its effect increases progressively if the weight is moved away from the central axis of the body.   It is a convenient method

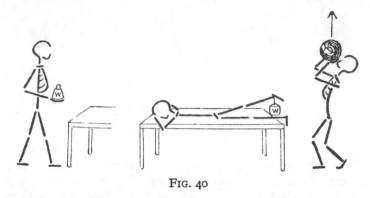

FIG. 40

and suitable for home practice after adequate instruction has been given.

EXAMPLES.   Lifting a weight held in the hand or attached to the foot or throwing a medicine ball are common examples.

Resistance by weights is also used for the technique known as Progressive Resistance Exercise.

PROGRESSIVE RESISTANCE EXERCISE

The use of Progressive Resistance Exercise for the restoration of muscle power and volume after injury was first described by de Lorme in 1945 although this method of promoting muscular development had been well known and used by professional muscle builders for a very long time.

Metal weights, which constitute the resisting force, are applied to the part of the body in question either by means of a bar-bell held in the hand or hands, a de Lorme metal boot or some similar device.   The poundage is determined by testing the repetition maximum (R.M.) for a given number of repetitions (page 30).   Lifting of the weight may involve either static (isometric) or dynamic (isotonic) muscle work according to the circumstances and the movement is slow and controlled.

Several ways of correlating the weight lifted and the number of repetitions have been used.   It appears that the regime most suitable and successful in the treatment of an individual patient varies very much with his age, temperament and the condition from which he is suffering.   It is essential that his instruction is precise and that his efforts are well supervised. The following schemes are all based on the test for a 10 R.M. and represent a power programme. Imperial measures can be replaced by metric units.

de Lorme & Watkins
10 lifts with ½ 10 R.M.
10 lifts with ¾ 10 R.M.
10 lifts with 10 R.M.

Zinovieff (Oxford Technique)
10 lifts with 10 R.M.
10 lifts with 10 R.M. minus 1 lb.
10 lifts with 10 R.M. ,, 2 lbs.
10 lifts with 10 R.M. ,, 3 lbs.
10 lifts with 10 R.M. ,, 4 lbs.
10 lifts with 10 R.M. ,, 5 lbs.
10 lifts with 10 R.M. ,, 6 lbs.
10 lifts with 10 R.M. ,, 7 lbs.
10 lifts with 10 R.M. ,, 8 lbs.
10 lifts with 10 R.M. ,, 9 lbs.

30 lifts 4 times weekly.
Progress 10 R.M. once weekly.

100 lifts 5 times weekly.
Progress 10 R.M. daily.

MacQueen
10 lifts with 10 R.M.
10 lifts with 10 R.M.
10 lifts with 10 R.M.
10 lifts with 10 R.M.
40 lifts 3 times weekly.
Progress 10 R.M. every 1–2 weeks.

The endurance programme is based on the use of relatively low resistance and high repetition regime.

Progressive resistance exercise can be used in principle for the development of most muscle groups but it is at present more often used for the Knee Extensors than any other group. Some suggestions with regard to suitable positions and methods are therefore described in relation to these muscles on page 192. 】

4. *Resistance by Weight and Pulley Circuits.* The use of a rope and pulley allows the force exerted by a weight to act in any direction (see Pulleys, p. 15), therefore the muscles need not be required to work against the resistance of both gravity and the weight. The effect of gravity can be counterbalanced if the movement takes place in a horizontal plane. This provides a useful method of arranging resistance for weak muscles when the limb is heavy.

EXAMPLE. In *sitting* the resistance of gravity to the Knee Extensors is approximately 5 kg. If these muscles are unable to straighten the knee against this resistance, they may still be able to perform the exercise adequately when, in *side lying*, the leg is supported horizontally and a resistance of, perhaps, 4 kg. is applied.

As the angle of pull of the rope by which it is applied, and therefore the resistance itself, must vary during the course of a movement, a resistance can be offered to the muscles which matches the variation of their power in different parts of the range more accurately than that supplied by means of a weight applied directly to the part or by a spring.

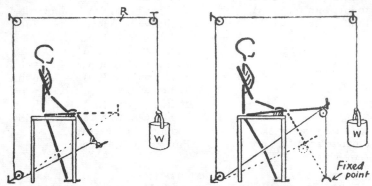

FIG. 41.   Two Methods of giving Weight and Pulley Resistance for the Knee Extensors.   The relaxation stop R is shown on the left

Assuming that a particular muscle group is most powerful in mid-range it is there that the resistance is applied at right angles.   Both the power of the muscles and the force of the resistance will diminish on either side of this point.

To ensure relaxation and lack of strain on the joints between movements a *relaxation stop* is incorporated on the circuit by means of a clip or knot which prevents the rope from passing the pulley, or by arranging for the weight to be supported at the end of the movement.   Psychologically, it is of the greatest importance for the patient to be able to see the weight moving as the result of his work and to know and record the poundage lifted.

5. *Resistance by Springs and Other Elastic Substances.*   The resisting force of a spring increases progressively as it is stretched or compressed according to the type of spring used.

Although convenient to arrange, the use of springs for resisting muscular contraction must be regarded as a somewhat crude method as it is virtually impossible to match their resistance to the capacity of the muscles with regard to both power and range of movement.

When springs are used the speed of movement must be carefully controlled by the muscles both in contraction and during controlled relaxation as the accumulated energy in an extended spring makes its natural speed of recoil very great.

Other extensible materials such as rubber elastic of various widths and thicknesses behave in a manner similar to that of springs, but they are not so durable. The elastic properties of Sorbo rubber are apparent on pressure, and rubber sponges, Dunlopillo and rubber balls

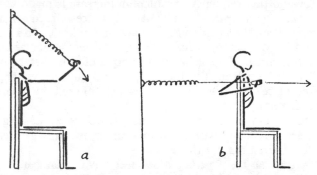

FIG. 42. Spring Resistance for the Elbow Extensors
(*a*) with shoulder extension, (*b*) with shoulder flexion

afford varying resistances which are particularly useful in developing the gripping muscles of the hand.

6. *Resistance by Substances which are Malleable.* Substances such as putty, clay, some kinds of wax, Plasticine and wet sand can be moulded into different shapes. The resistance they offer to this change in form is variable and can be used both for strengthening and for mobilising the hands.

7. *Resistance by Water.* The resistance offered by water increases with the speed and the surface area of the part moved. When the movement is vertical, buoyancy adds to the resistance on the way down and cancels out much of the resistance on the way up.

Progression

As the power of the muscle increases, the resistance must be increased proportionately.

There are four main methods of increasing resistance to muscle action. Each method may be used singly or in combination with any other method:

1. Increase in poundage or weight of the resisting force.
2. Increase in leverage of the resisting force.
3. Alteration in the speed of movement.
4. Increase in the duration of the exercise.

1. *Increase in Poundage or Weight.* For example: it is found that a muscle group, able to achieve full-range contraction against a weight of 2 kg. when it is applied at a specific point, can contract at a specific speed and for a specific duration. As the muscle power increases, the

weight is increased proportionately to 2.5 kg., 3 kg. or 4 kg., while the other conditions remain constant.   The actual amount of the increase is variable according to the particular muscle group, its rate of progress to recovery and the frequency at which an increase is made.

2. *Increase in Leverage.*   The total resistance offered by a given weight depends on the position of its point of application in relation to the fulcrum.   (Moment of Force = Weight × Perpendicular Distance from the fulcrum.)   The greater the perpendicular distance of the point of application from the fulcrum, i.e. the joint at which movement takes place, the greater the resistance offered by the weight (see p. 10, Levers).

EXAMPLE.   The effect of a resistance, which is constant, given to the Shoulder Abductors with the arm straight, is much greater when applied at the wrist than at the elbow.

3. *Alteration in the Speed of Movement.*   Muscular contraction is most efficient when it takes place at an optimum or natural speed. This speed varies according to the form and structure of the muscles concerned, the resistance, and the individual.   Increase or decrease in this natural speed of contraction increases the effect of the resistance when the muscle works concentrically, but when it works eccentrically, the slower the movement the greater the effect of the resistance, i.e. concentric work is easiest at natural speed, eccentric work at high speeds.

For example: it is easier to climb a steep hill at your own speed than at one dictated by a companion who may prefer to go faster or slower than you do, but it is easier to come down rapidly.

4. *Increase in the Duration.*   As muscles warm up to their task of overcoming a resistance, they become more efficient and therefore the effect of the resistance decreases and the exercise seems easier.   If, however, it is continued a sufficient number of times, fatigue reduces the efficiency of the muscles and the resistance therefore appears greater.

For example: sawing a log of wood may seem to become easier as you warm up to it, but it becomes hard work by the end of an hour.

Effects and Uses of Resisted Exercises

(*i*) Muscle power can only be maintained or increased by contraction, and in these exercises the working muscles are strengthened and hypertrophied in response to the tension created in them by the resistance.   Their power and endurance is increased.

Resisted exercises are used to build up weak muscles and so to restore the balance of muscle power which is essential for stability and co-ordinated movement.

(*ii*) The blood flow to the working muscles is increased in proportion to the amount of work they are called upon to do thus providing the materials for repair and hypertrophy.

Although the flow is impeded during the actual contraction, the amount of blood contained in the muscles immediately after contraction may be as much as ten times as great during strenuous exercise as the amount contained during rest.

This increase in the blood flow to the muscles continues for some time after exercise, bringing oxygen and nutrition to the part and assisting the removal of metabolic products.

(*iii*) A general rise in blood pressure frequently anticipates exercise and may be increased by the mental effort required to perform these exercises correctly.

(*iv*) Heat, which is produced as the result of strenuous muscular activity, stimulates the heat-regulating centre causing vaso-dilatation in the skin. This follows a constriction of these vessels which occurs in the first place to compensate for the increase in the blood flow to the muscles. If there has been sufficient exercise, the skin feels warm and possibly moist and appears pink, indicating that heat is being lost from the surface to balance the gain from muscle activity and so keep the body temperature within normal limits. The degree of moisture depends largely on the temperature, humidity and movement of the atmosphere.

INVOLUNTARY MOVEMENT

REFLEX MOVEMENT

Reflex movement is involuntary and may be defined as the motor response to sensory stimulation. These reflex movements are protective in character or concerned with the repetition of movement patterns which have become automatic or habitual. Although the stimuli which give rise to reflex movements do not usually gain conscious recognition the patient is aware that reflex movements of the body *have taken place.*

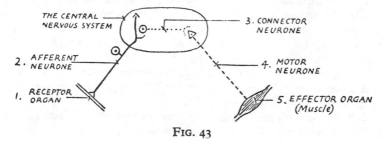

FIG. 43

The Reflex Arc

The reflex arc is the pathway of impulses which give rise to reflex activity. In its most simple form it consists of two neurones, an afferent neurone which leads from a sensory receptor organ to the C.N.S. and an efferent neurone leading from the C.N.S. to the effector organ (muscle fibres). Few reflex arcs are as simple as this, most of them consisting of a chain of neurones in which one or several connecting neurones lie between the afferent and efferent neurones.

Reflex activity can be stimulated and used to improve or facilitate movement or the maintenance of posture.

The Stretch Reflex

This is a spinal reflex activated by stretching a muscle. When an innervated muscle is stretched it responds by contracting and developing tension to counteract the stretching force; this provides a means of promoting activity in muscles when voluntary effort is ineffective or too weak to do so. Quick stretching stimulates the muscle spindles which are proprioceptive receptors so that they discharge impulses which reach the A.H.C.'s by mono-synaptic pathways. Tension in a contracting muscle is increased by the application of a resisting force and the quality of the contraction is improved. Contraction of muscles in response to stretch is accompanied by a reciprocal inhibition of antagonistic muscles to permit movement.

The Righting Reflexes

These are a series of reflexes concerned with the maintenance and restoration of equilibrium. Pushing the patient off balance elicits a series of mass movements designed to restore balance and save him from falling. This is well illustrated in *Practical Exercise Therapy* by M. Hollis.

The Postural Reflexes

The erect posture is maintained by a complex series of reflexes known collectively as the Postural Reflexes; these are described on p. 246.

Effects and Uses of Reflex Movement

1. The initiation of reflex movement provides a means of promoting activity of the neuromuscular mechanism when voluntary effort is ineffective or insufficient for the purpose. It is used in cases of flaccid paralysis and brain damage to facilitate the initiation of movement and to combat the effects of inactivity.

2. Normal joint movement and the extensibility of muscles is maintained by this type of movement when spastic paralysis makes voluntary movement impossible.

3. Circulation is improved by the contraction of muscles and movement of joints achieved during these movements.

4. Temporary relaxation of spastic muscles is obtained following repeated movements of this type by means of reciprocal innervation. This may provide the opportunity for the development of voluntary ability to perform movement in cases of spastic paralysis.

5. Postural reflexes are conditioned to reproduce a satisfactory pattern of posture by repeated use of these patterns. This is the basis of postural re-education.

6

RELAXATION

MUSCLES which are relatively free from tension and at rest are said to be relaxed. Tension develops in muscles as they work during contraction and this tension is reduced to a variable degree as the muscles come to rest during relaxation.

Muscle Tone

Under ordinary circumstances living muscles are never completely free from tension, as they retain a quality of firmness known as muscle tone even when they are as relaxed as possible.

Muscle tone, which represents a state of preparedness in resting muscles, is now thought to be maintained through the activity of the muscle spindle circuit. The efferent fibres of this small fibre nervous reflex pathway transmit impulses which produce a sustained contraction of the small intrafusal muscle fibres of the muscle spindles, while the large extrafusal fibres concerned in the production of voluntary movement remain relaxed.

Postural Tone

The contraction which persists in the muscles concerned with the maintenance of posture (chiefly the anti-gravity muscles) is called postural tone. Postural tone is maintained and regulated by a reflex mechanism, the fundamental basis of which is the myotatic or stretch reflex, although the higher centres also exert a controlling influence. Any stretching of the muscles by an external force, such as the force of gravity, stimulates sensory receptors situated within the muscles themselves and so gives rise to a discharge of motor impulses to the same muscles. These motor impulses bring about a contraction of a sufficient number of the muscles' motor units to increase the tension sufficiently to enable the effects of the force which produced the stretching to be counterbalanced.

As tension in these muscles is increased in response to stretching of their constituent fibres by an external force, and in proportion to the degree of stretching to which they are subjected, it follows that the use of measures tending to reduce or eliminate the effect of this force assists in promoting their relaxation.

The degree and location of postural tone varies with any alteration in posture. It is greater in the upright positions, in which the force of gravity tends to stretch the muscles more strongly, than it is in recumbent positions, in which the effects of the force of gravity upon them is adequately counterbalanced by full support of the body. Those recumbent positions which provide full support for all segments of the body are therefore most suitable for obtaining general relaxation.

Voluntary Movement

Specific muscles contract as they work to initiate or control movement, but at the completion of the movement in question they relax and come to rest. There is a recognised biological principle that activity of living cells tends to be followed by inhibition of that activity. Contraction in any one group of muscles is accompanied by a reciprocal relaxation of the antagonistic group to allow movement to take place smoothly. These facts are of importance during consideration of methods designed to obtain relaxation of a particular group of muscles.

Mental Attitudes

Mental attitudes such as fear, anger and excitement give rise to a general increase in muscular tension which serves a useful purpose by preparing the muscles for rapid or forceful action.

Normally this tension, developed to serve a useful purpose, is relaxed when the need for it no longer exists, but in some cases it persists and becomes habitual which may lead to alterations in normal posture.

Recognition of a state of tension followed by voluntary relaxation of the muscles in which it is present provide a means of helping the patient to economise in nervous energy, and in cases where the tension has resulted in the reduction of the normal range of movement in a joint, an increase in mobility can be achieved.

As fear in one form or another is the most usual cause of persistent tension, the physiotherapist must do her best to reassure the patient and to gain his confidence and co-operation. An atmosphere conducive to rest, both mental and physical, contributes much to success in helping the patient to acquire the art of voluntary relaxation.

Degrees of Relaxation

The degree to which muscular tension can be reduced is very variable and it is better to regard the term 'Relaxation' merely as an indication that some reduction in tension has taken place. It is often possible to estimate the degree of relaxation achieved by gentle passive movement or by palpating the muscles, as for instance during massage, and the fact that a patient falls to sleep during treatment is ample proof that the method of obtaining general relaxation has been successful.

Pathological Tension in Muscles

A marked, persistent increase in muscular tension or tone is a feature of many pathological conditions which affect the nervous system. Lesions of the higher motor centres, and those which interfere with the normal function of the nervous pathways which connect them with the spinal reflex arc, commonly result in an abnormal state of muscular tension which varies from hypertonicity to spasticity or rigidity. A temporary reduction in this tension in the affected area can be achieved in some cases by suitable means which promote relaxation, and this allows re-education of any functional activity which remains to take place.

TECHNIQUE

GENERAL RELAXATION

Support, comfort and a restful atmosphere are basic conditions for general relaxation and may prove effective without additional methods.

a. *Support*

Various forms and modifications of the *lying* position are used, to achieve full support of the body, the relative suitability of each one varying according to the condition of the patient and to individual preference. The weight of the body is thus effectively counterbalanced by the uniform upward pressure of a reciprocal surface, or by suspension, in a position of semi-flexion which obviates all mechanical tension on muscles or ligaments.

(i) *Lying Supine.* A firm surface is essential, and if resilient also, as in the case of a good spring mattress, it is ideal, as it will mould itself to the body contours and give even pressure and comfort. At all costs plinths or beds which sag are to be avoided as they cramp the thorax and so throw additional strain on the inspiratory muscles. A head

pillow is required which is sufficiently soft to prevent the head from rolling to either side, and to be well moulded to support the neck posteriorly. A small pillow

FIG. 44. *lying supine* for Relaxation

under the knees relieves tension on the Hamstrings and the ilio-femoral

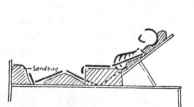

FIG. 45. *half lying* adapted for Relaxation

FIG. 46. *half lying.* Another method

ligament, and consequently allows the pelvis to roll backwards so that the lumbar spine is straightened and supported. The feet are held in the mid-position by a sandbag or similar device, and each arm, slightly abducted at the shoulder and flexed at the elbow, rests on a pillow.

(*ii*) *Half Lying*. This is similar to the previous position but breathing is easier as there is less weight on the back and abdominal pressure on the under surface of the Diaphragm is reduced.

An armchair makes quite a good substitute for a plinth or bed, the thighs are fully supported and the feet rest on the floor, or a footstool, or a T-shaped footrest.

(*iii*) *Prone Lying*. The head is turned to one side and may rest on a small pillow, if more comfortable. A firm pillow under the hips and the lower abdomen prevents hollowing of the back, and for women it should extend higher to avoid too much pressure on the breasts; the

FIG. 47
prone lying as for Relaxation

lower leg is elevated so that the knees are slightly bent and the toes free. A degree of medial rotation at the hips, causing the heels to fall apart, still further induces relaxation of the legs. Many find this position comfortable and use it for sleeping; others dislike it because of the rotated position of the head.

(*iv*) *Side Lying*. The measure of relaxation obtained is governed by

FIG. 48. *side lying* for Relaxation
(view from above)

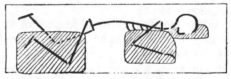

the efficiency with which the shoulder and pelvic girdles are stabilised. The arm and leg which are uppermost may be rested on the supporting surface instead of on pillows, but some of the weight then falls on the trunk and this impedes respiration. The head pillow supports the neck and head in alignment with the body, and must not be too high. The majority of people sleep on the side, but few are conscious of the part suitable positioning for relaxation plays in promoting it.

b. *Comfort*

In addition to support and individual preference in positioning, for which some suggestions have already been made, the ingredients of comfort include freedom to breathe deeply, warmth, abdominal quiescence and a mild degree of physical fatigue. Removal of constrictive clothing, such as corsets and belts, is essential and any garters, buttons or suspenders liable to cause pressure must be removed. The room should be warm, but should have a free supply of fresh air; in winter additional warmth can be supplied by light but warm blankets, a covered hot-water bottle at the feet, an electric blanket or by non-luminous infra-red irradiation, but care being taken to avoid over-heating, as this leads to restlessness. For home use a warm bath gives the most even and pleasing type of heat, but its soothing effect must not be ruined subsequently by vigorous rubbing with a towel. A light well-balanced meal, rhythmical physical activity of short duration, such as a brisk walk in the open air, and attention to emptying the bladder before treatment are all conducive to general relaxation.

c. *Restful Atmosphere*

As physical and mental relaxation are interdependent, an effort must be made to secure a state of mental rest. The treatment-room should be as quiet as possible, as many people for whom training in relaxation is prescribed are highly susceptible to the disturbing influence of noise. A few are worried by complete silence, but in general it is the high-pitched intermittent sound produced close at hand which is to be avoided; the continuous low-pitched 'hum' of distant traffic tends to be soothing. Bright lights and strong colours, such as red and bright yellow, are said to be stimulating, whereas a room with low well-diffused light with for instance green and peach furnishings gives a soft and warm glow and provides an ideal setting for relaxation. This is indeed a counsel of perfection, but much can be done with screens and shades used with a little imagination, even in a busy department!

The most difficult and important factor in the creation of a restful atmosphere, and one which determines the ultimate success or failure of the treatment, is the manner and bearing of the physiotherapist. She must inspire confidence, as fear, in one form or another, is at the root of much of the tension which she can help to relieve. Her appearance must be tidy and her dress suitable; she must be punctual and move calmly without hurry or hesitation. Her manner must be courteous, pleasant and understanding and her voice low-pitched and clear. A simple explanation of the routine and any instructions required are given to the patient in language and terms which he can understand, so that any anxiety or fear of the unknown is removed. It must be remembered that situations and routines with which one becomes very familiar often appear strange and terrifying when encountered for the first time. Conversation, apart from these instructions, should direct the patient's thoughts to contemplation of restful and pleasant topics.

Confidence in the physiotherapist and the treatment is gradually built up over a period of time; immediate results are not to be expected and are rarely achieved, often because of psychological factors beyond the control of the physiotherapist or patient. In successful cases a habit of relaxation is built up in place of a habit of tension, but the formation of new habits takes time. Regular and frequent practice on the part of the patient is essential, until finally he becomes an expert in the art of 'letting go' or relaxing, and the normal rhythm of life, in which activity alternates with relaxation, can be re-established.

d. *Additional Methods of promoting Relaxation*

Tension may persist in spite of the provision of conditions conducive to relaxation, in which case additional methods to help the patient may be employed. Very little should be attempted at first, the period of time being extended as the ability to relax improves.

Consciousness of Breathing. Under conditions of quiet and comfort the patient's mind may remain active and turn to mundane problems and anxieties, with associated physical tension; in this case it may help him to concentrate on his own rhythm of breathing, which must be deep with a slight pause at the end of expiration. Expiration is a phase of relaxation and should be accompanied by a feeling of 'letting go' in the whole body.

Progressive Relaxation. A method by which relaxation may be achieved progressively was devised and practised by Jacobson of Chicago, and something similar appears in modern literature on the Yoga System as the 'Savasana' or 'Still Pose'.

FIG. 49
'Savasana'—'The Still Pose'

Contrast Method. Difficulty in appreciating the sensation of relaxation is not uncommon; the patient does not know that the muscles are tense or what to do in order to relax them. This can often be taught by demonstrating the contrast between maximal contraction and the degree of relaxation which follows it, the patient being told to contract any group or series of muscles as strongly as possible and then to 'let go' and 'continue to let go'. Success may be achieved by another method by which the patient is urged to step up this preliminary contraction until he is so tired that he has to let go; there is a large element of suggestion about this as it is unlikely and undesirable that a state of fatigue should actually be produced. This method follows the biological principle that activity of living cells tends to be followed by inhibition of that activity.

Routine contraction followed by relaxation is carried out in each area of the body, the attention travelling in logical sequence from limb to limb and to the trunk and head including the neck and face muscles until all areas can remain relaxed at one and the same time. Much practice may be necessary before this is accomplished, and it is not unusual for the muscles of the leg, for instance, to again become tense while attention has been focused on relaxation of the face muscles. Before the routine has been completed, the patient frequently drops off to sleep and general relaxation is obtained. When possible he should be allowed to wake naturally; alternatively, he must be wakened gently in sufficient time for getting up and dressing to be unhurried. Later, the patient learns to relax the muscles at will from the state of tension in which they are normally maintained, and without previous voluntary contraction.

Physiological Relaxation. This method of relieving tension was devised by Laura Mitchell, M.C.S.P., Dip.T.P., in 1957. It is based on the physiological principle of reciprocal relaxation.

The position of tension of the whole body is defined in detail, *viz.* raised shoulders, bent-up elbows and hands, head and trunk flexed, etc. The patient changes the position of every joint in turn, by exact voluntary orders which he is taught to give to his own body, e.g., 'Stretch the fingers out long', 'Stop', 'Feel the straightened-out fingers and the fingertips touching the support'.

In this way, the patient induces, firstly, reciprocal relaxation in the muscles that had been working to maintain the tense positions, and then in the opposite group which he used to change that position. He registers the new position of the joints and skin pressures associated with them because these two senses reach the cortex. In this way, he changes the pattern of tension of the whole body to one of ease by means of a method which he can use by himself at any time, and so can stop mounting tension.

A full description of this method and its application to various conditions, e.g., chest, antenatal, etc., is given in *Simple Relaxation* by Laura Mitchell, 2nd edition, 1980.

Passive Movement. Rhythmical passive movements of the limbs and head may assist the degree of general relaxation in some cases. These movements are generally given as a sequel to massage. Group movements of joints, e.g. flexion and extension of hip, knee and ankle, are preferable, but a very high standard of performance on the part of the physiotherapist is required to obtain results. The rhythm of small pendular movements pleases some patients.

The ability to promote a state of relaxation depends very largley on the individual physiotherapist and the particular patient with whom she is dealing, and details of successful methods employed vary widely. Ideal conditions are rarely obtainable and, indeed, are hardly desirable, for many patients must eventually learn to relax where and when the opportunity presents itself, e.g. in the train or on a mountain top after a strenuous climb. General relaxation can sometimes be carried out effectively in groups, as in the case of pregnant women, who tend to relax easily, and with some asthmatic and bronchitic sufferers who have had previous individual instruction.

LOCAL RELAXATION

General relaxation takes time and is not always essential or desirable. Methods of obtaining local relaxation depend to some extent on the cause and distribution of the tension.

Preparatory to Massage and Passive Movement

Massage and passive movement both presuppose relaxation of the area under treatment. Relaxation is obtained of a specific area by the application to that area of the general principles already described for the whole body. A general attitude of rest, however, will assist the process, e.g. the abducted and flexed arm supported by a table or slings is more inclined to relax when the patient lies or reclines in a chair, than when he sits bolt upright.

For the Relief of Spasm

Spasm due to pain is protective and is most effectively reduced by the relief of the pain which caused it. However, if it persists because of fear of pain, techniques which ensure pain-free movement are often successful. Hold-relax (see p. 89) is applicable in these circumstances, or pendular movements which start in the free range and gradually increase in amplitude may restore confidence and achieve relaxation.

The relief of pathological spasm resulting from lesions affecting the central nervous system is only temporary unless some voluntary control remains and can be re-established. Temporary relief is useful to permit the re-development of voluntary control which is masked by the spasm and to maintain joint range and circulation in the affected area. The initiation of reflex movements by the use of the stretch reflex applied at the same time as a command for the patient's voluntary effort of contraction can be used for this purpose but care must be taken to ensure that spasm which is useful is not reduced by hyperactivity of the antagonistic reflex unless sufficient voluntary power is present, e.g. extensor spasm of leg which makes it possible for the patient to stand.

In preventing and combating Adaptive Shortening

Persistent tension or hypertonicity of muscles acting upon one aspect of a joint produces a state of muscular imbalance which leads to adaptive shortening of the tense muscles and progressive lengthening and weakening of the antagonists on the opposing aspect of the joint. Both agonistic and antagonistic muscles are inefficient when this situation develops. Relaxation techniques for the shortened muscles and strengthening techniques for their antagonists are followed by integration of their reciprocal action to establish the increase in the range of movement.

7

PASSIVE MOVEMENT

These movements are produced by an external force during muscular inactivity or when muscular activity is voluntarily reduced as much as possible to permit movement.

Classification
    a. Relaxed Passive Movements, including accessory movements.
    b. Passive Manual Mobilisation Techniques
        (*i*) Mobilisations of joints
        (*ii*) Manipulations of joints
        (*iii*) Controlled sustained stretching of tightened structures

Specific Definitions
a. (*i*) *Relaxed Passive Movements*
    These are movements performed accurately and smoothly by the Physiotherapist.   A knowledge of the anatomy of joints is required. The movements are performed in the same range and direction as active movements.   The joint is moved through the existing free range and within the limits of pain.
    (*ii*) *Accessory movements*
    These occur as part of any normal joint movement but may be limited or absent in abnormal joint conditions.   They consist of gliding or rotational movements which cannot be performed in isolation as a voluntary movement but can be isolated by the physiotherapist.
b. *Passive Manual Mobilisation Techniques*
    (*i*) *Mobilisations of joints*
    These are usually small repetitive rhythmical oscillatory, localised accessory, or functional movements performed by the physiotherapist in various amplitudes within the available range, and under the patient's control.   These can be done very gently or quite strongly, and are graded according to the part of the available range in which they are performed.
    (*ii*) *Manipulations of joints performed by*
        a. Physiotherapists
    These are accurately localised, single, quick decisive movements of small amplitude and high velocity completed before the patient can stop it.

b. Surgeon/Physician

The movements are performed under anaesthesia by a surgeon, or physician to gain further range. The increase in movement must be maintained by the physiotherapist.

(iii) Controlled sustained stretching of tightened structures

Passive stretching of muscles and other soft tissues can be given to increase range of movement. Movement can be gained by stretching adhesions in these structures or by lengthening of muscle due to inhibition of the tendon protective reflex.

PRINCIPLES OF GIVING RELAXED PASSIVE MOVEMENTS

Relaxation. A brief explanation of what is to happen is given to the patient, who is then taught to relax voluntarily, except in cases of flaccid paralysis when this is unnecessary. The selection of a suitable starting position ensures comfort and support, and the bearing of the physiotherapist will do much to inspire confidence and co-operation in maintaining relaxation through the movement.

Fixation. Where movement is to be limited to a specific joint, the bone which lies proximal to it is fixed by the physiotherapist as close to the joint line as possible to ensure that the movement is localised to that joint; otherwise any decrease in the normal range is readily masked by compensatory movements occurring at other joints in the vicinity.

Support. Full and comfortable support is given to the part to be moved, so that the patient has confidence and will remain relaxed. The physiotherapist grasps the part firmly but comfortably in her hand, or it may be supported by axial suspension in slings. The latter method is particularly useful for the trunk or heavy limbs, as it frees the physiotherapist's hands to assist fixation and to perform the movement. The physiotherapist's stance must be firm and comfortable. When standing, her feet are apart and placed in the line of the movement.

Traction. Many joints allow the articular surfaces to be drawn apart by traction, which is always given in the long axis of a joint, the fixation of the bone proximal to the joint providing an opposing force to a sustained pull on the distal bone. Traction is thought to facilitate the movement by reducing interarticular friction.

Range. The range of movement is as full as the condition of the joints permits without eliciting pain or spasm in the surrounding muscles. In normal joints slight over pressure can be given to ensure full range, but in flail joints care is needed to avoid taking the movement beyond the normal anatomical limit.

As one reason for giving full-range movement is to maintain the extensibility of muscles which pass over the joint, special consideration must be given to muscles which pass over two or more joints. These muscles must be progressively extended over each joint until they are finally extended to their normal length over all the joints simultaneously, e.g. the Quadriceps are fully extended when the hip joint is extended with the knee flexed.

Speed and Duration. As it is essential that relaxation be maintained throughout the movement, the speed must be uniform, fairly slow and rhythmical. The number of times the movement is performed depends on the purpose for which it is used.

A full description of the technique of giving relaxed passive movements to individual joints will be found in Chapter 14.

Effects and Uses of Relaxed Passive Movements

(i) Adhesion formation is prevented and the present free range of movement maintained.   One passive movement, well given and at frequent intervals, is sufficient for this purpose, but the usual practice is to put the joint through two movements twice daily.

(ii) When active movement is impossible, because of muscular inefficiency, these movements may help to preserve the memory of movement patterns by stimulating the receptors of kinaesthetic sense.

(iii) When full-range active movement is impossible the extensibility of muscle is maintained, and adaptive shortening prevented.

(iv) The venous and lymphatic return may be assisted slightly by mechanical pressure and by stretching of the thin-walled vessels which pass across the joint moved.   Relatively quick rhythmical and continued passive movements are required to produce this effect.   They are used in conjunction with elevation of the part to relieve oedema when the patient is unable, or unwilling, to perform sufficient active exercise.

(v) The rhythm of continued passive movements can have a soothing effect and induce further relaxation and sleep.   They may be tried in training relaxation and, if successful the movement is made imperceptibly and progressively slower as the patient relaxes.

Principles of Giving Accessory Movements

The basic principles of relaxation and fixation apply to accessory movements as to relaxed passive movements. Full and comfortable support is given and the range of the movement is as full as the condition of the joint permits.   They are comparatively small movements.

A description of the technique of giving accessory movements will be found in Chapter 14.

Effects and Uses of Accessory Movements

Accessory movements contribute to the normal function of the joint in which they take place or that of adjacent joints.

In abnormal joint conditions there may be limitation of these movements due to loss of full active range caused by stiffness of joints from contracture of soft tissue, adhesion formation or muscular inefficiency. Accessory movements are performed by the Physiotherapist to increase lost range of movement and to maintain joint mobility. Hence they form an important part of the treatment of a patient who is unable to perform normal active movement.

Principles of Passive Manual Mobilisations and Manipulations

These techniques, together with their effects and uses, cover a very wide field which is beyond the scope of this book. Specific reference to books by Maitland, Grieve, Kaltenborn and other authorities on the subject is given in the bibliography.

Manipulations performed by a surgeon or physician are usually given under a general or local anaesthetic which eliminates pain and protective spasm, and allows the use of greater force. Even well-established adhesions can be broken down; but when these are numerous, it is usual to regain full range progressively, by a series of manipulations, to avoid excessive trauma and marked exudation. Maximum effort on the part of the patient and the physiotherapist must be exerted after manipulation to maintain the range of movement gained at each session, otherwise fibrous deposits from the inevitable exudation will form new adhesions.

Principles of Giving Controlled Sustained Stretching of Tightened Structures

The patient is comfortably supported and as relaxed as possible in an appropriate position. With suitable fixation the part is grasped by the physiotherapist and moved in such a way that a sustained stretch can be applied to the contracted structures for a period of time within a functional pattern of movement. Mechanical means can be used, e.g. turnbuckle plaster.

A description of the technique of giving some commonly used controlled sustained stretchings will be found in Chapter 14.

Effects and Uses of Controlled Sustained Stretching

(i) Steady and sustained stretching may be used to overcome spasticity patterns of limbs, e.g. a hemiplegic patient. The slow stretch produces a relaxation and lengthening of the muscle.

(ii) A steady and prolonged passive stretch can overcome the resistance of shortened ligaments, fascia and fibrous sheaths of muscles as, for example, in controlled stretching and progressive spintage of talipes equinovarus.

PART II

8

AN INTRODUCTION TO NEUROMUSCULAR FACILITATION

THE Neuromuscular Mechanism initiates and achieves movement in response to a demand for activity. To 'facilitate' is to 'make easy or easier', and Neuromuscular Facilitation is the process by which the response of the Neuromuscular Mechanism is made easy or easier.

The Demand for Activity

The demands of voluntary effort are normally capable of producing efficient and purposeful movement. These demands are weakened by any factor which reduces (*a*) the patient's ability to exert voluntary effort, (*b*) the conductivity of the nervous pathways used by the impulses initiated by voluntary effort. A weakened demand may fail to elicit any response from the Neuromuscular Mechanism or be incapable of producing a satisfactory response.

Facilitation makes the response easier so that the weakened demands of voluntary effort are effective for the production of efficient and purposeful movement. The techniques of facilitation supply the demand necessary to elicit a satisfactory response and to improve the conductivity of the nervous pathways used.

The Response of the Neuromuscular Mechanism

The muscles are the effector organs of the Neuromuscular Mechanism and its response involves the initiation and control of muscular contraction. The ability to respond and the character of the response are determined by:

a. The integrity of the motor unit.
b. The excitability of the Anterior Horn Cell (A.H.C.).
c. The factors which influence the A.H.C.
d. The conductivity of the pathways of impulses influencing the A.H.C.s.
e. The nature of the demand.

a. *The Integrity of the Motor Unit.* The motor unit may be regarded as the functional unit of the Neuromuscular System; its activity is controlled by its cell (A.H.C. or motor cell of the brain stem)

74

which, when stimulated, discharges impulses to the muscle fibres which respond by contracting. As muscular contraction results from activation of the motor unit its integrity is an essential factor in implementing a response. Death of the unit's cell or destruction of the muscle fibres result in permanent inactivity of the unit, injury to the fibre results in temporary inactivity but regeneration is possible in favourable conditions.

b. *The Excitability of the A.H.C.* Activation of motor units depends on stimulation of the A.H.C.s. Impulses reach them from many sources but the effect they produce depends on the excitability of the cell at the time they arrive. A strong stimulus is required to stimulate cells with a high threshold of excitability but those with a low threshold respond to a relatively weak stimulus. The threshold of a cell is reduced by repeated stimulation and by the arrival of sub-threshold stimuli which, although they fail to achieve stimulation, progressively lower the threshold of the cell and facilitate its response to subsequent stimuli. An increase in the threshold results from lack of stimulation and trauma caused by some disease processes and it may be so great that the cell becomes incapable of responding to any normal stimulus and is therefore said to be dormant. Repeated bombardment of dormant cells by strong stimuli may, however, succeed in reducing their threshold sufficiently to make them capable of responding to stimulation, in which case re-activation of the motor units is achieved.

Stimuli reaching the A.H.C.s influence large groups or 'pools' of cells, some of which respond by firing, and others by a reduction in their threshold of excitability. The stronger the stimulus the greater the effect produced and the wider the sphere of influence. An increase in the excitability of cells in an area of the C.N.S. is referred to as an increase in Central Excitation and is a means of facilitating the response of the Neuromuscular Mechanism and of stimulating A.H.C. which have previously remained dormant.

c. *The factors which Influence the A.H.C.s.* The A.H.C.s are influenced by impulses which reach them from many sources in the body and the C.N.S. The character of the impulses may be excitory or inhibitory and it is the predominance of one or the other type at any one time which determines the effect they produce. Stimulation of the cells is achieved by excitory impulses which constitute a stimulus of threshold value, a sub-threshold stimulus fails to stimulate the cells but serves to reduce their threshold.

The sources of the impulses are the initiating areas of the C.N.S. and the Sensory Receptor Organs. Normally all the initiating areas co-operate in discharging impulses necessary for the production of movement and they are profoundly influenced by sensory impulses.

Any lesion or circumstance which interferes with the discharge of impulses influencing the A.H.C.s leads either to a lack of response or to

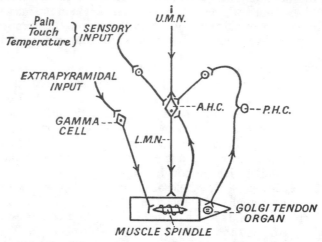

FIG. 50   Factors influencing the Anterior Horn Cells

an alteration in the character of the response.   Techniques of facilitation are designed to compensate for any deficiency by increasing the demand from sensory sources to obtain a satisfactory response and facilitate it by repeated activity.

d. *The Conductivity of the Nervous Pathways of Impulses Influencing the A.H.C.s.*   These pathways may consist of a single neurone (monosynaptic pathway) or more often of two or more neurones linked together at synapses to form a chain.   The energy required for the passage of impulses along the fibres is supplied by the fibres themselves, but the impulses are impeded by the resistance of the synapses. Disuse of the pathways increases synaptic resistance, and pressure or crushing of fibres either prevents or reduces their conductivity.   Repeated use of pathways lowers synaptic resistance and facilitates the passage of impulses provided the volley of impulses is sufficiently strong to break through in the first instance.   When normal pathways are permanently blocked the use of alternative pathways can be developed if there is sufficient demand for them as many undeveloped pathways are available in the C.N.S.   As specific pathways are used for the production of specific movements it is important that the patterns of movement used to obtain facilitation should be those which the patient requires most urgently, i.e. those of his normal functional movements or as nearly related to these as possible and that the pattern should be the same each time the movement is repeated.

e. *The Nature of the Demand.* The performance of normal functional activities utilises both voluntary and reflex movements and the demand for activity is initiated from both voluntary and sensory sources. When the demands of voluntary effort are ineffective or too weak to obtain a satisfactory response from the Neuromuscular Mechanism an increase in the demand from sensory sources can be substituted. A demand applied by stimulating sensory receptors initiates reflex movements to re-inforce the demands of voluntary effort and ensure a satisfactory response which can be facilitated by repetition.

9

PROPRIOCEPTIVE NEUROMUSCULAR FACILITATION

THE techniques of Proprioceptive Neuromuscular Facilitation rely mainly on stimulation of the proprioceptors for increasing the demand made on the neuromuscular mechanism to obtain and facilitate its response.

Treatment by these techniques is very comprehensive and involves the application of the principles of Proprioceptive Neuromuscular Facilitation to every aspect and in every phase of the patient's rehabilitation. This method of rehabilitation was developed by Doctor Herman Kabat, M.D., Pd.D., and Miss Margaret Knott, B.S., at the Kabat-Kaiser Institute between 1946 and 1951, and the philosophy of treatment and the techniques used are described in a book entitled 'PROPRIOCEPTIVE NEUROMUSCULAR FACILITATION. Patterns and Techniques', by Margaret Knott, B.S., and Dorothy E. Voss, B.Ed.

Doctor Kabat lectured on the subject at the first World Congress of Physical Therapy in 1953, and Miss Knott demonstrated her methods both then and in 1959 in connection with a course at the London Hospital. Much interest has been shown in Proprioceptive Neuromuscular Facilitation in this country and many physiotherapists from Britain have visited The California Rehabilitation Center at Vallejo, U.S.A., where Miss Knott was the Head Physical Therapist, and have learnt the techniques and something of the methods of treatment.

These techniques and the method of treatment in which they are used aim to obtain the maximum quantity of activity which can be achieved at each voluntary effort and the maximum possible number of repetitions of this activity to facilitate the response. The physiotherapist requires both skill in the performance of the techniques and a thorough understanding of the method of treatment to obtain the best results from the patient.

The techniques are suitable for use in the treatment of many conditions and provide an effective means of obtaining and accelerating the patient's rehabilitation. Some are described briefly here to serve as notes for those who have already had some practical teaching and to provide others with a basis for understanding when they are seen.

NOTES ON THE TECHNIQUES OF
PROPRIOCEPTIVE NEUROMUSCULAR FACILITATION

Treatment by these techniques aims to summate the effects of facilitation to increase the response of the neuromuscular mechanism. Proprioceptive stimulation is the principal means used to increase the demands made by voluntary effort, the initiation of some reflex reactions and physiological principles concerned with the interaction of antagonistic muscles are also used in some techniques. Resistance and stretch are applied manually to muscles working to perform patterns of mass movement, and dynamic commands give verbal stimulation to the patient's voluntary effort. Maximal resistance is considered to be the most important means of stimulating the proprioceptors, and techniques concerned with its application to patterns of mass movement are basic. Techniques of emphasis are designed to correct imbalances.

BASIC TECHNIQUES

I. PATTERNS OF FACILITATION

Mass movement patterns are used as the basis upon which all the techniques of Proprioceptive Neuromuscular Facilitation are superimposed because mass movement is characteristic of all motor activity. The patterns of movement used are spiral and diagonal and they are closely allied to those of normal functional movement; they may be observed in everyday use, e.g. in taking the hand to the mouth, and in work or sports, e.g. chopping wood or kicking a football. There are two pathways of movement for each major part of the body, i.e. Head–neck, lower Trunk, upper Trunk, Arm, Leg, and as movement can take place in either direction, each pathway provides two antagonistic patterns.

Components of Movement

Each pattern of movement has three components, the pathway is specific and in the line of action of the main muscle components responsible for the movement. Two components of the movement are angular and the third is rotatory, the latter being of major importance because it gives direction to the movement as a whole. Each pattern is named according to the movements which take place at the proximal joint or joints of the part moved, e.g. *Flexion-adduction with lateral rotation* of the Leg, or *Extension with rotation to the Right* of the lower Trunk. Movement in distal joints follows the direction of that in the proximal joints but intermediate joints may move in either direction, e.g. in *Flexion-adduction with lateral rotation* of the Leg the Foot dorsiflexes, adducts and inverts, the Knee either flexes (with Knee flexion) or extends (with Knee extension) during the movement or it can remain locked in extension.

Movement in Pattern

The pattern of movement starts with the major muscle components at the limit of their extended range and is completed when they are as shortened as possible.   The range of the rotatory component is only partial but essential, rotation starts the movement and gives it direction.

Neck Flexion with   Neck Extension with
rotation to the right   rotation to the left

FIG. 51   Neck Patterns

Flexion–abduction with   Extension-adduction
lateral rotation (right arm)   with medial rotation
                                (right arm)

Flexion -adduction with   Extension-abduction
lateral rotation   with medial rotation
(right arm)   (right arm)

FIG. 52   Arm Patterns

Upper Trunk.
Flexion with rotation
to the left (Chopping)

Upper Trunk.
Extension with rotation
to the right (Lifting)

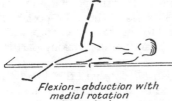

Lower Trunk.
Flexion with rotation
to the left

Lower Trunk.
Extension with rotation
to the right

FIG. 53   **Trunk Patterns**

Flexion-abduction with
medial rotation
(right leg)

Extension-adduction with
lateral rotation
(right leg)

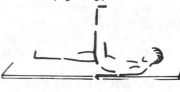

Flexion-adduction with
lateral rotation
(left leg)

Extension-abduction
with medial rotation
(left leg)

FIG. 54   **Leg Patterns**

Effects and Uses

As these patterns of movement are specific and closely allied to those of functional movements they can be repeated to facilitate movements which the patient requires most urgently.   They are more effective for facilitation than so-called straight movement as they are in the line of action of the muscles which work to produce them and the latter are more efficient in these pathways than in any others.   By applying maximal resistance and adjusting the sequence of movement during the performance of these patterns the action of weaker muscle components can be re-inforced by that of stronger groups which are their normal synergists.

The preceding diagrams indicate the position at the end of the movement assuming that intermediate joints remain still with the exception of Fig. 53 which shows lower trunk flexion with hip and knee flexion and movement is pivoted at proximal joints.   The limbs or area moved is shown in heavy type.

2. MANUAL CONTACTS

Pressure of the physiotherapist's manual contact with the patient provides a means of facilitation and is the only satisfactory way of applying maximal resistance to movement in patterns of facilitation.

The Application of Manual Contacts

Touch contributes to facilitation by stimulating the exteroceptors. Manual contacts must be (*i*) purposeful, (*ii*) directional, (*iii*) comfortable.

(*i*) Purposeful.   Pressure must be firm, so that the patient is aware of it, and applied directly to the patient's skin whenever possible. Pressure is given with the palm of the hand to ensure even contact with a wide area of skin, preferably over muscles and tendons taking part in the movement.

(*ii*) Directional.   Manual pressure is applied *only* in the direction of the movement to resist the action of the muscles taking part and to give direction to the patient's effort.   When there is loss of skin sensation the position of the hands may have to be adjusted.

(*iii*) Comfortable.   Manual contacts which are uncomfortable or which produce painful stimuli must be avoided as they inhibit contraction and may lead to the initiation of unwanted movements.

3. THE STRETCH STIMULUS AND THE STRETCH REFLEX

Proprioceptors situated in the muscles (muscle spindles) are stimulated by stretching, which increases the intramuscular tension.   Stimulation of the muscle spindle elicits a reflex contraction of the muscle provided the stimulus is of threshold value and the reflex arc is intact.   Bombardment of dormant A.H.C.s by impulses initiated from the spindles increases central excitation and facilitates stimulation of these cells.

The Application of the Stretch Stimulus

The muscles to be worked are put on full stretch, all components of the pattern being considered, so that tension is felt in all muscle groups.

The Application of the Stretch Reflex

A sharp but controlled stretch of the muscles at the limit of their extended range is given and synchronised with a dynamic command for the patient's maximum voluntary effort to perform the movement.   In this way the patient's effort adds all it can to the stimulus of stretching.

Now (stretch) . . . PULL!

Summation of the stimuli initiated by the spindles, in response to stretching of the muscle, and of those initiated by voluntary effort is obtained by rhythmical repetition of this technique until the maximum response obtainable is achieved.   Use of this technique in patterns of facilitation makes it possible to stretch the muscles effectively in all their components of action.

Effects and Uses

Provided the reflex arc is intact and the stretch stimulus and stretch reflex are applied correctly and with sufficient frequency, a response is assured except in cases of spinal shock.   Stretch is therefore a valuable means of initiating contraction and, when applied to weak muscles, increases their response and so accelerates the strengthening process.

4. Traction and Approximation

Traction and approximation (compression) may be effective in stimulating proprioceptive impulses arising from joint structures.

(*i*) Traction. Manual contacts make it possible to maintain traction throughout the range of movement.   It is most effective when used in flexion movements probably because any weight lifted would normally exert traction in proportion to its weight.

(*ii*) Approximation.   Compression of joint surfaces against each other simulates the normal circumstances which arise during weight-bearing or pushing, it is therefore more effective for facilitating extension movements.

5. Commands to the Patient

The physiotherapist's voice is used as a verbal stimulus to demand the patient's maximum voluntary effort.   Brief, simple, accurate and well-timed instructions suitable for his age, character and ability to co-operate demand the patient's attention and effort at the right time and indicate the type of reaction required from him, even if he does not understand the language! Accuracy in commanding is essential:

HOLD!   .   .   . for isometric contraction
PULL or PUSH!   .   „ isotonic   „
Relax .   .   .   . „ relaxation

The physiotherapist must make sure that her commands are carried out to the maximum of the patient's ability.

6. NORMAL TIMING

Timing is defined as the sequence of muscle contraction occurring in motor activity, and the production of co-ordinated movement presupposes the ability to achieve normal timing. In functional movements timing usually proceeds from distal to proximal because it is the distal parts, i.e. hands and feet, which normally receive most of the stimuli for activity. Proximal control develops first, then, during the process of learning co-ordination and purposeful movement, distal control is established.

Normal timing in patterns of facilitation is from distal to proximal and, provided rotation begins the movement, it proceeds in this direction in the normal subject. The movement as a whole progresses smoothly so that if each joint is blended with that at others, it is completed first in distal, then intermediate and finally in proximal joints. As movement is completed in each joint the muscles which have produced it (by their isotonic contraction) continue to contract isometrically until the movement as a whole is completed.

When normal timing cannot be achieved timing for emphasis is used as a means of correcting imbalances. Normal timing may be defeated by the application of too much resistance to a particular component of the movement with the result that its efficiency is decreased, e.g. too much resistance given to the foot in leg movements.

7. MAXIMAL RESISTANCE

Maximal resistance is defined as the greatest amount or degree of resistance which can be given to muscular contraction. Maximal resistance to an *isometric contraction* is the greatest amount of resistance which can be applied without breaking the hold. Maximal resistance to an *isotonic contraction* is the greatest amount of resistance against which the patient can perform a smooth co-ordinated movement through full range.

The Application of Maximal Resistance

In facilitation techniques maximal resistance is applied manually to movements and holdings in patterns of facilitation.   All three components of the movement are resisted maximally at every stage of the movement.   Variations in the strength of each component and in different parts of the range must be taken into account.

Effects and Uses

Maximal resistance demands 'all the muscles can do', i.e. all their available motor units are activated throughout the range of movement. Stimulation of the muscle spindles and a maximal increase in intramuscular tension leads to a spread of excitation to adjacent muscle groups by means of irradiation.   The demands of the resistance determines the extent of this spread of excitation and the pattern of movement the particular muscles affected by it.   Maximal resistance is used in all techniques of Proprioceptive Neuromuscular Facilitation to increase excitation, to strengthen muscles, to build up endurance, to demand relaxation and to improve co-ordination.

8. RE-INFORCEMENT

Innumerable combinations of movements are required and utilised in everyday life and when great effort is required movement of one part of the body is associated and re-inforced by those of other parts. This can be observed in heavy work and sporting activities when strength or concentration are required.

Muscle components of a pattern of movement re-inforce each other automatically according to the demands of the resistance and when this is maximal re-inforcement extends beyond the muscle components of the pattern to other segments of the body, e.g. from arm to trunk or from one leg to the other.

The proprioceptive stimulation which results from tension in strongly contracting muscles leads to a spread or overflow of excitation in the C.N.S. by the process of irradiation, the purpose of which is to recruit the co-operation of allied muscles which, by contracting as synergists, increase the efficiency of the movement.

The Use of Re-inforcement

The maximal contraction of strong muscles is used to re-inforce the action of weaker allied muscles.   Re-inforcement always takes place *from strength*, therefore strong muscle components of a pattern are used to re-inforce weaker components of the same pattern and strong patterns re-inforce weaker patterns provided they are related.   Re-inforcement is used with timing for emphasis as a means of obtaining or emphasising the contraction of ineffective or weak muscles to correct imbalances.

TECHNIQUES OF EMPHASIS

Techniques of emphasis use the means of facilitation to correct muscle imbalances and restore the patient's ability to perform effective co-ordinated movement.

I. REPEATED CONTRACTIONS

Repetition of activity against resistance is essential for the development of muscle strength and endurance. The contraction of specific weak muscles or weaker components of a pattern is repeated in this technique while they are being reinforced by maximal isotonic or isometric contraction of stronger allied muscles.

Application of Repeated Contractions

a) *Normal Timing—isotonic muscle work:* A maximal isotonic contraction is obtained in the desired pattern and when the patient can go no further the stretch reflex is repeated in order to facilitate contraction of the weaker muscle groups. This enables the patient to move through range. Two or three repetitions of the stretch reflex may be used; thus: PULL UP!—NOW (stretch) PULL UP!—NOW (stretch) PULL UP! etc.

b) *Normal Timing—isotonic and isometric muscle work:* This is a more advanced form of repeated contractions. A maximal isotonic contraction is obtained in the desired pattern and the muscles are then held in an isometric contraction. This contraction is held against maximal resistance to obtain a build-up of excitation (by a gradual increase in resistance without breaking the hold). Then, without relaxing, the resistance is reduced slightly, the patient is instructed to move and the stretch reflex is repeatedly applied to facilitate movement throughout the remainder of the range; thus:

PULL UP!—HOLD! . . . PULL UP!—NOW (stretch) PULL UP!—NOW (stretch) PULL UP! etc.

The stretch reflex must be short and sharp, and contraction of the reinforcing muscles must be maintained throughout. The performance of the technique as a whole should be unhurried to give time for excitation to take place.

c) *Timing for Emphasis—isotonic and isometric muscle work:* The sequence of muscle contraction in the performance of movement is adjusted to provide the means of reinforcing the action of weaker components of a pattern or of a weaker pattern. The maximal contraction of strong muscle groups for use in reinforcement is obtained first, then movement is pivoted to the joint or joints over which the weaker muscles in question are effective. Three factors are essential:

a. *the stabilising part* is the area which is proximal to the joint or joints usually over which the weak muscles work.

b. *the pivot* is the joint or joints over which the weak muscles work and in which movement is repeated to emphasise their activity.

c. *the handle* is the part of the body which is distal to the pivot.

Movement proceeds through pattern against maximal resistance until it is completed in joints of the handle and reaches the strongest part of the range of muscles working in the stabilising part.   The muscles used to produce these movements then work isometrically against maximal resistance, those of the stabilising part to maintain stability, those of the handle to 'lock in' the joints so that it moves as a single unit.   While this isometric contraction is maintained by maximal resistance, movement is initiated at the pivot to obtain or emphasise the contraction of the weaker muscles. Weak distal components maybe strengthened by irradiation from strong proximal components and weak proximal components maybe strengthened by irradiation from strong distal components.

Effects and Uses

Repetition of activity of weaker muscles, reinforcement and timing for emphasis are used together in this technique.   Repeated contractions build up strength and endurance of weaker components of a pattern and co-ordinate their activity with those of stronger components of the same pattern.   They are used to correct imbalances of muscle strength, to demand relaxation of antagonistic muscles and to gain range of movement in the treatment of stiff joints.

2. SLOW REVERSALS

This technique is based on Sherrington's principle of successive induction, i.e. that immediately after the flexor reflex is elicited the excitability of the extensor reflex is increased.   This principle is applicable to voluntary movement and to the interaction of antagonistic groups in the performance of movement.   The contraction of strong agonist muscles or patterns is used as a source of proprioceptive stimulation for weaker antagonistic muscles or patterns.

Application of Slow Reversals

Movement in a strong agonistic pattern against maximal resistance is followed immediately and without relaxation by a reversal of the movement into the antagonistic pattern, which is also resisted maximally.   The reversal of the movement takes place smoothly with normal timing and no relaxation is allowed as the physiotherapist changes the position of her hands.   A sequence of slow reversals follows; movement always beginning in the stronger pattern and ending in the weaker.

Effects and Uses

The contraction of muscles of the weaker antagonistic pattern is facilitated by that of the stronger muscles of the agonistic pattern working against maximal resistance. Repetition of the movement with normal timing integrates the action of these weaker muscles with those of their normal antagonists and facilitates the process of learning. The technique is used to strengthen and build up endurance of weaker muscles or of two antagonistic patterns, to develop co-ordination and establish the normal reversal of antagonistic muscles in the performance of movement.

3. RHYTHMIC STABILISATION

Isometric contraction of antagonistic muscles is used in this technique to stabilise joints. Stability is maintained against resistance by a co-contraction of antagonistic muscles.

Application of Rhythmic Stabilisation

Rhythmic Stabilisation can take place at any point on the pathway of the pattern of movement. The patient is instructed to 'HOLD!' while the physiotherapist applies maximal resistance alternating rhythmically from one direction to the other. The rotatory component of the pattern is particularly important for 'locking in' the joint, and is therefore given special attention and the direction of the resistance must be changed smoothly to hold in the simultaneous contraction (or co-contraction) of all the muscles. The patient is commanded to 'HOLD' (against resistance in any direction) for if his effort is directional an isometric reversal of antagonists takes place and not a co-contraction.

Effects and Uses

Maintenance of a co-contraction of antagonistic muscles against maximal resistance builds up excitation; the response of the muscles is facilitated and their strength increased. Circulation is improved following Rhythmic Stabilisations, the energy of the contraction being released as heat as there is no movement.

Any part of the range of movement can be used for this technique, the part selected varies according to the circumstances, e.g. to increase excitation the strongest part of the range of the muscles' action is used; when pain is a problem any pain-free part is suitable; when there is joint stiffness the point at which movement is limited is selected and Rhythmic Stabilisation is followed by an attempt to increase the free range. All parts of the range are used successively when postural inco-ordination is present and the technique is repeated at each point to improve stability.

4. HOLD-RELAX

This is a relaxation technique designed to obtain a lengthening reaction of muscles whose action is antagonistic to the movement limited in range. It is effective, simple and pain-free.

Application of Hold-Relax

a. *Isometric contraction of the hypertonic muscles:* Movement in pattern in the direction of limitation takes place either passively or actively. When movement is active it is resisted maximally with normal timing but, whether active or passive, it continues to the point at which it is limited either by tension or pain. Having made sure that the position is pain-free, the physiotherapist changes the position of her hands and commands the patient to 'HOLD!' while she applies maximal resistance to the hypertonic muscles. This isometric contraction is held to obtain a build-up of excitation and then followed by the patient's voluntary relaxation of all the muscles, 'Let go' or 'Relax'. Time is allowed for relaxation to take place, then an attempt is made to move in the direction of limitation to gain an increase in range. Special attention is given to the rotatory component of both the holding and the movement. The technique is repeated as often as required and is usually followed by Repeated Contractions to consolidate any increase in range.

b. *Isometric contraction of the reciprocal muscles:* The technique is applied in a similar way to (a) but the muscles working antagonistically to the hypertonic group are made to contract isometrically, in order to gain reciprocal relaxation of the hypertonic group.

Effects and Use

Immediately following the isometric contraction of the hypertonic muscles the activity of their antagonists is facilitated (successive induction). When the antagonists are facilitated, the lengthening reaction of the hypertonic muscles is increased (reciprocal innervation). Hold-relax is used as a means of increasing the range of movement in joints or of obtaining pain-free movement when pain is a limiting factor.

5. RHYTHMIC INITIATION

This is a relaxation technique for specific application to the rigidity of Parkinson's Disease.

Application of Rhythmic Initiation

The limb is taken passively and rhythmically through the range of a pattern and when some relaxation has occurred the patient is instructed to assist in the movement. Several repetitions of active-assisted movement are carried out and progression is made to resisted movement. Finally the therapist's hands are removed and the patient is encouraged to maintain a free active movement.   The rhythm must not be lost during the changes from passive to active-assisted to resisted and finally free active movement.

Effects and Use

The rhythmical movement of this technique produces relaxation and thus helps the Parkinson patients to improve their ability to initiate movement.

Guidance as to the use of these techniques in the treatment of patients is given in Part II of *Proprioceptive Neuromuscular Facilitation.   Patterns and Techniques*, by Margaret Knott and Dorothy E. Voss (2nd edition, 1968).

FUNCTIONAL RE-EDUCATION
I. Lying to Sitting

THERE are many things a physiotherapist needs to know about her patient before she embarks on a planned scheme of treatment. Initially much of the information which is required emerges from clinical notes and from whatever form of routine assessment is in current use. Nevertheless, however efficient an assessment may be, it usually needs to be augmented or amended after the first few treatments when the physiotherapist knows the patient better. Throughout the treatment period reviews are needed to record progress and establish new priorities.

Assessment of functional ability needs special attention. It seems that the only reliable method of discovering precisely what a patient can or cannot do is for him to demonstrate a series of appropriate activities if possible in a situation which, to him, is as near normal as possible. Information which is not confirmed by practical demonstration can be misleading for a number of reasons, and it is of the greatest importance that both therapist and patient should have a clear picture and a record of the latter's capabilities, difficulties or failures; only with this knowledge can a realistic programme of treatment leading to independence be viable.

To motivate the patient, the specific purpose of each activity must be emphasised so that his effort is directed towards regaining abilities he needs. Achievements are recorded and are available for use during everyday living. Restoration of functions which are needed is the sole criterion of progress. Although physiotherapists may wish to record $x°$ of joint range, y units of muscle power or z mm of muscle bulk these need not concern the patient as they do not necessarily indicate functional efficiency of purposeful activity.

Re-education of function is of the utmost importance in achieving the patient's rehabilitation, and all the methods used in Exercise Therapy are directed towards this end. As each patient's problems differ from those of others no set routine is possible, but the method used is adapted and modified to meet the needs of the individual. All the patient's abilities are used to their maximum to minimise the effects of inactivity, to help him to help himself. Re-education of function requires the co-operation of all who come in contact with him. Each member of the rehabilitation team is a specialist in his own field, but integration of their efforts is essential to obtain the best results with the least possible delay, e.g. it is useless for the physiotherapist to teach the patient to move about the bed and sit up unaided if his friends, relations or nurses continue to lift him.

The physiotherapist plays a part in re-training effective breathing and gaining expectoration and can also help in achieving other functions in which muscular action is required, e.g. speech, swallowing and feeding, by using suitable techniques. It is her job to see that sufficient strength and range of joint movement is obtained as quickly as possible to perform the normal activities of daily living and avoid frustration arising from the patient's repeated unsuccessful efforts. This is a positive approach to the patient's problems and results are achieved more quickly than when assistance is given to movement and gradually reduced. Many adaptations of clothing, utensils and furniture made by the occupational therapists help the patient to independence while he gains the ability to do without them.

Some suggestions as to the training of basic functional activities are given here. Once the activities can be done independently the patient can practise them on his own or in a group to increase the speed of his performance and to build up endurance.

ACTIVITIES ON THE MAT/BED

Rolling — the roll over from lying supine to side lying
This requires a total flexion-with-rotation of the body which is initiated from and led by the head and neck. Strong limb activity is recruited to assist whenever it is available, e.g. *to roll forward and to the left*.

a. *trunk rotation* is facilitated by a strong pull on the left hand which grasps a fixture at the side of the bed. (Retraction of the left shoulder facilitates the protraction of the right.)

FIG. 55

b. *the right arm* may be used to pull, thrust or swing across towards the opposite hip.

c. *the left leg* can be hooked over the side of the bed and by flexing and adducting can assist rotation of the lower trunk and pelvis.

d. *with the knee bent* so that pressure on the right foot can lift and push the right side of the pelvis upwards and over, the rolling movement of the lower trunk can be completed.

A reversal of the movement returns the body to the supine position. A push off with the arm or retraction of the right shoulder initiates the return, but to ensure control, the head should remain forward until the final position is reached.

Purposes and use of the roll

a. To assist during nursing procedures. For bed-making, back inspection, etc. the patient must be rolled over to one side and if he can achieve this unaided or with minimal assistance he has the satisfaction of knowing that there is *something* he can do to lighten the load for those who care for him.

b. The patient gains a measure of independence as he knows that whenever he pleases he can perform a movement which is useful to him. He has the freedom to make the decision as to when he shall roll over to get a different view of his surroundings, ease the pressure on his back or stiffness of his legs; maybe he can also reach and use a more comfortable sleeping posture.

The activity is suitable for use in bed once the patient is reasonably proficient and in no danger of falling out of bed. Rolling can be safely practised on a floor mat with minimal supervision.

This roll is the first part of an integrated series of movements which leads directly to a sitting position and to getting out of bed. The patient needs to know this so that he can see the direction in which progress lies.

The roll described next requires total extension-rotation of the body. It will also bring the patient to lie on his side but continuation of the movement leads to prone lying position.

Rolling — the roll over from lying supine through side lying to prone or to roll forwards and to the left (alternative method)

The arm initiates and gives direction to the movement which enables the patient to roll forwards to lie on the left side and when the movement is continued the prone position is reached. The patient extends and rotates the head to watch the right hand as the arm is lifted to a position

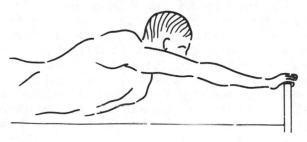

Fig. 56

obliquely across the face and reaching out towards the head of the bed. Extension-rotation of the upper trunk follows the arm movement and brings the body to the side lying position. When the hand grasps the head of the bed, or maybe the therapist's hand, and pulls, the roll over is facilitated. Before attempting the complete roll the therapist must check that the patient can tolerate the position of Fig. 56 lying prone. Skilful use of a firm supporting pillow on to which the patient can roll may make the position possible even for those with flexor deformity of the hips or with limitation of extension in the spine.

A reversal of the movement returns the patient to the supine position.

Purpose and use of the roll

a. The most important aspect of this activity and of the prone position, is that it helps to combat and counteract the effects of long-term recumbency in bed, sitting up in bed or reclining in a lounge chair. In all these circumstances the body posture is one of total flexion and most of the activities the patient needs to do are also flexor in character. Consequently there is a tendency for the normal range of extension to become limited especially in the lumbar spine and hip joints. Should this occur, the secondary curves of the spine are flattened out and movement in all directions is limited. This factor can create all kinds of problems once the patient attempts to stand and walk again. Other factors, such as pain and possibly age, can create similar problems for which the use of a modified version of the prone position may be appropriate.

b. For those unable to tolerate the final position this method may be easier or more suitable for turning on to one side than that described earlier. This total roll over provides another and different activity for patients who can roll right over to prone.

The following activity, which is called 'Bridging', is not part of the series of movements which leads to sitting and getting out of bed but it has been included at this stage because it is both suitable and appropriate for patients who are confined to bed as well as many others.

Bridging

From the crook lying position the pelvis is lifted to form the keystone to an arch the supports of which are the shoulders and the feet. The stability of the shoulders presents no problem, as downward pressure of the arms can be used as a bracket and a factor in reinforcing the extensor activity of the trunk. The stability of the legs in the crook position is not necessarily ready made and until it is established, aids such as a wall, footboard, or sandbag may be required to fix the feet, and a strap used to keep the knees from falling apart. By exerting downward pressure on the patient's knees (the lower leg must be vertical) and at the same time in the direction of the thighs towards the hip joints, the therapist facilitates the movement of extension through the legs to the hips and lower back to lift the buttocks from the bed.

Purposes and use of bridging

a. For the bed-bound patient bridging makes bedpan routines easier for everyone concerned.

b. By lifting the lower back from the bed, sensitive pressure areas are relieved of the body weight. When elements of rotation and side flexion are added to the lifting movement the weight can be transferred to one buttock or the other as it is lowered to the bed (preliminary training for transfers and ambulation).

c. Extensibility of both hips and the lumbar region are combined to combat the long-term effects of flexor situations (see Fig. 57) and the efficiency of the extensor muscles is maintained.

Fig. 57

d. The ability to bridge makes many dressing activities easier when they need to be carried out in bed, e.g. pulling up pants.

e. This activity provides the patient with the experience of feeling firm pressure on the soles of the feet and of a situation which demands considerable leg activity to support the body weight.

NOTE: When only one knee can be bent, bridging is still possible, e.g. an extended leg, perhaps fixed in plaster, may be supported on a low stool or sand-bag; or, both legs may be supported in extension so that the pelvis can be lifted and the body arched from heels to shoulders. The inactivity of an extended leg (as in recent hemiparesis) may defeat the effort to bridge but by holding the two together firmly, preferably in the crook position, it may be possible, and this also stimulates the affected leg to active cooperation.

Forearm support side lying

This position is usually reached by rolling to one side and then pushing up with the elbow to support the upper trunk with the whole forearm. A pause en route in side lying is sometimes more suitable. The position of the upper trunk is most stable when the supporting arm is vertical (from elbow to shoulder) and both shoulders lie on the same plane; stability of the pelvis is ensured by bending one leg (Fig. 58).

Fig. 58

Purpose and uses

a. The position is used en route from lying to sitting.

b. Some find it convenient for reaching across to a bedside table without sitting up.

c. It is a relatively relaxed position suitable for use on the floor or out of doors, possibly for reading or looking at the view.

d. Pressure through the shoulder joint (approximation) stimulates activity in the whole of the shoulder region, therefore it may prove useful during the treatment of some shoulder conditions. Note that the reaction to pressure does not appear to be sustained for long periods.

Prone lying with forearm support

This position may be reached from side lying with forearm support, the free elbow being moved to a position shoulder width from its fellow so that both shoulders are supported. The pelvis and legs continue the movement until the body lies prone. A push up with the elbows from prone lying is another method. The upper arms must be vertical to ensure

FIG. 59

balance in the position with minimum effort and the weight should be evenly distributed along the full extent of the forearm and hand (Fig. 59).

Purpose and uses

a. Considerable activity of the extensor muscles of the head, and through to the upper trunk, is needed to support the head in alignment with the upper trunk so the position can be useful to counteract stooping posture when there is minimal loss of normal extensibility.

b Support being given to both arms stimulates all muscles of the shoulder region to stabilise the position. A rocking movement transferring weight from arm to arm is useful to promote activity in the treatment of some shoulder conditions.

c. Extensibility of the hip joints and lumbar spine is maintained; however, the position without some support under the hips is only suitable for the young and mobile.

d. Creeping movements which propel the body along the floor using the arms, pelvic movement and legs if possible provide strong co-ordinated movement which is related to that used for other methods of ambulation. A method of progression used by some babies and in infantry training where 'cover' is low.

Sitting — on the side of the mat/bed

From lying on one side propped up by the elbow (forearm support side ying) the body is pushed upright by extension of the elbow as the legs are lifted and swung over the side of the bed. During the movement the body is pivoted on one buttock until the sitting position is reached when the weight is equally distributed through both buttocks (Fig. 60).

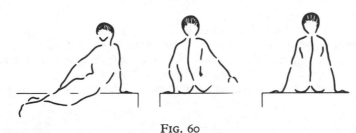

FIG. 60

The patient is taught to sit by correcting the pattern of his sitting posture with support, then maintaining it against resistance. If he tends to fall in a particular direction when the support is removed, he is pushed off balance in that direction to elicit the righting reflex and equilibrium reactions. He must, of course, be prevented from falling if these reactions are slow or inadequate.

Stability in sitting is ensured by pressure of the thighs to the mat/bed and the feet to the floor, if they can reach it. Sitting on the side of the mat/bed is usually a preliminary to standing up and moving elsewhere for dressing and other toilet activities. More people probably spend more hours sitting than in any other position. How they sit is not always beneficial but in general it is a useful position of great stability which leaves the arms free for innumerable purposes in the home, at work and for recreation. Sitting provides a welcome opportunity for many to take the 'weight off their feet'!

Hitching and Hiking

The ability to take the weight on the arms, lift and move the pelvis is essential for transfers for wheelchair patients, e.g. from bed to chair. Blocks, sandbags or short crutches help to make these easier for the

Hitching & Hiking   FIG. 61

patient to practise. Once support is secure on the arms, movement of the pelvis forwards, backwards and sideways with rotation is practised in preparation for lifting the buttocks from one place to another. Progression in any direction can be achieved by moving the hands and the buttocks alternately or the latter may be moved one after the other (like walking on the buttocks).

Transfers

The method of doing transfers varies very much with the individual patient and the circumstances. Useful ideas on the subject are given in most books on rehabilitation and they are clearly described in *Handling the Handicapped* by the Chartered Society of Physiotherapy.

The height and relative position of the bed, chair, etc., are of great importance in achieving transfers.

MOVEMENT AND STABILITY AT FLOOR LEVEL

Getting down to the floor

Not everybody needs to get down to the floor or ground but a surprising number of people like to be able to, e.g. to retrieve a book or a ball of wool which has fallen, plant seeds, play with small children or manage to do innumerable household jobs in the good old-fashioned way. Some reach the floor accidentally by falling and, even if they are unhurt, are so confused by the seemingly unfamiliar surroundings that they are afraid to try to get up or even call for help. It is an advantage therefore for every patient to have the experience of 'feeling at home' on the floor and to know how best to summon help if need be or to get up by themselves.

For safety and suitability a floor mat or thick carpet is ideal for learning to get down and practising moving from one place or position to another. The muscle work is extensive and varied so that strength, coordination, endurance and confidence can be built up without undue worry about balance or the fear of falling. Patients can practise at home once they are reasonably competent or they may gain additional benefit from working with a group in a physiotherapy department, possibly while they await specific individual treatment. Patients suffering from some painful conditions, e.g. Rheumatoid Arthritis are unable to tolerate mat activities although many of the activities can be achieved in a modified form.

The initial difficulty of getting to the floor often deters both patients and therapists but, like so many difficulties, this can usually be overcome with help and careful planning. Passive lifting and maximal assistance are only practical if strong and experienced helpers are available; but many patients can do a lot for themselves if they just know how to. Some

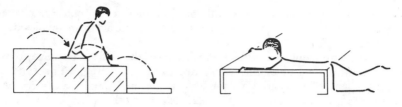

FIG. 62

suggestions follow which may prove useful in planning the most suitable approach for any particular patient (Fig. 62).

1. For the patient who can stand with support. Turn and stand to face the bed or chair, leaning forwards so that both hands can give support, then kneel and put one hand on the floor well away to the side, sit down towards it.

2. Transfer from a chair to a low stool, then to the floor. Any number of stools or wooden boxes can be arranged to form shallow steps. This method is especially suitable for bi-lateral amputee patients.

3. Roll prone on a high mat or wide divan bed, pivot round until the feet hang over the edge of the bed then slide backwards bending the knees until they rest on the floor. From the kneeling position sit on the floor.

Side Sitting

Unlike the push up to sitting on the side of the bed, the push up to side sitting on the floor includes little or no rotation as the trunk is pivoted to sit upright. The legs are bent and remain resting on the floor. To sit upright the arms may be used for support unless strong activity of the lateral trunk and abductor muscles on one side is available to free the hands for other purposes (Fig. 63).

FIG. 63

Purpose and uses

a. This is an elegant way to sit either on the floor or out of doors for those who find it possible and comfortable. It can be practised safely and it is easy to return to a resting position.

b. Maintaining the position without the use of the arms emphasises the activity of the lateral trunk and abductor muscles on one side of the body. This may help to correct imbalances resulting from inefficiency of these muscles.

c. An ambulatory movement which allows the patient to move from one area of a room to another is initiated from side sitting. This can be useful when weight-bearing on the legs is contraindicated for any reason or for those who fall and need to reach a chair or other piece of furniture for help in getting up again. The 'scooting' movement is described as follows: the hands are moved towards the direction in which the patient wants to progress; they take the weight as the pelvis is lifted and drawn towards the hands before it is lowered to the floor; the legs help if they can and are then bent before the progression continues. This method of 'ambulation' may be successful when only one arm and the leg on the same side are available for use and a similar movement can be used to move up the bed. Initially the therapist can control and if necessary assist progression by grasping the pelvis firmly from *behind* to make sure the patient's effort achieves success.

Prone Kneeling

Prone kneeling or the 'four foot position' may be reached from prone lying when flexion is initiated by bending the head forward to put the chin on the chest, then by walking the hands backwards as the hips and knees bend. Fixation of the feet against a wall or by a sandbag makes this easier. The position, however, is more often reached by turning forwards and over from side sitting. The position is mechanically stable when arms

FIG. 64

and thighs are vertical but widespread and co-ordinated isometric activity is needed to maintain it. This activity can be increased considerably by the use of suitable stabilising techniques, e.g. rhythmic stabilisation (Fig. 64).

Purpose and uses

a. This is the starting position for 'crawling' which gives the patient mobility at floor level in any direction he wishes. It may prove very useful for patients with vertigo and others who cannot bear weight on the feet for the time being.

b. Partial weight-bearing through the hip joints (although they are in a position of flexion) is a step towards weight-bearing in erect positions.

c. Partial weight-bearing on the arms stimulates activity in the shoulder area which leads to the development of the strength and mobility required for so many functional activities.

d. Many useful activities are, or can be, carried on at ground level, e.g. playing with small children, cutting out material for dressmaking, planting seeds and weeding the garden, and some people still sweep, scrub and polish on hands and knees! Incidentally, the trunk activity required to return to side sitting makes a change and is a welcome rest.

Crawling

This may be regarded as movement in a position and as it is such an important and useful activity a brief description is included here.

When balance and stability have been established in prone kneeling patients can begin to practise lifting a hand or a knee from the floor to balance 'on three legs'. This makes it possible for the crawling movement to take place in any chosen direction as the weight-free limb can be lifted and replaced in a new position before taking the weight once more. The sequence of limb movement and support should be allowed to develop naturally whenever possible as precise instructions as to which and where a limb should be moved often confuses the patient. During practice, rest

FIG. 65

periods can be interspersed with activity by sitting to one side or the other in side sitting position (Fig. 65).

Purposes and uses of crawling

a. Crawling activities build up co-ordination of the whole body including reciprocal movement of the arms and legs as required in walking. The direction of the crawl, i.e. forwards, backwards, sideways determines the distribution and emphasis of the neuro-muscular activity employed.

b. Because the spine is weight-free in the horizontal position the potential range of movement in these joints is increased, therefore this activity is useful for mobilisation and/or for learning control of excessive mobility.

c. A measure of weight-bearing on arms and legs stimulates activity in the region of these joints, by approximation of joint surfaces, and this can contribute to the retraining of the function of the limbs, e.g. crawling backwards is used to regain knee flexion and arm elevation.

d. Crawling provides a safe and effective means of moving from one area of a room to another for those who have very poor balance in erect positions. Those who are not too proud to use the floor not only achieve their purpose in moving but do so independently.

Kneeling

One can kneel down or get up to kneeling.

Before the patient attempts to kneel it is advisable to make sure that,

a. the surface on which to kneel is sufficiently comfortable for the patient to tolerate pressure on the knees;

b. there is sufficient range of knee flexion, i.e. a minimum of about 100°;

c. any furniture to be used for support is in the right position, firm and immobile. A chair or bed is better pushed back against a wall;

d. any other disability which affects the patient has been taken into account, e.g. restriction of ankle joint movement, painful toes. Toes inadvertently bent under or pressed against a hard surface can be extremely painful.

Kneeling down from standing

From standing facing a chair, or other suitable support, the patient leans forward to take some weight on one or both hands as the legs bend to put first one and then the other knee to the ground. Alternatively, by standing back further from the support both legs can be bent and both knees rocked to the ground together. When the knees are in position the rest of the body is brought into alignment in the erect position.

Kneeling down from sitting (on a divan bed or settee)

As the patient sits he turns to one side taking the weight on both hands; the turning movement continues as the knees come over the side of the bed and down until they reach the floor; the trunk remains prone and supported on the bed. Care must be taken to see that the knees come to the floor beside the bed (and not underneath it). Once the knees are settled on the ground the body is brought into alignment in the erect position, by hip extension and the help of the arms.

When patients first attempt kneeling the therapist can control the movement by grasping the pelvis firmly from *behind* thus giving confidence and indicating the direction of the movement by pressure of her hands.

Kneeling up from prone kneeling

By sitting back on the heels and then extending hips and knees the kneeling position is reached. The body weight is evenly distributed between the knees, the lower legs act as a bracket and the rest of the body is held erect. Throughout the movement the arms can be used for control or assistance if necessary.

Kneeling up from side sitting

The turn and lift of the pelvis as used to come to prone kneeling can be combined with extension in a continuous movement which terminates in the kneeling position.

Purpose and uses

a. The kneeling position is rarely maintained for any length of time as it is unpopular and uncomfortable for most people. However, when it can be assumed without undue discomfort it provides a link in the series of activities which leads the body from the horizontal to the vertical position.

b. To establish the vertical alignment of the trunk and thighs is the first active position, so far mentioned, which reuqires the trunk and the thighs to be balanced in vertical alignment. It is suitable for re-educating or correcting hip and lumbar control, e.g. hip and lumbar flexion tends to persist from the habitual circumstances due to prolonged sitting. To correct hip and lumbar flexion if it occurs two methods are suggested:

i. the patient is asked to stretch up in response to relatively light

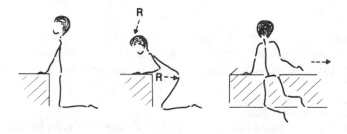

FIG. 66

pressure of the therapist's hand on the vertex of the head;

ii. to bring the body segments into line the hips must move forwards and up as the head and upper trunk move backwards and up. Patients learn where and how to move when the therapist indicates the direction by manual pressure in front of the hips and high on the back of the head. The only instruction needed is 'get up!' said in the nicest way!

c. To establish control when weight is supported on one leg (by the knee) may be regarded as a preparation for walking when the weight must be supported on one leg long enough for the other to be replaced in a new position. This also applies to replacing one leg to get up from kneeling.

Transference of weight from one knee to the other can take place rhythmically without disturbing the alignment of the body. Balance on one knee can also be practised, using the arms for support if and when they are required. Progression can be introduced by moving sideways with small 'steps'.

Half Kneeling

To reach this position from kneeling the body weight is supported on one knee while the other leg is lifted and brought forwards to put the foot on the floor. Even when the arms are used for support patients frequently find this movement difficult because the supporting hip fails to hold in extension and/or the range of flexion on one or more of the joints of the moving leg is insufficient to allow the leg to be folded as it is brought forwards (Fig. 67). From prone kneeling some find this easier as the supporting limb is stable and balance is no problem. The body can be

FIG. 67

raised once the legs are in position. From standing the half kneeling position can be assured either by stepping forwards to kneel or by stepping backwards to kneel on one knee. Good balance or some support is essential for stability.

Getting up from the floor

Each patient should be encouraged to discover the most suitable and effective method of getting up. Initially the therapist can offer advice and, if necessary, caution. The following methods may help to provide a basis for planning the activity.

a. From side sitting close to a large and stable chair the patient leans on the chair seat and with this support turns to kneel. One leg is then lifted and placed forwards to half kneeling before both legs push the body up to standing. While the arms still provide support a turning movement pivots the buttocks to sit on the chair.

b. A series of transfers using the hands to lift the body upwards and backwards, or upwards and sideways, to a low stool and then to another somewhat higher and finally to chair level is a useful method for those who have strong arms. Three 'lifts' of 6 inches bring the patient to chair level but any number of 'stairs' can be used.   Bi-lateral amputee patients find this method very satisfactory.

    c. From kneeling facing a divan bed of suitable height and with the body fully supported, a push on to the bed with one or both feet may be sufficient to lever the pelvis on to the bed.   The patient can then roll supine and sit up in one continuous movement.

FUNCTIONAL RE-EDUCATION

2. Sitting activities and gait

On chairs and other seats

An infinite variety of sitting postures are used habitually for sitting on a wide variety of seats. Ideally the design of the seat should always fit the physical characteristics of the individual who uses it and also be suitable for the purpose for which it is used. However, with the exception of those who need wheelchairs, people do not buy chairs as they buy shoes. A compromise is usually acceptable except for those who are obliged to spend many hours sitting on the same chair, e.g. some schoolchildren, office workers, long-distance drivers and the elderly infirm. Chairs and seats come in every shape and form, hard, soft, high, low, narrow, broad, small, large etc., as stools, chairs, benches, deck chairs, logs, rocks etc., seats to wait or rest on, seats for meals, toilet seats, seats for travelling, seats for working, seats for sporting activities and seats for relaxing. The young and active are sufficiently resilient to adapt themselves to whatever seating accommodation is at hand but, for the relatively inactive, advice and action from the therapist may be needed both as to the chair and the sitting posture. Simple methods of adapting the dimensions of unsuitable chairs are in common use, e.g. raising or lowering seat; what is all important is that somebody is, in the first place, sufficiently knowledgeable and observant to know what needs to be done.

The sitting position is reached by getting up from lying, as from bed; by getting up from the floor or by sitting down from standing. The fundamental position (as described by gymnasts) demands active stability and balance of the head and trunk in the erect position. This is also an ability every patient needs to possess prior to walking because trunk stability provides the essential background for effective movement of the extremities. When sitting for any length of time some kind of support is required to maintain the normal alignment of the body, e.g. a chair back and/or armrests. When a back support is vertical and without arm support the weight of relaxed arms and shoulder girdle tends to draw the body forwards into total flexion with the result that the buttocks slide forwards on the chair seat; this results in prolonged over-stretching of the back extensors with loss of the secondary curves of the spine together with compensatory hyperextension at the atlanto-occipital joints provided the patient is awake and wants to look ahead. The effects of this are only

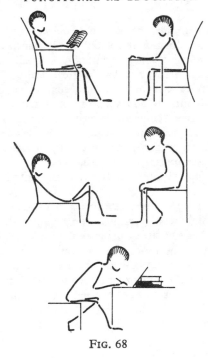

FIG. 68

transitory for the resilient young but for the weak, elderly or immobile restriction of thoracic movement, abdominal compression, reduction in the normal extensibility of the spine with hyperextension in the atlanto-occipital joint can create or aggravate problems. Sitting erect with back support and armrests or inclining the body forwards from the hips to rest the forearms on a table provide good support and are suggested as attitudes of alertness. When both back and head are inclined backwards and supported the attitude suggests relaxation.

For relaxation

When a chair has been selected for or adapted to fit the patient's requirements and his physical characteristics he must learn to sit well back into it to make full use of the support it provides. All too often the body is allowed to sag into flexion and the pelvis is pushed forward towards the front of the seat. Some find this posture comfortable and relaxing for a short time but it may lead to problems for the weak or very elderly who slide into this position when they fall asleep in the chair. A seat which is inclined backwards may help but unfortunately this makes standing up from the chair more difficult.

Sitting for work

In a work situation both the pattern of the seat which is available and its relative height and position in relation to the bench or table influence the stress factor of the worker profoundly. Small adjustments, often evaluated by trial and error, can make a great deal of difference. While sitting, movements of the trunk are mainly complementary to those of the head and arms. By turning both the head and the body the area of vision is extended, e.g. to greet a colleague entering from a door behind the sitter. Similarly the possible range for hand activities is considerably enlarged by the addition of body movement, e.g. by leaning forwards, the patient can reach the floor to pick up objects or tie up shoes.

There follows four examples of useful chair activities.

a. Bending forwards with a turn from sitting and raising

This activity combines the purpose of reaching to the floor to the right (with the left hand) and of sitting up and turning to look behind and to the left. The pattern of the movement is similar to that for the Forward Roll with Flexion (see p. 92). It may be advisable for the right hand to grasp the arm or base of the chair either for stabilisation or to facilitate the rotation. The movement may be reversed ending with a strong head and back extension-with-rotation to the right. Picking up a light object from the floor, such as a book, adds reality (Fig. 69: *i*).

b. Sitting with legs crossed

Many people like to sit with legs crossed at the ankles or thighs for comfort or neatness. To lift one leg across the other it must first be lifted from the floor. Help with the hands can be used sometimes if the movement presents difficulty: it may also be facilitated by firm pressure on the floor of the contralateral foot (extension) to elicit reciprocal activity to lift the leg (flexion). Dressing activities may also be assisted in this way by bringing the foot towards the hands. Rhythmical repetition of leg crossing may help to re-train reciprocal movement in preparation for walking or stair climbing (Fig. 69: *ii*).

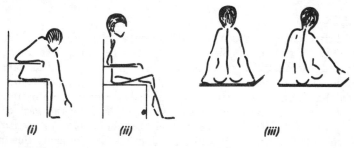

(i)   *(ii)*   *(iii)*

FIG. 69

c. Sitting, weight transference from buttock to buttock — leading to 'walking on the buttocks'

Anyone who sits for long needs to wriggle and shift their weight from time to time, especially on hard chairs or benches. Rocking the weight from one side to the other with the upper trunk erect and unsupported simulates the lower trunk activity which is used in walking. A forward walking movement on the buttocks towards the front of the chair seat adds a rotary movement of the pelvis and brings the patient to a position from which he can stand more easily. Some support given by the arms prevents swaying and reduces the frictional impedance of the chair surface (Fig. 69: *iii*).

d. Lifting the body weight forward towards the front of the chair seat, using the arms

The purpose of this and the previous activity (*iii*) is primarily to bring the body weight forwards over the base, i.e. the feet, in preparation for standing. The lift requires both strength and control in the arms whereas the 'buttock walk' can achieve the same purpose without them, e.g. in cases of severe Rheumatoid Disease. The supportive capabilities of the arms should have been assessed and built up, if necessary, before the patient is ready to concentrate on standing up; in any case the arms may be needed to use bars, crutches, sticks or some other supporting device for walking (Fig. 70).

To lift the body forwards the hands are supported on the arms of the chair, the side of the seat, or on non-slip wooden blocks on a bench or side

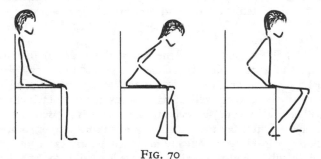

FIG. 70

of the bed. Few people have arms which are long enough to get a good push up from sitting level. As the arms take the weight the body is inclined forwards from the hips and the feet press towards the floor; extension at the shoulder joints then lifts and carries the buttocks to the front of the chair seat. Similarly, by reversing the shoulder movement, the patient learns how to sit well back into the chair. Practice in moving forwards and backwards in the chair repeatedly facilitates the movement and gives the patient the feeling of weight on the feet in readiness for standing.

Examples of activities which may be used to re-train the supportive function of the arms and legs from both lying and sitting positions are described in the next section.

Standing — Standing from Sitting

For many patients the ability to stand upright is a great morale booster and is regarded as a milestone of progress. However, from the point of view of being independent, there is little purpose in being able to stand or walk unless you can rise to the standing position unaided. Each patient has his own specific difficulties but there are a few factors which should be considered even before an attempt to stand is made. These factors include:

a. Suitable shoes

Most adults habitually wear shoes for weight-bearing as in standing or walking and they should be firm, comfortable and well-fitting. Wearing sloppy slippers or bare feet on a cold hard floor are a deterrent rather than a help, especially for the elderly.

b. Suitable clothing

Slacks or a track suit, which is easily pulled on, seem to be the most practical in lieu of long slippery nighties, dressing gowns or inadequately secured pyjamas; these can be the therapist's nightmare when the patient needs to be supported manually and they are a safety hazard at any time.

c. Range of joint movement

It is advisable to check that the range of movement in the ankles, knees, hips and lumbar spine is sufficient to permit the body segments to be brought into alignment for balance in the erect posture. Lack of range in any one of these joints will demand adjustments to maintain balance which will be easily recognised as postural faults. It is essential to identify the root cause of these faults so that they can be corrected or compensated. For example, a 'heel-raise', quickly made from cork, can compensate for restricted dorsiflexion of the ankle and make it possible to get a heel-strike without hyperextension of the knee and hip flexion. In this case there is a bonus effect as the pressure exerted on the heel acts as a stimulus to dorsiflexion.

d. Stability of support

Any apparatus used for support must be checked and tested for stability, e.g. chair, bars, furniture and floor mats.

For those of us who are able to stand whenever the occasion demands there is little or no need for thought, but for the patient who has been unable to get up for some time, the operation needs planning. With the need for independence in mind the patient must be permitted and encouraged from the start to take part in decisions concerning such things as the placing of the feet, whether to pull or push up with the arms and other relevant details. The feet are as close to the chair as possible and placed apart to bring the centre of gravity of the body over an effective base which is as large as possible; pushing up from the chair with at least one arm is to be encouraged since it is more realistic as far as the home is concerned, but to begin with the pull up on a bar means that the hand is in position to give support when the upright position is reached.

Moving to the Standing Position and returning to Sit

With the body weight, the feet and the hands in position on chair or bars, downward pressure with both hands and feet initiates total extension of the body which is continued until all segments are brought into vertical alignment and the patient stands. The therapist is at hand to give help or support when it is needed, being mindful of the fact that too much help delays the achievement of independence but that too little may ruin confidence if, as a result, things do not go smoothly. Only when the

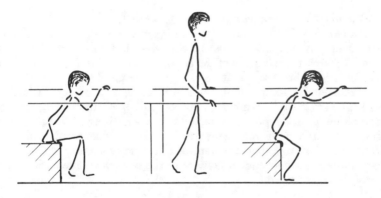

FIG. 71

therapist is satisfied that the patient can stand, balance in standing and return to sit, is it safe for him to practise alone. To sit down again the patient puts one hand on the arm of the chair (to test its presence and stability) then, leading with the head the whole body is flexed and then moved slightly backwards to sit. The buttocks can then be 'walked' or lifted to the back of the chair seat before the back is straightened.

Correction of some common mistakes in standing up
a. Failure to complete extension

The patient is asked to push the head up against the pressure of the therapist's hand placed firmly on the vertex. This often proves to be a quick and effective means to bring all body segments into alignment when the range of movement permits. When the knees and hips appear to be the main problem area manual pressure *in front* of the hip and *behind* the

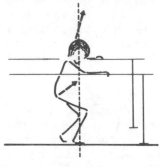

FIG. 72

knees alerts the patient's attention to both the site and direction in which movement is required (Fig. 72).

b. Failure to push down with the arms for support

Patients who use their arms to pull up to stand tend to pull upwards instead of pushing downwards on the bars thus losing the benefit of effective support and bracing of the back muscles. This is usually a panic reaction arising because the downward push required for support has not been explained or taught. It is likely to occur with patients who have used 'monkey poles' or other means of pulling themselves up in bed. Instruction in the supporting function of the arms is essential for many in order to teach them the management of frames, crutches or sticks at a later date. The flexion pull on a therapist's arm either for standing or walking does not lead to independent activity in the upright position and should always be discouraged.

c. Uneven distribution of weight on the feet

As the patient stands the body weight may not be brought forwards far enough to allow it to be evenly distributed on the whole of the foot or feet. When this happens the major part of the weight is taken on the heels and consequently the hips must flex to maintain balance. This can be put right by bringing the hips forward so that the weight is transmitted at the level of the transverse tarsal joints. A simple method is to ask the patient to lift the head and bring the hips forward and this request is reinforced when the therapist applies pressure on the *front* of the hips and high on the back of the head to indicate the direction of the movement required. This is in lieu of the 'tuck your seat in' type of request which is far from explicit and usually results in the patient bending his knees!

Therapists are often asked to 'get the patient on his feet' long before he has the ability to stand. In these circumstances the project is mainly, if not entirely, passive as far as the patient is concerned. The purpose of standing up is to elicit the postural reflex by approximation of joint surfaces and pressure on the soles of the feet, etc., maybe to promote drainage or as a psychological boost. Any abilities the patient can muster to help himself must be exploited, e.g. downward pressure on elbows or hands, inclining the body forward from the hips before rising to stand or bending to sit. Two helpers are usually essential and one of these should be a therapist experienced in this type of lifting so that the patient is given no cause to fear that he may fall. For very heavy or severely handicapped patients a standing table is a great help to start with and later on leg splints or body belts can make things easier in some cases. Whenever the patient manages to contribute something to his own support this is worthy of praise but when in fact he is totally supported by the therapists and contributes nothing it is unwise and unrealistic to try and encourage his effort by telling him he is doing splendidly.

Walking

Walking is a complex activity which requires the co-operation and control of the whole body. From a functional point of view the ability to walk is pretty useless unless the patient has first learnt to get up and stand. Most patients are eager to walk and regard the ability as something of a status symbol, so for them motivation is no problem. However, there are always some who doubt that they can succeed and exhaust themselves with fear and anxiety before even an attempt is made. Success is so important to a patient that every effort must be made to secure it by careful preparation.

Walking is the logical progression from the activities already described in previous chapters and including specific limb activities included in Chapter 12. Patients readily accept the necessity for practising preparatory activities provided they can see and understand that they lead towards walking itself.

To provide the conditions relative to normal functional walking the patient should be suitably dressed, women in slacks if possible, and wearing comfortable outdoor-type walking shoes. Sloppy slippers give the feet no support and may well slip off, causing discomfort and danger. Except for the very young, barefoot walking is unusual in the conditions which exist in this country; it is certainly uncomfortable and cold for the elderly.

Some general principles to be observed in teaching a patient to walk again are as follows:

a. The patient must learn the correct pattern of walking from the start. Movement patterns learnt and repeated accurately become habitual very quickly. Bad habits, as well as good ones, are established just as rapidly and they are difficult and time-consuming to eradicate.

b. Sufficient support and/or aids must be provided to allow a correct pattern of walking to be a practical possibility. In many cases the correct or optimum pattern of movement is only possible with the assistance of suitable support, e.g. parallel bars, crutches or sticks, to help balance or to reduce weight-bearing on one or both legs to an acceptable magnitude. Aids such as a toe-spring, heel-raise or prosthesis may be needed to compensate for neuromuscular or skeletal deficiencies.

c. The amount of support or aid must only be withdrawn or modified when the patient can demonstrate his ability to walk satisfactorily with less support or no aid. A demonstration of good walking for a few paces in a room is insufficient for testing purposes; endurance over longer distances and under other circumstances, such as out of doors or on carpets, must also be taken into account. Assuming that standing balance is assured before walking is attempted, a mechanical support such as parallel bars or the backs of two or more heavy chairs, is preferable to manual support. The therapist must, of course, be involved in the procedure to instruct and assist if necessary. A fixed support allows for greater concentration on the walking activity without the additional worry of moving and controlling crutches or sticks. The disadvantage of manual support is that patients learn to rely on the therapist and are often reluctant to change to other types of support which would allow greater independence.

Walking instruction

In many cases patients need little or no instruction and it is sufficient to make sure that it is safe for them to practise on their own to build up confidence and endurance. Even for those who have been unable to walk for some time because of a condition affecting the locomotor mechanism there is always a chance that they will walk instinctively once they are on their feet providing they have previously walked habitually. Therefore before embarking on instruction it is advisable to give the patient the opportunity to try to succeed merely with support and encouragement. If this method is successful much time and effort will be saved. Some patients only become ambulant the hard way with total re-education which demands patience and repetition of each phase; others may need correction and then practice of only one phase of the total walking pattern and the establishment of rhythmical movement.

It is not easy to find a relatively simple way to re-educate such a complex activity. In the brief description which follows only the activity of the lower limbs is mentioned but therapists will be well aware of the importance of efficient co-operation of the lower trunk muscles for providing the essential background of activity which is necessary for effective limb movement.

The mechanism of walking

The activity of the legs alternates during walking, i.e. one leg supports the body weight while the contralateral limb swings forwards to replace the foot in a new position ready to receive the body weight when it is transferred.   When this occurs the role of the legs is reversed.   It is an advantage for the patient to rise from the chair with one foot ahead of the other, i.e. in walk standing when the weight is equally distributed between the feet, to avoid making adjustments in the relative position of the feet before walking can begin.   For the purpose of description the term 'stance' indicates that the limb is weight-bearing in contrast to 'swing' in which it is weight-free.

Phase 1 — Stance

From walk standing body weight is moved forwards until the body is supported in vertical alignment over the forward foot; the line of gravity will reach the floor through the transverse tarsal joints.   The toes of the rear foot remain on the floor to help maintain balance.   This position of stance must be well learnt as progression is achieved by moving from one position of stance to another.   The position should be practised first with one foot in front and then with the other and its efficiency can be tested by lifting and replacing the toes of the rear foot.

Phase 2 — Swing and Heel Strike

The supporting function of the forward leg is maintained while the rear leg is lifted and flexed to clear the floor as it swings forwards; it is then extended at the knee and the foot is dorsiflexed to allow the heel to be brought to the ground, i.e. heel strike.   Thus this foot has been replaced

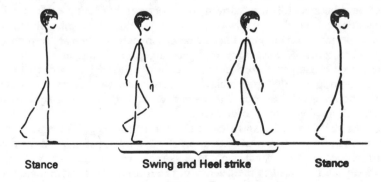

Stance   Swing and Heel strike   Stance

FIG. 73

in a new position ahead of the supporting leg and it must now be termed the forward foot. The balanced support of the other leg must not be disturbed during practice of the swing and heel strike. Sometimes there is difficulty in lifting the leg to clear the floor for the swing; in this case the patient can be asked to think of pressing the supporting leg hard towards the floor to encourage reciprocal flexion; this slightly tilts the pelvis laterally and also helps to reinforce the flexors. Usually it is the position of heel strike which causes the most difficulty; patients so often want to point their toes instead of putting the heel down; maybe they believe they should try to walk like a ballet dancer on stage! The heel strike is essential to initiate the normal rocker movement which transfers the weight to the forefoot and it also provides the stimulus for the leg extension activity and co-contraction needed to support the body weight.

Phase 3 — Weight Transference and Return to Stance

Then there is a return to stance position but with the other foot forward. The body weight is transferred from what is now the rear leg to be supported over the forward leg. Using the heel as a pivot the hip extensors of the forward leg are mainly responsible for initiating the forward shift of the pelvis in combination with lumbar and hip extensors of the rear leg during normal walking on level ground.

Once Phase 3 is completed Phase 2 follows and then these two phases are repeated alternately so that the patient moves from one stance to the other. Gradually all movements are blended in sequence to produce a rhythmical walking pattern. Phase 1 is introductory and is not repeated as such in the sequence; it is described here for purposes of training the stance positions.

Correction of Faulty Patterns of Walking

The body always does its best to achieve the purpose of an activity, i.e. walking, in this case. If it is prevented or impeded from using the habitual pattern it substitutes another (so-called 'trick movement'), e.g. a limping gait, and because this new pattern soon becomes habitual it often persists long after the need for it has disappeared. Pain, neuro-muscular inefficiency or limitation of joint range are common factors which are responsible for the automatic redesigning of a walking pattern and unless they are corrected or compensated the faulty pattern will persist. Adequate and efficient support, such as crutches or splints, can be used to compensate for deficiencies and ease pain temporarily but withdrawal of support too soon will inevitably lead to problems.

The skill of the therapist lies in the ability to recognise the key factor or factors responsible for the alteration of the normal pattern and then deal with it specifically. What is not always recognised is that many faults in walking can be traced to inefficiency of the muscles or lack of range in the lumbar region, i.e. the rigid spine, the pelvic tilt, as well as the more

obvious regions of hips, knees and feet.   The examples which follow may
be helpful to serve or suggest a line of thought.

a. Walking with flexed hips

This requires correction of the stance positions.   Lack of the normal
range of lumbar and hip extension, possibly due to prolonged recumbancy
or sitting slumped in a chair, can be a predisposing factor and merely asking the patient to stand erect often results in the patient bending the knees
to compensate for the hip flexion.   One method to help the patient's
efforts is for the therapist to give pressure in the direction in which movement is required, i.e. in front of the hip and high on the back of the head.
If the range of movement is severely limited, mobilisation of the relevant
joints must be attempted first.   Flexed hips, in combination with hyperextension of the weight-bearing knee, may be caused by lack of adequate
dorsiflexion range in the ankle joint, e.g. following Pott's fracture or spasm
shortening of calf muscles from any cause.   A heel-raise eliminates the
need for postural compensation and, incidentally, the pressure on the heel
provides a stimulus to dorsiflexion.

b. Lateral shift of the pelvis

This is a situation which frequently occurs when one leg has been
non-weight-bearing for some time.   It is easily observed because of the
uneven gait with lateral flexion of the trunk towards the side of the
affected leg.   The fault lies in the failure to transfer the weight over the
hip of the affected leg; therefore to preserve balance in Phase 2 the trunk
must lean sideways.   This type of gait can usually be corrected by practice
of the stance position until it is established and secure, then it can be
integrated with the total pattern of walking.   Another corrective activity
is sideways walking, with support of a handrail or a couple of chair backs,
in the direction of the affected leg, pausing when it is weight-bearing to
check that the whole body is in vertical alignment.   A useful test of
efficiency is to step up sideways on to a shallow stair-tread, or a large book,
and balance in the erect position.   Incidentally most hemiplegic patients
find this very difficult or impossible.

c. The flat-footed shuffle

Walking with the feet held rigid in dorsiflexion and possibly with
knees and hips slightly flexed is often associated with painful conditions
such as arthritis.   The protective tension which produces this pattern
increases the effort of walking and may well produce or even increase pain
by reducing the normal shock absorbing function of the many joints of the
lower limbs.   Mobilisation of the feet and lumbar region with instruction
in the use of all possible joint movement by adopting a 'lilting' gait often
helps to restore the 'spring' into walking.   The lilt is exaggerated at first

FIG. 74

and may be tried linking arms with a therapist or friend on either side to give support; later the lilt is reduced in degree to be less obvious. The provision of a 'Plastazote' insole or other device may increase foot comfort.

No one who has managed to walk a few steps forward should be misled into thinking that they can now be completely mobile without further effort. To be a functional walker the patient must be able to move freely and safely at home, then later on, out and about. Both mentally and physically the hazards to be overcome in normal everyday living are many and varied. Many patients quickly regain the confidence to attempt and succeed in doing all that they need and want to do, others less confident and adventurous can benefit from help and advice from a therapist. Practice in overcoming any particular stumbling block may be necessary but patients must be encouraged to face and solve their own problems as soon as possible.

At home, the floor surface may vary from carpets to polished floors and alas, sometimes, mats which seem to be designed to trip up the unwary. There is furniture to be used or avoided, room and cupboard doors to be opened and shut; toilet facilities such as basins, loo seats and baths to be utilised; steps, stairs or lifts to be negotiated and a variety of kitchen furniture to be used — to mention only a few circumstances to which the patients must adapt themselves.

Out of doors, pavements or other sidewalks are rarely smooth, horizontal or free from pedestrians, and road crossings in the face of traffic have been known to terrorise even the agile! Endurance, or rather the lack of it, may be a problem as suitable places to sit down and rest rarely occur at frequent intervals. Management of impedimenta such as handbags, shopping bags, briefcases or walking aids add to the hazard of moving about, especially when public transport, upon which many must rely, is used.

These are only a few of the problems which need to be considered before walking re-education (or gait training) is completed.

Suggestions for practising some walking activities are included in the **following chapter.**

Climbing Stairs or Ramps

This is often essential for the patient's independence. A shallow step or slope is attempted first and practice given to balancing with one leg on the step ready for weight transference. Movement both up and down and the management of crutches and sticks must be included. It is advisable to use a hand-rail, if there is one, in which case both crutches or sticks are held in the free hand. Frequent repetition of the activity is needed to build up endurance, increase speed and gain confidence.

FUNCTIONAL RE-EDUCATION

3. Limb activity

THE previous chapters have been devoted to a description of useful activities which involve the use of the whole body and which emphasise the importance of efficient trunk movement and stability. The extremities, i.e. the upper and lower limbs, are appendages of the trunk developed primarily for support and ambulatory mobility of the body as a whole. In the normal subject lower limb activity is still almost exclusively concerned with these functions; the upper limb also has an important and often forgotten role with regard to body support and movement which is immediately recognised and exploited when leg function is impaired for any reason, e.g. arm function used for transferring from chair to bed, crutches and handrails. However, in addition to these functions the adoption of the upright posture has freed the hands to a considerable extent for the development of a multitude of skilled activities.

Any disability, however localised it appears to be, affects the whole body to a greater or lesser degree. Therefore total restoration of function must be the aim of treatment in every case. Nevertheless measures which emphasise the activity of specific areas are appropriate at some stage of recovery.

Attention is drawn to the fact that the efficiency of limb function is profoundly influenced by and largely dependent on the co-operation of pelvic or shoulder girdle movement and stability. Body weight is transmitted to the legs through the pelvic girdle, the structure of which is admirably adapted for this purpose, i.e. the complete ring of bones between which only minimal gliding movement is permitted. Movement in lumbar and hip joints allows the pelvis as a whole to tilt and rotate to maintain posture and augment the range of limb movement. The shoulder girdle is incomplete and so permits a much wider range of movement in the proximal joints of the upper limb with the result that stability is a more complex problem. Muscles which control the shoulder and pelvic girdle are closely integrated with both trunk and limb muscles and their importance in relation to both movement and stability cannot be ignored.

Lower limb activities
Lower limb activity in the normal subject must be carefully observed

to make sure that patients with problems affecting these areas learn those activities they need for immediate use. Priority in re-education is given to the achievement of the basic leg function in the pattern and circumstances of activity required for normal independent living. In this context a summary of leg function is included.

Leg function
a. To support the body in weight-bearing positions

More often than not the area in contact with the supporting surface is the soles of the feet, as on standing erect, but one foot, the knees or knee can be substituted according to the circumstances. The legs may be used unilaterally, bilaterally or reciprocally. In the sitting position the feet and thighs are used to stabilise the position. Under normal circumstances joints are stabilised by the isometric co-contraction of antagonistic muscles, e.g. the quadriceps and hamstrings stabilise the knee joint, unless the latter is locked in full extension.

b. To lift or lower the body from or to the ground

Whatever the range of lifting or lowering demanded by the circumstances, the soles of the feet are the fixed point from which movement is initiated although the knee or knees may be substituted or recruited en route. The isotonic contraction of the leg extensors lift the body (by shortening concentrically) and control the movement of lowering (by lengthening eccentrically), e.g. getting from floor to chair, from sitting to standing or the reverse, climbing or descending stairs. Lifting and lowering the body during activities such as jumping and landing, or running and leaping only differ with regard to the speed and strength of the contraction which, of course, includes plantaflexors and toe flexors.

c. To propel the body in any direction

Movement is initiated from a fixed area of a foot (or knee as in crawling) and extensor activity is employed both for support and propulsion. The legs are used reciprocally (replacement of one foot to obtain progression involves some flexor activity).

d. The foot may be freed from weight-bearing for replacement in a new position, to gain momentum for a thrusting movement or to bring the foot within reach of the hands

These functions are all non-weight-bearing. The isotonic contraction of the leg flexors and dorsiflexors produce the movements necessary to replace the foot, e.g. in walking, running, stepping, climbing and also to bring it towards the hands for such activities as dressing when shoes or trousers are put on.

When considering these functions notice that:

a. The majority of functions are weight-bearing

Afferent stimuli, initiated by pressure on the soles of the feet and by consequent approximation in the joints of the leg, elicit a response which brings about either extensor activity for movement or a co-contraction for stability. The extensor muscles, which are normally powerful as they lift or lower the body weight in the upright position, habitually work together and reinforce each other's action. Working isotonically they lift (concentrically) or lower (eccentrically) the body weight and when working isometrically they co-operate with their antagonists to maintain stability of joints to balance the body.

b. Weight-bearing activities are initiated from a fixed foot (or feet)

The body is moved or supported on a foot which remains stationary and in contact with the ground. This means that the muscles involved work from what is anatomically described as 'with reversed origin and insertion'.

c. In non-weight-bearing the foot is free to move

The foot is freed from weight-bearing when it is lifted prior to replacement in a new position, e.g. to permit ambulation. Inspection of the foot and some dressing activities require the body weight to be supported by the buttocks or other areas to permit freedom of the foot. This situation is usually associated with flexor activity of the whole limb. It is worth noticing that, when the limb is dependent, traction stimulates flexion, i.e. to lift the foot, provided the traction is not prolonged.

In conclusion it is suggested that activities which are normally weight-bearing should be re-educated in a weight-bearing situation, i.e. with the foot fixed, with whatever degree of pressure on the feet that is tolerable in the circumstances and with the body in the erect position whenever possible. As functional movement is produced by the integrated activity of a series of muscle groups which habitually work together, this pattern of integrated activity is more likely to be effective in re-education. The activity of each group reinforced that of the other groups in the series, the stronger groups being more effective for reinforcing or recruiting the activity of those which have been weakened as the result of pain, disuse or other circumstances.

Retraining the Stability and Extensor Activity of the Legs

Man is a plantigrade animal and even in these days of mechanical transport he relies on the weight-bearing function of his legs for much of his mobility, provided he is not wheelchair-bound by necessity. As the undisputed aim of physiotherapy is the restoration of function as directly and as rapidly as possible it would seem logical to emphasise the importance of retraining stability and extensor activity of the legs in weight-bearing situations.

The term *weight-bearing*, as defined by therapists, presupposes that the total weight of the body is supported on one or both legs but for a multitude of reasons this may be contra-indicated for a time because of the patient's condition. When the magnitude of the pressure on the feet in erect positions exceeds that which is acceptable in the circumstances, it can be reduced by providing an *alternative support* for the excessive weight (partial weight-bearing), i.e. by taking some of the weight on the arms by using parallel bars, crutches, sticks or even the backs of two stout chairs, etc. When, for any reason, the body must remain supported horizontally the stimulus to an extensor reaction, i.e. suitable pressure on the sole of the foot with approximation, can be applied manually or by means of a board fixed at the bottom of the bed.

In all erect positions provision of a *controlling support* for the body, by the use of a handrail, bars or a wall, gives the patient the freedom to concentrate on the accuracy of the movement without the anxiety of maintaining balance; as he becomes more proficient this control is gradually withdrawn.

The few examples which follow are designed to indicate the application of the principles upon which specific retraining of leg function are based.

Non and partial weight-bearing

a. With the body supported horizontally a firm small pillow is placed under the knee to prevent hyperextension (which inhibits quadriceps contraction and puts a strain on the hamstring muscles). Pressure on the sole of the foot stimulates extensor activity as the patient is asked to press the knee to the pillow and the foot towards the therapist's hand, a footboard in the bed, a wall or other suitable structure (Fig. 75). Manual pressure is preferred at first to estimate the patient's ability to react to the stimulus or to judge the threshold of pain if this is a factor. Emphasis on heel pressure with the foot in dorsiflexion simulates the heel strike and elicits a stabilising reaction; pressure under the balls of the toes with plantaflexion elicits the more primitive total extensor thrust.

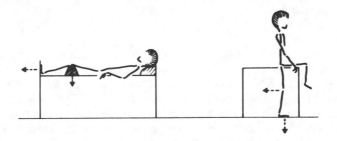

FIG. 75

b. A similar effect is achieved in the erect position for one leg when the body weight is supported at the buttocks or by one sound leg and an appropriate means of support.

c. From the sitting position leg extension and stability can be successfully practised in many parts of the range. A firm chair with armrests is most suitable; (*a*) the patient presses the thigh towards the seat of the chair (hip extension) and (*b*) the foot towards a wall or curb (plantaflexion) (*c*) with the heel pushing towards the floor as (*d*) the knee is straightened. Additional reinforcement is obtained by leaning back and pushing against the chair back. This simple activity needs careful teaching which is time well spent as it is frequently pain-free when other modalities elicit pain. It is particularly suitable for practice for the elderly patient who spends a considerable time sitting. It may be regarded as a substitute for quadriceps 'setting' or straight leg lifting which bear little relation to the patient's functional needs.

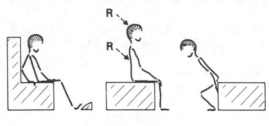

FIG. 76

d. Manual pressure applied in a forward and downward direction on the head or back of a patient holding the sitting position elicits activity in the soles of the feet and stabilising activity in all the leg muscles. Note the strong contraction of muscles round the ankle and foot.

e. When the patient lifts and transfers the buttocks forward towards the front of the chair the feet are fixed in the position for extension ready to stand up. The arm thrust can be used either as a partial support or to maintain balance.

Weight-bearing

a. Standing on the edge of a step or staircase with the heels free is a convenient way to emphasise the isotonic contraction of the plantaflexors, together with the isometric contraction of the quadriceps and hip extensors. The body is moved upwards and downwards vertically at the ankle joints. A reasonably rapid dropping of the heels boosts the contraction of the plantaflexors by utilising the stretch reflex. As the heels are lifted the patient is asked to brace the buttocks and pull them together to reinforce the contraction of the quadriceps (Fig. 77). The body weight can be

FIG. 77

adjusted on to either one or both feet or some weight may be taken by the arms which however are usually co-opted to ensure balance during the movement. This is a useful activity for home practice when knee flexion is contra-indicated, maybe because of effusion, or when the pattern of walking is marred by inefficiency of the calf muscles, a situation which is not uncommon following a prolonged period of non-weight-bearing or fixation in plaster.

b. Standing with his back in contact with a wall the patient bends his knees to slide his back downwards, still in contact with the wall and then straightens his knees to stand once more. The movement is repeated rhythmically in whatever range is possible and pain-free and the body weight can be distributed between the two legs as required (Fig. 78). This activity is useful for home practice when strength, mobility or smooth, co-ordinated movement is required. Care must be taken to avoid more flexion that can be controlled by the extensors.

c. A medicine ball, beanbag or other suitable object can be used for a similar 'bend and stretch' activity but balance is much more difficult without a wall. However, it adds variety as progress is made (Fig. 79).

FIG. 78

FIG. 79

Stepping Activities

a. Stepping up forwards is needed to go upstairs, get aboard a train or bus, reach the pavement after crossing the road, mount a ladder or enter some front doors.   If there are no stairs in the patient's flat, a stool or other stable support can be used for practice with the hands or hand pressed to the wall.   The importance of suitable handrails *and* their use cannot be over-emphasised as a safety measure and for building up the patient's confidence.

b. Stepping down forwards throws additional strain on the knee extensors because of the weight distribution of the body to maintain balance.   Many patients fear this movement and it is advisable to teach them to push their way downwards against the therapist's resistance, applied manually by supporting the pelvis anteriorly.   This gives a splendid sense of security and blocks the patient's view of a long descending staircase which he may find frightening.   Gradually the amount of resistance to the descent is reduced until the patient has the confidence to do without it altogether.   Practice for curbs and transport is helpful.

c. Stepping up and down sideways can be useful when only one handrail is available; the movement also helps to develop lateral stability of the leg and trunk.   Incidentally few patients with hemiparesis can achieve this type of stepping on to the affected leg.

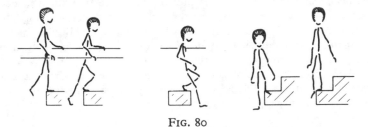

FIG. 80

To gain functional independence as early as possible when one leg is less efficient than the other, the more efficient leg is used to *move* the body weight while the less efficient plays a *supporting* role, i.e. the patient steps up *on* to the more efficient leg and *down from* it.   One patient's method of remembering this was as follows 'Go to heaven on the good and to hell on the bad!'

Retraining the Flexor Activity of the Legs

The leg flexors work with the extensors (co-contraction) to stabilise the legs for support of the body in erect positions; they lift the foot for replacement during reciprocal movements such as walking and running, and, with the co-operation of the trunk flexors, they bring the foot within reach of the hands for some dressing and washing activities.   Note that the isotonic activity of the flexors is always non-weight-bearing and that the foot is free to move. The few examples which follow suggest simple activities which can be facilitated, resisted or practised freely as required.

a. Total flexion of the leg on the trunk is easier to obtain from positions in which the leg and the lumbar region are fully extended immediately before flexion is attempted. Traction and the stretch stimulus will facilitate the movement.

FIG. 81

b. A strong extension thrust of one leg facilitates flexion in the counterlateral leg; this occurs in walking, running and stepping. The downward thrust of the forward leg to step up plus the backward stretch of the rear leg combine to achieve flexion to replace the foot in a new and forward position.

c. To reach the foot for putting on socks the patient usually sits and lifts the foot towards the hand and/or bends the body forwards. Forceful pressure of the counterlateral foot on the floor helps the lifting of the foot. It is usually sufficient to draw the patient's attention to the downward thrust of the foot to the floor but it can be resisted manually by the therapist to test if it works, or sometimes a cushion under the thigh reminds the patient of what he can do to help himself.

The leg activities described in this section are intended to suggest a line of thought as to the pattern and conditions of re-education rather than to provide a list of suitable activities.

Upper Limb Activity

The efficiency of arm activities is profoundly influenced by the movement and stability of the shoulder and the trunk. Scapular movement is essential to ensure that the face of the glenoid cavity is turned in the direction of the arm movement and the scapular muscles must provide stability to allow movement to be pivoted at the gleno-humeral joint. Correction of any deficiency in scapular range or stability must receive priority in treatment to avoid wasting time. Manual techniques are most effective as they can emphasise scapular rotation which is all-important in combination with elevation, depression, protraction and retraction. Obviously both isotonic and isometric contraction of the scapular muscles must be elicited.

Consideration of the normal functions of the arms in everyday living helps to suggest the pattern and type of activity the patient needs to achieve.

Four-legged animals use both fore and hind legs for support and ambulation. Having assumed upright posture man relies more on his legs for these functions to free the arms for the development of an amazing variety of manual skills. The arms, however, still play an important part by helping to support and move the body, especially when leg function is impaired; the pattern of this activity closely resembles that of the legs. Arm activities which rely on the skills of the hand which is free to move, e.g. dressing, eating, cooking, writing, use of tools for work or play have been well observed and analysed and therefore will not be considered here except to suggest that re-education should be realistic, therefore real objects which provide the right stimulus for the appropriate activity should be used, for a gripping movement of the hand is useless and unrealistic to a patient unless the action is purposeful. For example, try picking up an apple for inspection, holding it to take a bite and then releasing it for replacement on a plate.

Attention is drawn to the use of the arms to support and move the body as these functions are frequently taken for granted and omitted, especially in the treatment of some localised conditions.

Arm Function

a. *To support or help support the body in a variety of positions*

The long axis of the arm is vertical and the weight is transferred to the supporting agent, i.e. floor, table, chair arm, crutch or stick etc., through the hand or maybe the forearm or elbow. These weight-bearing situations stimulate the extensor thrust downward of the arm together with strong stabilising activity of the scapular muscles.

b. *To move or help move the body in any direction*

When the hands, forearms or elbows are weight-bearing and fixed, movement occurs proximally, e.g. pushing up to standing from a chair, transferring from chair to chair as when the legs are paralysed, or using a handrail to help mount stairs. The downward thrust of the arms is obtained by the action of the powerful extensors of the arm which include latissimus dorsi. When the hand is fixed by grasping (rather than by pressure) the body is moved towards the hand with a withdrawal action, i.e. elbow flexion with shoulder extension such as in pulling on a handrail going up steep stairs or getting on to a bus or train.

c. *To stabilise the position of objects*

One hand stabilises while the other is free to move, e.g. paper held in position for writing or bread for cutting. Similarly one arm may be used to stabilise an area of the body to improve the performance of another, e.g. supporting pressure downwards on one arm improves the effort to reach up with the other arm, also support of the elbows and/or forearm facilitates many skilled hand activities, e.g. as in writing.

Consideration of the supporting and moving functions of the upper limb justifies the need to emphasise their inclusion in the re-education programme. They are an integral part of the basic functional activities described in the previous two chapters, and, in the treatment of localised conditions affecting the arm, pressure on the heel of the hand with approximation of joints has far-reaching effects in combating the withdrawal reaction which tends to persist following painful injuries to the hand. Body movement away from the fixed and supported hand results in shoulder movement which is often pain-free when elevation of the arm under other circumstances is limited by pain.

A few examples of activities suitable for practice follow.

a. Pressing the heel of the hands to the chair or chair arm as if to lift the body from the seat can be practised at frequent intervals. The pressure can be increased by the therapist or by the patient himself pushing the body sideways towards the supporting arm.

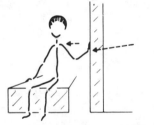 

FIG. 82

b. The patient leans on a table to take the weight of one or both hands and then moves the body forwards, backwards or sideways to vary the magnitude of the weight on the hands. If wrist or finger range of movement is limited some device is arranged to make pressure on the heel of the hand possible and pain-free.

FIG. 83

c. Prone kneeling and crawling activities provide the patient with a means of grading the amount of weight that the arm can support.

d. One hand is supported on a table or on the back of a heavy chair, then, by leaving the hand where it rests, the patient walks backwards bending at the hips to bring the arm towards elevation in relation to the trunk. This often provides a simple method of increasing the range of movement following stiffness in the shoulder region.

PART III

13

JOINT MOBILITY

SKELETAL movement occurs at the joints, the type and range of movement possible depending on the precise anatomical structure of the joint and the position of the muscles controlling it.

The slightly movable or cartilaginous joints all lie in the median plane and permit a limited degree of movement by compression of a fibrocartilaginous disc interposed between the bony surfaces, e.g. the pubic symphysis and joints of the vertebral bodies.

The freely movable or synovial joints predominate in the body and, with one exception, include all the joints of the limbs.

Structural Features

The adjacent areas of bone are covered with hyaline cartilage, which provides a relatively smooth, wear-resistant surface, allowing almost friction-free movements. The ligaments of white fibrous tissue are flexible and pliant and offer no resistance to the normal range of movement, but are inelastic and unyielding to prevent excessive or abnormal movement. Excessive stretching of this tissue stimulates the sensory receptors with which it is freely supplied, and causes pain and spasm in the muscles antagonistic to the force responsible for the stretching. The capsular ligament completely encloses the joint and supports the synovial membrane which secretes synovial fluid to lubricate the joint cavity, and, in all probability, to nourish the cartilage. Ligaments of the joint, consisting of localised thickenings of fibrous tissue, re-inforce the capsule, and accessory ligaments, which may be extra- or intra-capsular and stand clear of it, give additional strength. Tendons or fibrous expansions of muscles sometimes function in the capacity of ligaments. In some joints fibrocartilagenous structures and pads of fat are interposed to make the articular surfaces more congruent, or to act as buffers. They are usually adherent to the capsule at their circumference and are enveloped by the synovial membrane. Sensory stimuli from the joint record pain, pressure and the knowledge of position in space and are carried in the nerves which supply the muscles working over the joint. Nutrition is received from the blood vessels in the vicinity. Joints are stabilised by the balanced contraction of muscles, and are activated by the co-ordinated working of opposing groups. They can also be moved passively by an external force when the muscles are relaxed.

Classification

Joints may be classified according to the movement they permit.

Uni-axial. Movement takes place about one axis: in a hinge joint it is flexion and extension (e.g. inter-phalangeal joints), in a pivot joint it is rotatory (e.g. atlanto-axial joint).

Bi-axial. Movement takes place about two axes: an ellipsoid joint allows the four angular movements, flexion, extension, abduction and adduction, and a combination of these four called circumduction (e.g. wrist), and a saddle joint such as the carpo-metacarpal joint of the thumb is similar.

Poly-axial. Movements about many axes occur in ball and socket joints: they are the four angular movements, circumduction and rotation (e.g. hip).

Plane. Small gliding movements only are allowed, probably being more or less poly-axial in character (e.g. acromio-clavicular joint).

Some joints permit small accessory movements in certain positions which cannot be performed voluntarily.

Under normal conditions joint movements are usually limited by tension of the opposing muscles, contact of soft tissues or tension of ligaments.   For example, abduction of the hip is limited by the tension of the Adductor Muscles, flexion of the hip with the knee bent is limited by contact of the thigh with the abdomen, and extension is limited by the tension of the Flexor Muscles and the ilio-femoral ligament.   The active range is usually greater than the passive range of movement owing to the reciprocal relaxation of the antagonistic group of muscles.

LIMITATION OF THE RANGE OF JOINT MOVEMENT

Injury or disease may affect each or all of the structural components of a joint and lead to a reduction in the normal range of movement. The factors which commonly cause limitation are:

(*i*) Tightness of skin, superficial fascia or scar tissue.   This limits both the active and passive range.

(*ii*) Muscular weakness or inefficiency.   Weakness or flaccidity of muscles limits active range if the power of the muscles is insufficient to overcome the resistance offered by the weight of the part moved. Tightness or spasticity of muscles limits or prevents both active or passive movement, as the muscles antagonistic to the movement are unable to relax and allow it to take place.

(*iii*) The formation of adhesions.   These limit both active and passive movement.   Adhesion formation occurs following the output of a sero-fibrinous exudate into the region of the joint or into the joint itself. The joint structures become soaked in this exudate and if it is not speedily removed the fibrinous constituents of the exudate 'glue' the collagenous fibres of the ligaments and tendons together. The fibrinous 'glue' constitutes the adhesion, which is relatively soft at first and easily broken, but later, when the adhesions are consolidated, they contract to form scars. In this way the limitation of movement may be progressive. In the case of the shoulder joint, for example, adhesion formation may limit movement considerably, the capsule being 'glued' in folds, if the joint is allowed to remain in the same position for too long.

(*iv*) Displacement or tearing of an intracapsular fibrocartilage or the presence of a foreign body in the joint. Limitation of both passive and active movement may be present in this case, when either are accompanied by intense pain as the result of which the joint becomes locked by muscular spasm.

(*v*) Cartilaginous or bony destruction. The pain which arises may limit both active or passive movement and the articular surfaces will not slide easily upon one another. Bony or fibrous ankylosis limits movement altogether. Bony obstruction, such as in myositis ossificans, limits range in the direction of the obstruction.

(*vi*) Sometimes no organic cause can be found when the patient is unable to move a joint.

The Prevention of Joint Stiffness

Whenever possible it is the physiotherapist's duty to prevent a joint from stiffening, and thereby save the patient pain and the possibility of a permanent disability. The period of rehabilitation can be considerably reduced in many cases and a return to work made possible. The motto that 'Prevention is better than cure' was never more apt than when applied to stiff joints.

Methods of prevention vary to some extent with the cause of the potential stiffness. Tightness of skin, fascia and scars must be combated by hot pack, soaking or massage. Muscular efficiency must be maintained by resisted exercise to prevent atrophy from disuse. Suitable strong muscles working against maximal resistance can be utilised to secure overflow of effort and ensure contraction of muscles working across immobilised joints, e.g. after knee injury or surgery Quadriceps and Hamstrings can be activated by strong contraction of hip and foot muscles of either leg. In addition the patient must be taught to initiate and practise voluntary static contractions of these muscles at frequent intervals. 'Five minutes in every hour' is the slogan. Coarse muscles such as Quadriceps, Deltoid, Gastrocnemius and Glutei waste very rapidly without sufficient resistance to their contraction. In cases of flaccid paralysis passive movement maintains joint range and the extensibility of muscles, one or two full-range movements, within physiological limits, performed twice daily being sufficient for the purpose. Where muscular imbalance is present splintage may be required. Joint range can be maintained in spastic paralysis by initiating reflex movement. Any forcing of passive movement or strong resistance is contra-indicated following recent injury to the elbow region because of the danger of myositis ossificans.

The formation of adhesions in the collagenous tissues of tendons, ligaments and fascia must be prevented by attempting to control the level of serofibrinous exudate. This may be achieved by reducing circulation in the area, by removing the cause of the increased exudation, or by increasing the removal of exudate. Firm bandages, rest, chemotherapy, cold packs or cooling lotions are effective means of treatment. The position of rest is of some importance, as it is designed to ensure an equal degree of tension on all fibres of the capsule. If a portion of the capsule is slack and prone to fall into folds, adhesions form very readily and glue these folds into tucks, therefore the knee joint is rested for example in 20 degrees of flexion and the shoulder joint is partially abducted.

Except in cases of bacterial infection, persistent effort must be made to assist the removal of the exudate or swelling before adhesions become organised, even if the affected joint has to be rested for a time to prevent further exudation. Elevation of the part, elastic bandaging and rhythmical active exercise of muscles and joints in the vicinity assist the venous return and ensure the free movement of tendons passing over the affected joint. Other methods of improving the circulation, such as contrast baths, massage and heat, may also be employed if required. Careful active movements of the affected joint are begun as soon as possible and should progress rapidly. These movements maintain the power of the working muscles, ensure the freedom of tendons, and enable the pattern of movement to be remembered. Passive movements can also be used but they are more likely to give rise to minor trauma of the affected joint with consequent further output of exudation, and their effect on the circulation is minimal.

MOBILISING METHODS

Limitation of the range of movement impairs the function of a joint and the muscles that move it. Measures which increase the range of movement must, therefore, go hand in hand with those which build up sufficient muscle power to stabilise and control that movement. As instability and lack of control lead directly to further injury, it is absolutely essential to ensure that every degree of mobility gained can be controlled by muscular action. Active exercise, which leads to an increase in range, works the muscles and reminds the patient of the pattern of movement, is the treatment of choice; in some cases, however, relaxation and passive or manipulative methods precede or assist its performance.

1. *Relaxation*

Where spasm causes limitation of movement relaxation leads to an increase in range.

2. *Relaxed Passive Movements*, including accessory movements

Relaxed passive movement maintains but does not increase mobility. It is used when active exercise in the same range is impossible or contra-indicated. Freedom of accessory movement is necessary to maintain or regain full joint function.

3. *Passive Manual Mobilisation Techniques*

(*i*) Mobilisations of joints.

(*ii*) Manipulations performed by physiotherapists or surgeon/physician.

(*iii*) Controlled Sustained Stretchings.

These techniques increase mobility in joints and are followed by active exercise to maintain the increase. Where the manipulations are carried out by a surgeon or physician, it is an advantage to the physiotherapist to be present so that she sees the range of movement to be maintained, and can treat the patient as soon as possible after he comes round from the anaesthetic.

4. *Active Exercise*

Assisted Exercise. Rhythmical movement, in which muscular contraction and assistance combine at the limit of the free range against the resistance of the limiting structures, is often successful in increasing the range. The patient's co-operation and strict supervision by the physiotherapist are essential to achieve results.

Free Exercise. This is a valuable method as the exercises can be learnt and carried out at frequent intervals by a co-operative patient. This co-operation, and accurate instruction to ensure the correct movement, are essential. Pendular movement is used with an attempt to increase the amplitude, or a series of contractions or 'pressing movements' are performed at the limit of the range. Circulation is also increased.

Resisted Exercise.   Techniques of Proprioceptive Neuromuscular Facilitation are most effective for rapid mobilisation of stiff joints. Relaxation techniques are used to obtain a lengthening reaction of tight muscles and strengthening techniques for their antagonists. Control of the newly gained range of movement is established by slow reversal techniques.   In some cases rhythmic stabilisation followed by contraction into the range which has previously been limited may be more suitable.

Objective, Occupational and Diversional Activities such as ball exercises, scrubbing and hiking may fall into any one of the three previous categories.   They interest the patient, increase the circulation and the variety of natural movement may help to 'shake loose' joints which do not respond to other methods; in any case they are always a valuable adjunct to more localised treatment.

14

TECHNIQUE OF MOBILISING JOINTS

THE aim of mobilisation may be either to maintain the present range of movement in a joint or to increase it. Relaxation, Relaxed Passive Movements including accessory movement, Passive Manual Mobilisation Techniques, Assisted, Free, Assisted-Resisted and Resisted Exercises or General Activities all have a part to play in the mobilisation of joints in one case or another. The technique of Relaxation has already been considered, Manipulations under an anaesthetic are the province of the doctor or surgeon and the techniques of Proprioceptive Neuromuscular Facilitation which are recommended as the most effective method of using resisted exercise, are described in Chapter 9. With regard to all Free Exercises it is important to emphasise that a mobilising effect results not so much from the choice of a particular exercise but depends very largely on the manner in which it is performed. Full-range movement at natural speed with emphasis at the limit of the range and repeated many times and at frequent intervals seems to be most effective, but sometimes a more rapid movement or a sustained contraction are also used.

Assessment of Progress

Measurement of the present range of joint movement (see p. 29) is essential before treatment begins and at specified intervals afterwards to permit assessment of progress. If progress is unsatisfactory the method of treatment must be modified or changed, and if it is still ineffective further investigation of the cause of the limitation must be made.

JOINTS OF THE FOOT

The many joints of the foot all contribute to its ability to adapt itself for walking on uneven surfaces, and to its resilience. With the exception of the transverse tarsal and subtaloid joints the range of movement at the intertarsal, tarsometatarsal and intermetatarsal joints is very small and cannot be localised to a single joint

RELAXED PASSIVE MOVEMENTS OF THE FOOT

Interphalangeal Joints of the Toes

Each of these joints can be moved separately with the patient *sitting* or *lying* with the foot relaxed. The bone proximal to the joint moved is fixed, traction is given in the long axis of the joint and the full free range of flexion and extension is performed with a slight pause for overpressure at the end of each movement. Extension usually requires emphasis, as curling of the toes frequently limits this movement.

Metatarsophalangeal Joints of the Toes
½ ly.; Toe flex. ext. abd. add. and ⊙ (pass.)

Passive movements of each joint may be done separately or all five joints may be moved simultaneously, in which case the fingers of the physiotherapist's fixing hand lie under the arching shafts of the metatarsal bones and her thumb rests on the dorsum of the foot. Her other hand grasps the proximal phalanges, gives traction and then performs the movement. Alternatively the distal phalanges may be grasped, and, while the toes are kept straight by traction, the movements are performed at the metatarsophalangeal joints, usually with emphasis on flexion. This alternative method is preferable as it more nearly approaches the correct functional movement of the toes in gripping the floor. For abduction and adduction all the toes are moved together either medially with regard to the body, or laterally. The great toe may need special attention.

The Transverse Tarsal Joints
½ ly.; 1F. inv. and ev. (pass.)

One of the physiotherapist's hands fixes the patient's ankle in dorsiflexion to prevent the lateral movement which may take place in this joint during plantaflexion. The other hand grasps round the distal row of the tarsus and the bases of the metatarsal bones from the lateral border of the foot and then inverts and everts the forefoot. Traction and overpressure are given in the usual way.

Ankle Joint
crk. ½ ly.; 1 Ank. dorsiflex. and plantaflex. (pass.)

Tension on the Calf Muscles must be slackened to avoid limitation of dorsiflexion, therefore some position in which the knee is bent must be selected. Half lying with the patient's knee bent over a firm pillow or across the physiotherapist's knee, leaving the heel unsupported, is a suitable starting position. The physiotherapist's fixing hand grasps immediately above the joint while her other hand grasps round the foot at the level of the tarsal joints to perform the movement. Overpressure during dorsiflexion may be given with this hand in the same position or by means of traction on the heel with the forearm on the sole of the foot. The plantar structures must not be strained by pressure on the forefoot.

Accessory Movements of the Foot

Metatarsophalangeal Joints of the Toes

Some accessory rotation, side to side, and anteroposterior gliding movements are possible when the joints are distracted.

Intermetatarsal Joints of the Foot

These movements cannot be performed actively except in con-

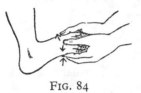

Fig. 84

junction with other movements. Gliding movements between the distal ends of the bones performed passively help to keep the foot resilient. Upward pressure of the physiotherapist's fingers bunched behind the heads of the metatarsal bones on the sole of the foot, in combination with a stroking movement performed with her thumbs on the dorsum, moulds the anterior transverse arch of the foot into what should be its normal non-weight-bearing position (Fig. 84).

The Subtaloid Joint

Movement here usually accompanies inversion and eversion so that the heel falls in the same plane as the forefoot. With the leg resting horizontally the heel is grasped with both hands, as in a clamp, and while traction is maintained on the tendo-calcanaeum a side-to-side gliding movement on a vertical axis is performed. Fixation of the talus by means of pressure on the lateral malleolus with the fingers, and on the medial aspect of the talus with the thumb, while the calcanaeum is moved on it by the other hand, is another method which may be used.

Controlled Sustained Stretching of the Foot

Stretching of tightened structures is required for deformities such as talipes equino-varus. For this condition the baby's knee is bent and protected by the mother while the ankle and heel are grasped so that the physiotherapist's thumb rests on the talus. Using this as a fulcrum for the movement the forefoot is then drawn into abduction and eversion. When this movement is relatively free it is followed by that of dorsiflexion, during which traction is given on the calcaneum in an attempt to approximate the little toe and the anterior aspect of the tibia.

Assisted Exercises for the Foot

Manual assistance can be given to all the muscle groups which move the joints of the foot by using the same grasps as those used for giving passive movements of the joints.

Self-assistance given by means of a rope and pulley or a treadle machine is most useful for home practice.

EXAMPLES OF FREE EXERCISES FOR THE FOOT

Rhythmical exercises which are performed at a speed which allows time for additional pressure at the limit of the free range are used for group treatment and for home practice. A special effort on every 2nd or 3rd beat provides variety and reduces fatigue.

e = easy
a = effort
b = more effort
c = much more effort

FIG. 85   Effort Pattern for Rhythmical Movement

Exercises during which the foot is free from weight usually precede those in standing.

Non-weight-bearing Exercises

1. For the Ankle Joint

a. *Legs crossed sitting; 1 Foot dorsiflexion and plantaflexion.*

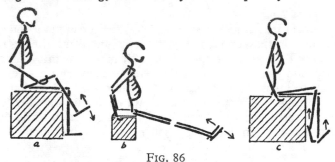

FIG. 86

b. *inclined long sitting; alternate Foot dorsiflexion and plantaflexion* (Treadle Movement) (Fig. 86b).

c. *sitting; alternate Heel and Toe raising* (Fig. 86c).

2. For the Transverse Tarsal and Subtaloid Joints

d. *Legs crossed sitting (Foot dorsiflexed); Foot inversion and eversion.*

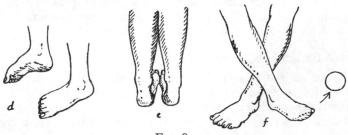

FIG. 87

e. *close sitting; Foot inversion and eversion (inner and outer border raising).*

f. *Ankles crossed sitting; Foot inversion and eversion* (Sweeping Movement).

3. For the Metatarsophalangeal Joints

g. *sitting (Toes resting on book); Toe flexion and extension at these joints, with pressure on balls of Toe.*

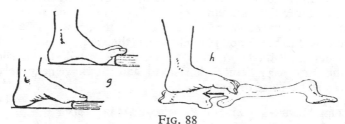

FIG. 88

h. *sitting; Foot shortening by flexion at the metatarsophalangeal joints.* (Draw up stocking under medial longitudinal arch.)

i. *sitting; Toe parting and closing.* (This may be done in water or sand.)

Weight-bearing Exercises

j. *reach grasp high Toe standing (wall bars); Heel raising and lowering.*

k. *reach grasp standing (on rocking board); Foot inversion and eversion.* (See saw movement of board.)

l. *high standing; walk up inclined form.*

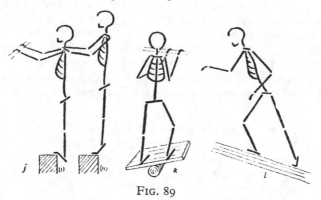

FIG. 89

ACTIVITIES TO INCREASE MOBILITY OF JOINTS OF THE FOOT

Common activities such as walking, running and, later, skipping, dancing and hiking are also good mobilising exercises when the feet are used correctly. Walking and running on uneven ground are specially recommended, as the feet are constantly required to adapt themselves to a varying surface and this requires movement at most or all of the many joints.

THE KNEE JOINT

The joints between the femoral and tibial condyles permit flexion, extension, and rotation in semi-flexion.   The latter is possible in this position only when the lateral and medial ligaments, which lie some-what posterior to the joint, are slackened as the knee is bent.   Gliding movements in all directions are possible at the patello-femoral joint when the Quadriceps Femoris is relaxed, and this movement must be free to allow the knee to bend.

ACCESSORY MOVEMENTS AT THE PATELLO-FEMORAL JOINT

Whenever freedom of movement of the patella cannot be maintained by means of repeated contractions of the Quadriceps Muscles the bone must be moved passively.   With the knee fully extended and the muscles relaxed, the patella is grasped between the first finger and thumb of both hands and glided up and down and from side to side.

RELAXED PASSIVE MOVEMENTS OF THE KNEE JOINT

Between all the Articular Surfaces of the Knee Joint
a. *ly.; 1 Hip and K. flex. and ext. (pass.)*
With the patient in *lying* and relaxed the physiotherapist in *walk standing* gives support under the thigh with one hand and with the other hand grasps round the ankle and gives traction.   The hip and the knee joints are then moved into full flexion during which the physiotherapist's hand, which is under the thigh, glides to a position in front of the knee to give overpressure at the end of the movement. As the hip and knee are extended, this hand is again moved to its original position to prevent any jarring of the knee at the conclusion of the movement.

b. *s. ly.; 1 Hip and K. flex. and ext. (pass.)*
Either the leg which rests on the plinth or the one which is upper-most may be moved.   In the latter case the leg must be fully supported throughout the movement in the hands, in suspension, on a re-education board or in water.

c. *½ crk. ly.; 1 K. rot. (pass.)*
For rotation at the knee the thigh is supported vertically with the knee flexed to a right angle.   The physiotherapist supports the thigh with one arm and grasps round the heel with the other hand so that the

sole of the foot rests on her forearm, or, she may grasp round the lower leg just above the ankle.

To localise movement to the knee joint either *side lying* or *prone lying* are the most suitable starting positions for the patient.

ASSISTED AND ASSISTED-RESISTED EXERCISE FOR THE KNEE JOINT

(i) s. ly.; 1 K. flex. and ext. (ass.)

Manual assistance may be given for the Flexors or Extensors of the Knee from *side lying* with the limb supported in the hands or on the surface of a plinth. In the latter case it is convenient to support the other leg in slings, but when the hands are used for support the leg remaining on the plinth is bent up to increase the stability of the trunk. The pattern of movement used should be that of withdrawal of the leg followed by thrust, as in this way the stabilisation of the origins of the muscles working over the knee is adapted progressively to the circumstances of the movement.

During the thrusting movement the physiotherapist's hand is placed under the ball of the great toe in order to gain advantage from the proprioceptive stimulation of pressure on this area. The movement is repeated rhythmically many times and, whenever possible, resistance to the movement is gradually introduced to encourage greater activity on the part of the muscles (Fig. 90).

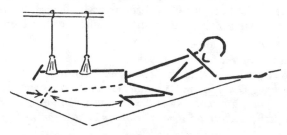

FIG. 90

(ii) pr. ly.; alt. K. flex. and ext. (auto-ass.)

Auto-assistance can be arranged in the *prone* position, and is particularly suitable when the hip is arthrodesed. A pillow under the pelvis to get a degree of flexion will, however, help the movement if the hip is free.

A rope is attached to the heel of the stiff leg by some suitable device and passed over a pulley on the wall facing the patient, the other end of the rope being attached to the other leg. The rope is kept taut throughout by the reciprocal movement of the lower legs, the assisting leg being near full extension when the other reaches the limit of flexion. Alternatively the patient may operate the assistance by

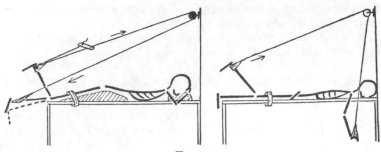

FIG. 91

hand.   Maximum assistance and overpressure are given at the limit of flexion by a right-angled pull on the rope at this point.

Except in special circumstances, these assisted exercises are only of use when movement is very limited or the patient is not allowed to bear weight.

Free Exercises for the Knee Joint

These may be non-weight-bearing, partial weight-bearing or full-weight-bearing according to the condition and the stage of treatment at which they are used.   Rhythmical movements with active overpressure at the limit of the range are essential.   In full-weight-bearing exercises, when the body weight is used to assist flexion the power and control of the Extensor Muscles must be sufficient to restore the joint to full extension.

Non-weight-bearing Exercises (Fig. 92)
    a. *lying; One Hip and Knee flexion and extension.*
    b. *side lying; One Hip and Knee flexion and extension.*
    c. *prone lying; alternate Knee flexion and extension.*
    d. *high sitting; alternate Knee flexion and extension.*

Partial Weight-bearing Exercises (Fig. 93)
    e. *Bicyling* on free or stationary bicycle.
    f. *Rowing* on rowing machine or inclined form.
    g. *long sitting; receive and pass ball.*

Weight-bearing Exercises (Fig. 94)
    h. *reach grasp Toe standing; double Knee bending and stretching, with bobbing movements.*
    i. *crouch position; alternate Leg stretching, with or without spring.*
    j. *prone kneeling; sit back on Heels.*

Activities to increase Mobility of Knee Joint
Correct movement in walking must be learnt and practised as soon as possible, and later, walking up- and downstairs and uphill and down-

hill, breaststroke swimming and other activities involving running and jumping should be encouraged when possible.

FIG. 92

FIG. 93

FIG. 94

THE HIP JOINT

The joint between the spherical head of the femur and the aceta-
bulum is poly-axial and very stable. The range of movement can
become limited in any or all directions but the most usual deformity
is a combination of flexion, adduction and lateral rotation. Emphasis
in mobilising is, therefore, on extension, abduction and medial rotation.

RELAXED PASSIVE MOVEMENTS OF THE HIP JOINT

ly.; 1 Hip abd. and add., med. and lat. rot., flex. and ext. (pass.)

The leg which is not to be moved is fully abducted and fixed, either
by a sandbag or by bending the knee over the side of the plinth, and
the patient relaxes. With the forearm supinated, one of the physiotherapist's hands supports under the thigh, and with the other pronated she supports the lower leg at the ankle joint. Traction is given
and the leg is moved into abduction (about 30° from the median plane)
and adduction. Medial and lateral rotation can be performed by giving
traction on the heel and rolling the knee inwards and outwards with a
stroking movement (as in using a rolling pin).

Support under the thigh and round the ankle or foot is given for
flexion, the hand under the thigh moving as the knee is bent into a
position in which the fingers support the knee laterally and the thumb
gives overpressure on the front of the knee. This pressure is directed
towards the patient's shoulder. The leg is then extended by allowing
the heel to come to the plinth first and then straightening the lower leg.
Extension is still incomplete in this position and the patient must be
moved to *side lying* or *prone lying* for the additional 15° which is
possible.

A combination of abduction and lateral rotation, adduction and
medial rotation can be done in both hips simultaneously from *crook
lying*, and the four angular movements can be combined as a hip rolling,
in which case the knee is held in flexion.

ASSISTED EXERCISES FOR THE HIP JOINT

Grasps similar to those used for relaxed passive movements enable
the physiotherapist to assist the patient's own efforts to move.

As the limb to be moved is heavy, suspension and the use of roller
skates are valuable means of assistance. Suspension for flexion, extension, abduction and adduction may be either axial with manual
assistance, or pendular, and the use of tension springs gives a feeling of
buoyancy and prevents any jerking as the direction of the movement is
reversed. In acute cases, where movement is very limited, vertical
suspension at the knee and foot helps relaxation and avoids the centri-

petal pull of the rope, which presses the joint surfaces against each other, in the axial method. The point of suspension should be high in this case, to flatten the plane of movement as much as possible.

Extension is emphasised in *side lying*, the stationary leg being bent up to fix the pelvis by the tension of the Hamstrings (Fig. 95, left).

For abduction one or both legs can work in *lying* or *prone lying*, the legs being as nearly in alignment with the body as possible to get pure abduction (Fig. 95, centre).

Skates can be used in a similar way either on the floor or on hinged and sloping boards.

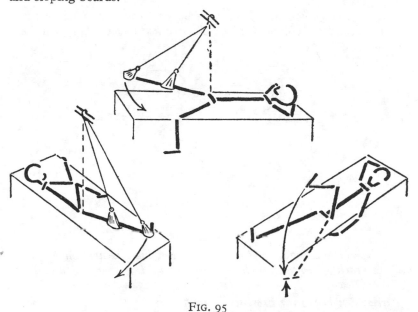

FIG. 95

Rotation is most effective when combined with angular movements, medial rotation with abduction, lateral with adduction. In flexion, the leg can be suspended so that the thigh is vertical and the lower leg horizontal and a rotatory movement assisted manually with traction. In extension, traction can be given and movement assisted manually.

EXAMPLES OF FREE MOBILITY EXERCISES FOR THE HIP JOINT

Movement in these joints is usually associated with movement in the spine and in the knees. A combination of hip and knee flexion with lumbar flexion and backward tilt of the pelvis provides a fixed origin for the Hip Flexors and relief of tension on the antagonistic muscles (the Hamstrings), whereas extension of the hip and knee with lumbar extension and a pelvic tilt forwards provides for maximum efficiency of both the Gluteus Maximus and the Hamstrings and a release of tension on the Hip Flexors (including Rectus Femoris).

To increase mobility, full-range movement performed with active overpressure and frequent repetitions is required. In non-weight-bearing exercises resistance to the movement can be added to increase the effect.

Non-weight-bearing Exercises (Fig. 96)
  a. *side lying; one Hip and Knee bending, stretching and Leg carrying backwards.*
  b. *grasp high half standing; Leg swinging forwards and backwards.*
  c. *prone lying (Knees straight, Toes tucked under); Leg medial and lateral rotation.*

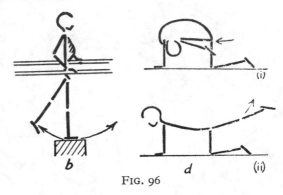

FIG. 96

  d. *prone kneeling; one Hip and Knee bending and stretching.*
  e. *reach grasp high half standing; one Leg swinging across and sideways.*

Partial Weight-bearing Exercises (Fig. 97)
  f. *heave grasp high half standing; Arm stretching and one Knee bending.*
  g. *crouch position; step or spring to stride prone falling.*

Weight-bearing Exercises (Fig. 98)
  h. *grasp standing; change to fallout sideways position.*
  i. *half kneeling, or step standing; forward pressing.*
  j. *crouch position; change to stretch standing.*
  k. *stride standing; Pelvis and Trunk rotation.*
  l. *standing; step and hop with one Leg swing sideways.*

Activities suitable for increasing Hip Mobility
  Examples of these are walking, running, climbing stairs, cycling, rowing, breast-stroke swimming and golfing.

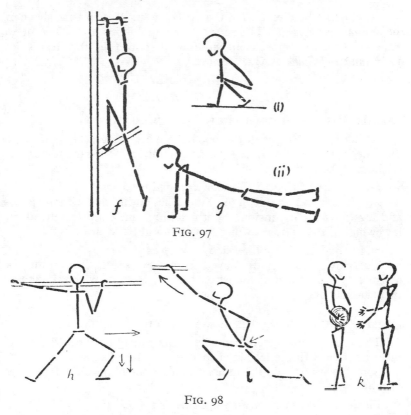

FIG. 97

FIG. 98

THE JOINTS OF THE PELVIS

The movements in these joints are very slight and are associated with those in the hip and lumbar spine.

During pregnancy, however, the pelvic joints become more mobile as the result of the slackening of their ligaments, and allow a rotation of the hip bones on the sacrum which increases the capacity of the pelvis. These ligaments tighten again during involution and the joints regain their stability.

THE JOINTS OF THE VERTEBRAL COLUMN

Movement between any two adjacent vertebrae is very limited, but the sum of these small movements results in the production of a considerable range in the spine as a whole. The movements permitted vary in the regions according to the shape and thickness of the interarticular discs, the direction of the articular surfaces and the shape of the spinous processes. The spine can be mobilised as a whole or in regions. Assessory movements are not described in this text. See *Mobilisations of Spine* by G. P. Grieve.

(A) THE LUMBAR REGION

Relaxed Passive Movements of the Lumbar Region

Owing to the weight of the body these are most easily performed in suspension, the best leverage being obtained by fixing the upper part of the body and moving the lower.

s. ly. (P. and L. susp.); Lumbar flex. and ext. (pass.)

For flexion and extension the patient lies on his side with the pelvis and legs in axial suspension. With the hips and knees extended the lower half of the body is swung forwards and backwards.

ly. (P. and L. susp.); Lumbar s. flex. (pass.)

The pelvis and legs are moved from side to side, fixation may be assisted by pressure at the waist on the side towards which the movement takes place.

Assisted Exercises for the Lumbar Region

These are usually given manually as the patient performs the movement actively with the legs in suspension or from *hanging*.

Some positions hold the lumbar spine at the limit of the free range of movement.

Flexion.   *crk. sitt., lg. sitt., stp. sitt. or stp. kn. sitt.*
Extension.   *sit. ly., ly.* (pillow under waist).

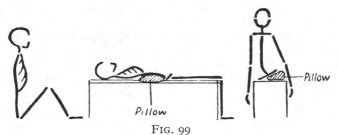

FIG. 99

Side flexion.   *s. sitt., sitt.* (pillow under one buttock).

Examples of Free Exercises for the Lumbar Joints

a. (i) *crook lying* or
    (ii) *grasp crouch sitt.; Pelvis rolling.*

b. *stride long* or
   stride crook sitting; Trunk bending forward and raising.
c. ½ *reach grasp step standing; Trunk bending forward and arching
   backward.*
d. *prone kneeling; Trunk side bending.* (Wag Tail.)
e. *half standing (Foot support sideways); Trunk bending sideways.*
f. *hanging; Leg swinging sideways (from waist).*

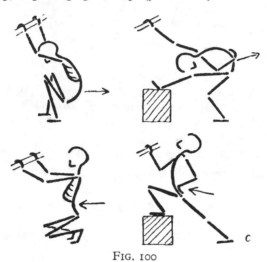

FIG. 100

(B) *THE THORACIC REGION*

Flexion, extension and side flexion are all limited in this region
but rotation is free.   The tendency to adopt a flexed position and so
to restrict the movement of the ribs in inspiration makes extension and
straightening of major importance.

Passive movements in this region are rarely used.   The movements
are most easily performed as active assisted exercises.

Assisted Exercises for the Thoracic Spine

During these exercises the lumbar region must be controlled as far
as possible by the starting position.   In the upright position the weight
of the head and shoulders has a telescoping effect on the spine; when
this weight is removed from it by traction or by using the horizontal
position the spine tends to straighten and elongate and the range of
movement is increased.

Active extension is assisted by traction on the tightened anterior

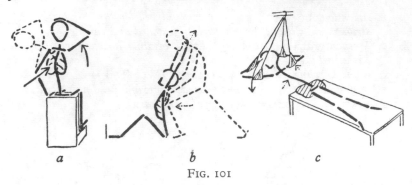

FIG. 101

structures and by a deep inspiration (Fig. 101*b*); side flexion can be localised and assisted when the trunk is suspended horizontally in extension (Fig. 101*c*).

EXAMPLES OF FREE EXERCISES FOR THE THORACIC SPINE

Relaxation in *crook lying* and deep breathing help to straighten the spine.

 a. *stretch Wrist support stoop kneel sitting; Trunk pressing downward.*
 b. *inclined prone kneeling; Leg lift crawl .*
 c. *prone kneeling; Trunk turning with loose Arm swinging.*

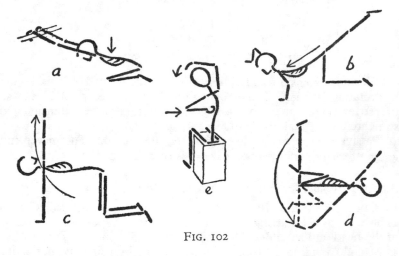

FIG. 102

 d. *yard crook or Leg lift lying; Trunk rotation.*
 e. *under bend ride sitting; Trunk side bending.*

(C) THE CERVICAL REGION

Movement in this region and that at the atlanto-occipital joint are virtually inseparable. Flexion, extension and lateral flexion are free but rotation is limited except at the atlanto-axial joint.

RELAXED PASSIVE MOVEMENTS OF THE HEAD AND NECK

The patient lies relaxed on a low plinth with head supported by the physiotherapist's hands cupped round the occipital bone, as she sits with legs astride and elbows resting on her knees. Traction is given in the long axis of the spine prior to all movements.

CONTROLLED SUSTAINED STRETCHING

Controlled sustained stretching can be used in the treatment of Torticollis. The child's head is grasped between the hands and his shoulders are fixed by the mother. Traction is given first to stretch the neck, which is then bent to one side and then rotated in the opposite direction, thus obtaining the maximum stretch on the shortened sterno-mastoid muscle. The child's mother is usually taught to perform the stretching movement so that it can be repeated at frequent intervals during the day.

ASSISTED EXERCISE FOR THE HEAD AND NECK

When the shoulder girdle is fixed, manual assistance can be given to all movements by the physiotherapist or by the patient himself.

FREE EXERCISE FOR THE HEAD AND NECK

Rapid full-range movements of the head tend to give a feeling of giddiness and so these exercises should be done in the patient's own rhythm, often with a rebound or a pressing movement at the limit of the range and in bouts of short duration. The shoulder girdle may be fixed or the movement can be continuous with that of the rest of the spine, preferably with the objective interest of seeing or touching some object.

a. *low grasp sitting; Head bending, stretching, side bending, rolling and turning.*
b. *prone kneeling; Head bending, stretching, side bending, rolling and turning.*
c. *standing; throwing and catching beanbag, quoit or ball.*
d. *sitting or crook sitting; Trunk bending to put right Ear on left Knee and raising with Head turning to right.*

P.N.F. Hold-relax techniques are very effective for neck mobilisation as they can be localised to specific points, i.e., atlanto-occipital, atlanto-axial, lower cervical joints.

(D) THE WHOLE SPINE

Many activities using heavy balls, Indian clubs, sticks and hoops promote a wide range of trunk movement.

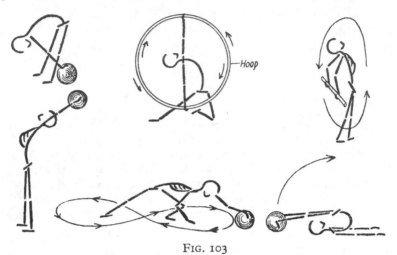

FIG. 103

THE THORAX

The ribs move in respiration and with the thoracic spine. When the range of the respiratory excursions is reduced, the thorax may be either expanded and unable to relax, or tense and unable to expand. In the first case, mobility can be improved by relaxation and breathing exercises which emphasise expiration, and in the second, relaxation and breathing exercises to improve the efficiency of the inspiratory muscles are required.

Expiratory Exercises

These are general breathing exercises with emphasis on expiration and relaxation. The patient is taught to reverse the effort of breathing so that expiration becomes a muscular act and inspiration the recoil from it. Inspiration must be easy and as shallow as possible, expiration is prolonged and assisted by pressure on the antero-lateral aspects of the lower part of the thorax. General relaxation is practised between each exercise at first, as controlled breathing is very tiring and requires much concentration. Exercises to mobilise the shoulder girdle and thoracic spine are also used and are timed to assist the movements of the new pattern of breathing.

EXAMPLES OF EXERCISES TO INCREASE THE EXPIRATORY RANGE

  a. *half lying; general relaxation.*

  b. *half lying; Diaphragmatic breathing, emphasising relaxation of abdominal wall on inspiration and contraction on expiration.*

  c. *half lying; breathing with pressure during expiration on lower ribs by the patient's own hands, a strap or by the physiotherapist's hands.* Coarse vibrations may also be given to increase the effect of the pressure.

  d. *half lying; breathing with Hip and Knee bending to press on chest during expiration.*

  e. *relaxed stoop sitting; Trunk raising with inspiration and relaxing on prolonged expiration.*

  f. *sitting; Trunk turning with loose Arm swinging, breathing out and relaxing during turn, breathing in coming forwards.*

Inspiratory Exercises

These may be required to affect the whole thorax (general) or a specific area (local).

General. To increase the respiratory range generally, the muscles of inspiration must be exercised progressively and freed from the opposition of tight anterior structures, notably the Pectoral Muscles, and the weight of the head and shoulders which may cause stooping posture. Mobilisation of the thoracic spine and shoulder girdle, correction of posture and relaxation are essential in addition to teaching the patient how to use the whole chest and so train a new and better habit of breathing. Deep inspiration is taught in the patient's own time with the trunk supported, relaxed and straight. *Half lying* is preferred, as pressure on the back is insufficient to impede movement at the costo-vertebral joints and the Diaphragm is freed from excessive abdominal pressure.

Movement in all parts of the thorax is encouraged by pressure on specific areas such as the lower ribs anteriorly or posteriorly (Diaphragmatic, Basal or Lower Costal Expansion), or under the arms (Axillary or Lateral Costal Expansion), or over the sternum (Apical Expansion). Exercises in which the arms are rotated laterally, or elevated, and the spine is extended assist expansion of the thoracic cage, and when suitable, activities which make the patient laugh and get out of breath increase the respiratory excursions. Resisted leg exercises increase intra-abdominal pressure and stimulate diaphragmatic movement.

EXAMPLES OF EXERCISES TO INCREASE THE INSPIRATORY RANGE

  a. *crk half lying; relaxation and general deep breathing.*

  b. *crk half lying; Lower Costal Expansion—against resistance of webbing strap. 'Enlarge all the way round.'*

  c. *relaxed; crook sitting; Back arching with deep inspiration.*

d. *sitting; Arm rotation outwards with deep inspiration.*
e. *relaxed sitting; Arm lifting and Trunk raising with inspiration as in yawning and stretching.*
f. *skipping, running or swimming to 'Get out of breath'.*

Local. The patient may be required to localise respiratory movements to a specific area, to affect the underlying lung tissue. Correct posture and alignment are established first, and the area is localised by firm manual pressure against which the patient must try to push and withdraw. Concentration and patience are required, therefore practice must be frequent but of short duration.

THE SHOULDER GIRDLE

Limitation of scapular movement and lack of stability is a not infrequent cause of pain and delay in re-mobilisation of the shoulder joint. Efficient scapular movement permits the position of the glenoid cavity to be adapted to meet the circumstances of shoulder movement as it progresses through range, and scapular stability provides a stable background. Limitation may be due to spasm, e.g. in hemiparesis, or to muscle weakness, e.g. following immobilisation of the arm as the result of pain or traumatic injury. Mobilisation of the scapula is achieved by specific movements against resistance, i.e. elevation (forwards or backwards) with lateral rotation and depression (forwards or backwards) with medial rotation, followed by prolonged holding.

EXAMPLES OF FREE EXERCISES TO MOBILISE THE SHOULDER GIRDLE

a. *sitting; Shoulder shrugging.*
b. *prone kneeling; upper Back rounding and flattening.*
c. *bend sitting; Shoulder girdle rolling.*
d. *sitting; Arm medial and lateral rotation.*

THE SHOULDER JOINT

The head of the humerus articulates with the glenoid cavity of the scapula at the gleno-humeral or shoulder joint. In free movements of the arm, movement at this joint is always associated with that at the joints of the shoulder girdle and it is only under artificial conditions that they can be localised, as, for example, when the shoulder girdle is fixed by external pressure or when gleno-humeral movement is severely limited pathologically.

Limitation of range in the shoulder joint is often associated with pain or limitation of neck movements or with scapular inefficiency. The key factor in shoulder joint mobilisation is an increase in medial and/or lateral rotation as these movements are almost invariably

limited.   In these cases attempted elevation of the arm usually results
in excessive movement of the scapula, i.e. a shoulder shrugging movement, to compensate for shoulder deficiency; once the synergic action
of the scapular muscles is established, whatever shoulder movement is
possible follows.   This alteration in the normal pattern of movement is
referred to as a reversal of scapulo-humeral rhythm.   To correct this
a hand placed firmly over the scapula encourages stabilisation of the
bone during the initiation of the arm movement and leads to more
satisfactory results.   Exercises which involve the use of both arms
reciprocally or symmetrically, are also useful to assist scapular stability.
It is interesting to observe that the normal sequence of movement
remains unaltered when diagonal spiral patterns are used to re-educate
movement as the synergic action of the scapular muscles is timed to
precede movement at the shoulder joint.

Relaxed Passive Movements of the Gleno-humeral Joint

With Shoulder Girdle fixed

ly. or ½ ly.; S. abd., add., flex. ext. (circum.), lat. rot., med. rot (pass.)

The patient's back and head are supported to ensure relaxation,
the point of the shoulder being free at the side of the plinth, to prevent
the necessity of altering the position to obtain full extension.   One of
the physiotherapist's hands fixes the shoulder girdle by pressure on the
acromion and lateral third of the clavicle, the other grasps just above
the elbow, which is bent to a right angle, and supports the patient's
forearm on her own forearm.   Traction is given to depress the head of
the humerus in the glenoid cavity as the arm is moved into abduction
(about 80°) with sufficient lateral rotation to bring the forearm into the
same plane (see Fig. 104).

Flexion and extension can be done in either abduction or adduction
In abduction, flexion is across the body and extension backwards over
the side of the plinth, traction being given in the plane of the scapula.
The natural pattern of arm movement, in which the elbow is flexed

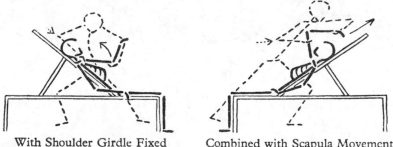

With Shoulder Girdle Fixed   Combined with Scapula Movement

(Fig. 104) Shoulder Flexion and Extension

with shoulder extension and extended with shoulder flexion, is followed. It is not necessary to fix the shoulder girdle for rotation movements, and these, too, can be performed in either abduction or adduction with the patient's elbow flexed to a right angle. One of the physiotherapist's hands acts as a fulcrum and gives traction above the elbow, while the other uses the forearm as a lever to produce the movement.

Combined with Scapula Movement (Fig. 104)

The arm is grasped at the elbow and across the wrist, the movements being the same as with the shoulder girdle fixed, except that abduction is extended and combined with maximum lateral rotation to obtain full elevation. Elevation through flexion is usually combined with elbow extension.

Examples of Assisted Exercises for the Shoulder

The range of movements in the shoulder may appear to be greater than they are when they are augmented by movements in the spine. For example, the hand can be lifted higher during elevation through flexion by extending the lumbar spine, and the elbow can be raised by side bending to the opposite side, while lateral and medial rotation are increased apparently, by extension and flexion of the spine respectively. Spinal movement can be controlled by suitable starting positions for the exercises or by using both arms simultaneously, either together or in opposition.

The shoulder girdle may be fixed or free during manual assistance which can be given in conjunction with the mechanical support of

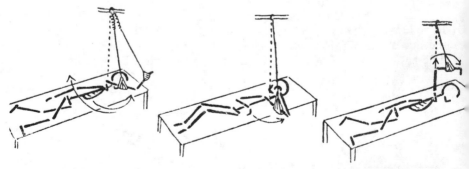

Flexion and Extension   Abduction and Adduction   Rotation

Fig. 105

slings, using *side lying* for flexion, extension and rotation, and *lying* for adduction and abduction. In *lying*, flexion of the elbow, so that the patient holds the rope, shortens the leverage but ensures the lateral rotation which is essential for abduction. *Side lying*, with the forearm supported so that the upper arm is vertical, is used for rotation, traction prior to movement being given by pressing the scapula to the trunk and a counter pull above the elbow.

Flexion and extension can be self-assisted by clasping the hands or supporting under the elbow, and the buoyancy of water will help abduction when the body is upright and submerged. Rotation is encouraged by rubbing the back vigorously with a short towel held vertically.

EXAMPLES OF FREE EXERCISES FOR THE SHOULDER JOINT (Fig. 106)

a. *stoop stride sitting; Arm swinging forward and backward.*
b. *half reach fallout standing; one Arm swinging backward, forward and circling.*
c. *Arms crossed sitting; one Arm lateral rotation with swinging obliquely forwards and upwards.*

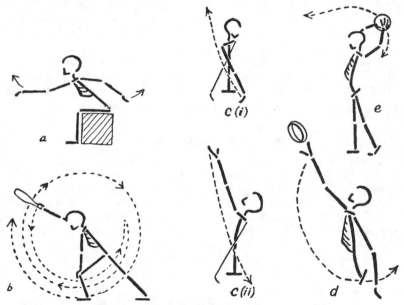

FIG. 106. Free Exercise for the shoulder

d. *stride standing; Arm swinging across, sideways and sideways-upwards and circling.*
e. *walk standing; overhead throw.*
f. *walk standing; throw and catch quoit.*

Strengthening exercises given in the pain-free range are of great importance in the treatment of stiff shoulders as the Deltoid muscle is coarse in texture and wastes rapidly.

ACTIVITIES FOR THE SHOULDER

Many household activities such as polishing, cleaning windows, scrubbing floors, hanging clothes on a line and household decorating are useful in promoting movement and strength in the shoulder region. Recreational activities such as netball, basketball, deck quoits and handball encourage movement with objective interest.

THE ELBOW JOINT

The humerus articulates with both the radius and the ulna at the elbow. The trochlea surface of the humerus and the trochlea notch of the ulna form the medial part, the capitulum of the humerus and the circular facet on the head of the radius form the lateral part of the joint. In full extension the supinated forearm is abducted to about 10° at what is known as the 'carrying angle', but in flexion it lies in the same plane as the upper arm. During flexion, however, there is normally a slight medial rotation of the humerus so that the fingers are directed towards the middle of the clavicle.

Stiffness resulting from traumatic injury is mobilised by free exercise only in the early stages, the emphasis being on the maintenance of flexion, which is essential to bring the hand to the mouth and is usually performed against the resistance of the force of gravity.

RELAXED PASSIVE MOVEMENTS OF THE ELBOW JOINT

½ ly.; Elb. flex. and ext. (pass.)

The lower end of the humerus is supported by one of the physiotherapist's hands while the other grasps across the wrist, fingers anteriorly, thumb posteriorly. When movement is localised to the elbow joint the forearm is usually supinated throughout and full extension is ensured by upward pressure of the hand grasping above the elbow, allowance being made for the 'carrying angle'.

It is preferable, however, as a general rule, to follow the natural movements of the arm as a whole, combining extension of the shoulder, with flexion of the elbow and supination to bring the fingers towards the clavicle, and following this by flexion of the shoulder, with extension of the elbow and pronation.

ASSISTED EXERCISES FOR THE ELBOW

Mechanical assistance is unsuitable for this joint because of the

danger that it may develop into passive traction, which is contra-
indicated in many cases.   Manual assistance can be given with care,
and a mild form of self-assistance is encouraged by the patient 'creeping' or 'walking' the fingers up and down a wall or across a table.

EXAMPLES OF FREE EXERCISES FOR THE ELBOW

In the early stages of treatment the passive traction exerted by the
force of gravity can be eliminated by suspension or by the support of

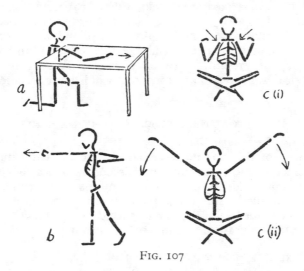

FIG. 107

a polished table or re-education board.   Associated movements of the
shoulder, forearm and hand assist the action of the muscles which pass
over both joints, and these should be encouraged.

    a. *Arm support sitting or half kneeling; Elbow flexion and extension.*
    b. *walk standing; Arm flexion and extension, 'Punching' movement.*
    c. *cross sitting; Arm swinging to touch Shoulder and tap floor.*
    d. *stride standing; Arm bending and stretching in all directions,*
       rhythmically.

THE RADIO-ULNAR JOINTS

At the superior radio-ulnar joint the head of the radius rotates in
the osseo-fibrous ring formed by the annular ligament and the radial
notch of the ulna.   There is a fibrous connection between the shafts of
the bones which may be referred to as the middle radio-ulnar joint
and at the inferior joint the ulnar notch of the radius, carrying the

hand with it, glides round the head of the ulna.   When the elbow is extended the movements of pronation and supination are usually accompanied by medial and lateral rotation at the shoulder joint, therefore to localise the movement to the radio-ulnar joints the elbow is flexed to a right angle and the upper arm is held still.

RELAXED PASSIVE MOVEMENTS OF THE RADIO-ULNAR JOINTS

B. sup. sitt.; pron. and supin. (pass.)
The upper arm is fixed and the elbow flexed to a right angle.   With her forearm in line with that of the patient, the physiotherapist grasps as if to shake hands, extending her index and second fingers across the anterior aspect of the wrist to stabilise this joint.   With the other hand she supports round the patient's elbow.   Traction is given in the long axis of the forearm and the movement is one of rotation about this axis.

ACCESSORY MOVEMENT AT THE INFERIOR RADIO-ULNAR JOINTS

At the Inferior Radio-ulnar Joint
The head of the ulna moves relatively backwards on the radius during pronation and relatively forwards during supination.   As the movement is only free in the mid-position, this accessory movement is performed in that position with the patient's elbow flexed and supported.   The lower end of the radius is fixed with one hand while the head of the ulna is grasped and moved by the other.

ASSISTED EXERCISES FOR THE RADIO-ULNAR JOINTS

Manual assistance can be given to the movement while grasping the lower end of the bones.   Associated movements of the hand, i.e. making a fist with supination, and opening the hand with pronation, assist the movement.
Additional leverage is obtained for mechanical assistance when the patient grasps a stick in the hand (Fig. 108a).

EXAMPLES OF FREE EXERCISES FOR THE RADIO-ULNAR JOINTS (Fig. 108 *b* & *c*)

    a. *Forearm support sitting; pronation and supination.*
    b. *Forearm support sitting; pick up cards from a pack and turn them to face upwards on a table.*
    c. *walk standing; bounce a ball and 'throw and catch' a beanbag.*

Activities to increase the Range of Pronation and Supination
Many household activities encourage movement in these joints, such as screwing and unscrewing, using a screwdriver, turning door handles, and wringing out a dishcloth.

a   b   c

FIG. 108

THE JOINTS OF THE HAND

The prime function of the hand is to grip, and movement in its numerous joints enables it to be moulded to the wide variety of shapes and sizes with which it comes in contact. The ability to oppose the thumb in *abduction* is essential for a satisfactory gripping action.

RELAXED PASSIVE MOVEMENTS OF THE HAND

The Wrist Joint

A. supp. sitt.; Wr. flex. and ext., abd. and add., circum. (pass.)

The patient sits on a chair with the elbow semi-flexed and supported and the forearm supinated. The physiotherapist supports and fixes the forearm above the wrist with one hand, and grasps the patient's hand from the ulnar side with the other, her thumb straight and lying comfortably on the back of the hand and her fingers in the palm. Traction is given and then the wrist is flexed and extended.

It is important to observe the natural movement of the fingers which accompanies these movements, i.e. flexion of the fingers with extension of the wrist and vice versa, in response to tension of the tendons passing across the wrist. A small degree of pronation permitted with extension of the wrist and supination with flexion will also allow the natural pattern of movement to be followed.

Abduction and adduction are done with the same grasp; note that the range of adduction is greater than that of abduction.

Circumduction is performed in either direction by combining the four angular movements.

The Carpometacarpal Joints

(i) *of the Fingers.* A gliding movement at these joints is associated with movement at the intermetacarpal joints, which is very slight on the radial side of the hand but freer on the ulnar side.

Two adjacent metacarpal bones are grasped and moved forwards and backwards on each other; all these joints may be moved simultaneously, the palm being moulded to form an arch and then flattened.

(*ii*) *of the Thumb.* Owing to the shape of the articular surfaces, flexion at this joint is accompanied by medial rotation and is then called opposition. The ball of the thumb can be opposed to each finger when it is *abducted* and *opposed* (flexed and medially rotated).

With one hand the physiotherapist grasps round the carpal bones to fix the wrist and to support the forearm, and with the other hand gives traction on the thumb prior to flexion with medial rotation (opposition) and extension, both of which occur in the plane of the palm of the hand.

Abduction and adduction are at right angles to the plane of the palm of the hand and when all the angular movements are carried out in sequence circumduction results, i.e. opposition, adduction, extension, abduction.

The Metacarpophalangeal Joints

When each joint is moved separately the metacarpal bone is fixed and the proximal phalanx grasped. Traction is given and the joint is moved through its full range of flexion, extension, abduction, adduction and circumduction. It is important to notice that flexion at these joints directs the fingers across the palm of the hand towards the thenar eminence.

With the exception of the thumb, all these joints can be moved together, in which case the physiotherapist fixes the patient's hand and wrist with one hand and grasps the tips of all four fingers with the other. Traction is given and the movement performed with the fingers straight. Flexion must be at the correct angle and abduction and adduction are achieved by moving all the fingers first to the radial and then to the ulnar side. Circumduction combines these movements.

A considerable degree of separation of the joint surfaces takes place during traction and an accessory movement of rotation can be performed. During this movement care must be taken to ensure that traction is always in the long axis of the joint, otherwise strain or dislocation may result.

The Interphalangeal Joints

Each of these joints can be moved separately by fixing the bone on the proximal side of the joint and moving the bone which is distal to it. As the tendons inserted distal to these joints also pass over the neighbouring joints, the latter must be positioned to eliminate tension which would otherwise prevent full range movement. All the interphalangeal and metacarpophalangeal joints of the fingers can be flexed and extended together. The physiotherapist grasps round the wrist with one hand and places the other on the dorsum of the patient's fingers, so that her fingers point in the same direction as those of the patient. The metacarpophalangeal joints are fully flexed first and then, as the proximal and finally the distal interphalangeal joints follow, the metacarpophalangeal joints are extended to give room for the finger tips and reduce the tension of the long extensor tendons. Extension in the proximal and distal interphalangeal joints follows progressively.

Ease of movement is achieved by following the natural pattern and allowing extension of the wrist with flexion of the fingers and vice versa.

Accessory Movements of the Hand

The Wrist and Mid-carpal Joints

With the patient's hand in pronation the physiotherapist grasps round the lower end of the radius and round the distal row of carpus. Traction is given in the long axis of the forearm and then the patient's hand is moved vertically upwards and downwards on the forearm.

The Metacarpal and Intercarpal Joints

The heads of two adjacent metacarpal bones are firmly grasped and they are moved in an antero-posterior direction upon each other. Movement between the 4th and 5th is relatively free compared with that between the 2nd and 3rd. Following this the palm is moulded and hollowed to form an arch and then flattened.

The Metacarpophalangeal Joints

The head of the metacarpal bone is firmly fixed and the proximal phalanx grasped between the thumb and fingers. Traction is given in the long axis of the joint and considerable separation of the articular surfaces results and small gliding movements in an antero-posterior direction are permitted. When the joint is slightly flexed a considerable degree of rotation is possible.

The Interphalangeal Joints

These joints are formed between the proximal and middle row of phalanges, and the middle and distal row of phalanges. The head of one phalanx and the base of the adjoining phalanx are held firmly and traction is given separating the joint surfaces. Rotatory, side to side, and antero-posterior movements can be given.

Assisted Exercises for the Hand

Manual assistance can be given using grasps similar to those used for relaxed passive movements. Mechanical assistance is unsuitable, although sometimes a light elastic recoil is arranged to assist wrist or finger extension in cases where flexion contracture is likely to occur.

EXAMPLES OF FREE EXERCISES FOR THE HAND

As the hand is a functional unit, there is little doubt that move ments which use the hand as a whole are the most beneficial in promoting mobility. Movements for individual joints in the fullest possible range can be given, preferably with the hand immersed in warm water or after wax treatment. Care must be taken to see that neighbouring joints are correctly positioned, i.e. fingers flexed to gain full extension of the wrist.

a. *sitting; grasping a stick.*

b. *sitting; flexion and extension at the metacarpophalangeal joints* (keeping the interphalangeal joints extended, draw the tips of the fingers and thumb together, then flatten the hand and spread the fingers).

This and many other movements are very satisfactory when done with the objective aim of gathering in or spreading out some substance in a tray, such as sand, rice or beans.

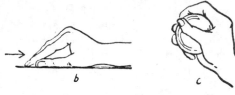

FIG. 109

c. *standing; fit Hand round a soft ball, squeeze it repeatedly and then let go.*
d. *sitting; grasp rolling pin* (or pole about 2 inches in diameter) *and roll it forwards and backwards on the thighs.*
e. *sitting; tie and untie knots.*
f. *sitting; transfer matches from one box to another about 6 inches away, each match is picked up separately, the first being held between the thumb and 1st finger, the second between the thumb and 2nd finger and so on.*

PART IV

15

MUSCLE STRENGTH

INTRODUCTION

ACTIVE movement of the skeleton is brought about by the contraction of voluntary muscle. This muscle tissue has contractile properties which are activated by nerve impulses, to supply the effort required to move or stabilise the body levers.

STRUCTURAL FEATURES

The structural unit of voluntary or skeletal muscle is the muscle fibre (large extrafusal), which is cylindrical in form and averages from 20 to 40 millimetres in length, and $\frac{1}{10}$ to $\frac{1}{100}$ of a millimetre in diameter. It is enclosed in an elastic sheath called the sarcolemma.

Some fibres appear 'red', due to a rich blood supply and the presence of a pigment. Their contraction in response to stimulation is slow, but can be sustained for a considerable time without fatigue. This type of fibre, therefore, predominates in the anti-gravity muscles which are primarily concerned with the maintenance of posture, e.g. Soleus.

Other fibres, paler in colour, and called 'white', respond rapidly to stimulation but are easily fatigued. These form the greater part of muscles which are primarily responsible for movement, e.g. Gastrocnemius.

Muscle fibres, lying parallel to each other, are grouped together and surrounded by connective tissue to form bundles, and many bundles are bound together by denser connective tissue to form the substance of a muscle. Muscles are attached at both extremities to bone, cartilage, or fascia, by fibrous tissue which is continuous with the connective tissue investing the muscle. This fibrous tissue contains elastic non-contractile elements and may be concentrated to form a narrow cord, or spread out to form an aponeurosis.

The more proximal of these attachments, which usually remains relatively fixed when the muscle contracts, is known as the origin, to distinguish it from the insertion, which is the attachment at which the power of contraction is concentrated to produce movement of the body levers. Either attachment, however, may be free to move towards the centre of the muscle, or the insertion may remain relatively fixed and the structure of origin moved, in which case the muscle is said to work with reversed origin and insertion.

The form of a muscle varies according to its function. A wide range and speed of movement is produced by the contraction of long fusiform muscles in which the fibres are all relatively parallel to, or in series with, each other and the tendon of attachment. By this arrangement the number of muscle fibres included is relatively few and limited by the length of the muscle, with the result that no great power can be exerted, as the power of muscle contraction is directly proportional to the number of fibres stimulated. The number of fibres is much increased, in the case of muscles designed primarily for powerful contraction, by the inclusion of fibres arranged obliquely or at right angles to the line of pull of the muscle as a whole. The forces of contraction are compounded at the point of attachment (see p. 2), but the range of movement is obviously limited.

Muscles are supplied by nerves which contain both motor and sensory fibres. Each motor fibre has a cell in the anterior horn of the Spinal Cord or in the nucleus of a Cranial nerve which can be influenced from a variety of sources. The fibre or axon of this lower motor neurone divides on reaching the muscle into from 5 to 150 branches each of which terminates in a motor end-plate beneath the sarcolemma of a muscle fibre. A motor neurone and the muscle fibres it supplies constitute a motor unit. The unit is activated by stimulation of its cell which discharges impulses for transmission to the muscle fibres which respond by contracting. When stimulated the muscle fibres contract to their maximum capacity in the circumstances, i.e. the maximum contraction which results from a single stimulus is summated by subsequent stimuli arriving at a sufficiently high frequency. The number of motor units activated at any one time determines the strength of the contraction of the muscle as a whole and the strength of the contraction is determined by the resistance offered to the contraction.

Sensory receptors, which record the tension of passive stretching, the degree of contraction, pain and deep pressure, are found in muscles and tendons, and impulses recording these are conveyed to the Central Nervous System. The receptors sensitive to stretching of the muscle are component parts of the muscle spindles which lie between and parallel to its fibres and the muscle responds to stimulation of its stretch receptors by an increase in intra-muscular tension. The function of the spindles and their nervous connections also serves to increase the efficiency of motor unit activity. Stretch receptors in tendons are stimulated by prolonged stretching which results in inhibition of muscle contraction. Sensory fibres from receptors in the fibrous tissue which surrounds joints travel in the same nerves which supply the muscles which pass over the joints, and a reflex contraction of these muscles in cases of strain is an important factor in preventing joint injury.

TYPES OF MUSCLE WORK

Muscle work involves an increase in intra-muscular tension; when this is accompanied by a change in the length of the muscle the contraction is said to be isotonic. When intra-muscular tension is increased without a change in the length of the muscle the muscle work is isometric.

There is a change in the length of a muscle when it works to produce movement in opposition to an external force, and when it works to resist movement produced by an external force which gradually overcomes it. When the attachments of a working muscle are drawn towards the centre of that muscle, it works concentrically, i.e. towards the centre, or 'in shortening' (Fig. 110). When the attachments are drawn away from the centre, as its resistance is overcome by the external force, the muscle works eccentrically, i.e. away from the centre, or 'in lengthening' (Fig. 111).

There is no alteration in the length of a muscle which works to stabilise a joint, the power of its contraction being exactly equal and opposite to the forces which oppose it. In this case the attachments of the muscle remain stationary and it is said to work statically.

1. *Isotonic*
    a. *Concentric Muscle Work*

Muscles working concentrically become shorter and thicker as their attachments are drawn closer together and joint movement results. A patient doing concentric muscle work performs a movement, and in so doing overcomes some force which offers resistance, such as friction, gravity, manual pressure by the physiotherapist, or some form of mechanical resistance.

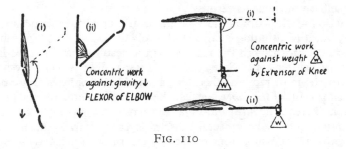

FIG. 110

The physiological cost of this type of work is high, as only about a quarter of the energy liberated during contraction is available as mechanical work. Some is used to overcome the initial inertia and some is converted into heat. Concentric muscle work is used to build up muscle power, and although most everyday movements involve the use of all types of muscle work, it seems to be more natural, and to require least concentration, to use the concentric type.

b. Eccentric Muscle Work

Muscles working eccentrically become longer and thinner as they pay out and allow their attachments to be drawn apart by the force producing the movement.

The physiological cost of this type of muscle work is low, probably only about a quarter of that required for concentric work, therefore a muscle recovering from paralysis may sometimes be persuaded to contract to resist before it will attempt to produce movement. Considerable concentration is required during exercises designed to work

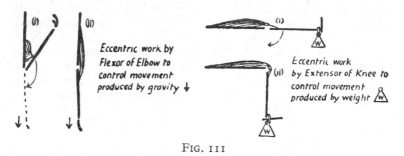

Eccentric work by Flexor of Elbow to control movement produced by gravity ↓

Eccentric work by Extensor of Knee to control movement produced by weight

FIG. III

the muscles in this way. This is probably to control the speed of the movement, as eccentric work in natural movements is usually fairly rapid.

2. Isometric or Static Muscle 'Work'

The length of the muscle remains the same throughout the muscle work and no movements results.

Static muscle work is more economical than either of the previous types, but it is fatiguing if sustained, probably because of hindrance to the circulation through the muscle, as the result of an increase in the intramuscular tension. Static muscle work against maximal resistance provides the most rapid method for gaining hypertrophy of muscles at a *particular point of the range* because the resistance demands the greatest possible increase in intra-muscular tension.

Static work of the postural muscles is used to train the pattern of good posture. Posture is maintained by muscle work which is somewhat similar, but is not fatiguing because of the low metabolic rate at which the muscle fibres work, and the special nature of their reflex control.

RANGES OF MUSCLE WORK

The range of muscle work is the extent of the muscular contraction which results in joint movement.

Full Range

The joint is moved as the muscles work from the position in which they are fully stretched, to the position in which they are fully contracted, concentrically, or, from the position of full contraction, to the position of maximum extension, if they are working eccentrically.

Under ordinary circumstances muscles are rarely required to work in full range, but in emergencies they may have to do so. Active full-range exercises are used for patients as they maintain joint mobility, increase the circulation and ensure that the emergency reserve of power and mobility is preserved.

Inner Range

The muscle works either concentrically from a position in which it is partially contracted (approximately half-way between the limits of full range) to a position of full contraction, or vice versa if it works eccentrically.

Exercise in inner range is used to gain or maintain movement of a joint in the direction of the muscle pull, and to train some extensor muscles responsible for stabilising joints.

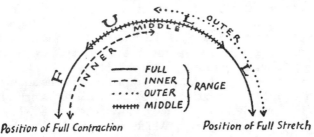

Position of Full Contraction   Position of Full Stretch

FIG. 112

Outer Range

The muscles work concentrically from the position in which they are fully stretched to a position in which they are partially (half) contracted, or vice versa if working eccentrically.

The outer range of muscle work is used extensively in muscle re-education as a contraction is initiated more easily from stretch in most muscles.

Middle Range

The muscles are never either fully stretched or fully contracted. This is the range in which muscles are most often used in everyday life and in which, generally speaking, they are most efficient. Exercises in this range maintain muscle tone and normal power, but full joint movement is never achieved.

THE GROUP ACTION OF MUSCLES

Muscles do not work singly, but in groups, and it is the harmonious working together of several groups which results in co-ordinated movement.

1. The Prime Movers, or Agonists, are the group which bring about the movement by their contraction.

2. The Antagonists, which are the opposing group, relax and lengthen progressively so that the movement is controlled but not impeded.

3. The Synergists are the muscles which work or relax to modify the action of the prime movers. They may alter the direction of pull or, in the case of prime movers which pass over more than one joint, they fix or move the joint in which the main action is not required into the position which is most advantageous.

4. The Fixators are muscles which work to steady the origin of the prime movers or the synergists.

EXAMPLE. In flexion of the fingers, as in making a fist, the Flexors of the Fingers work as prime movers to perform the movement. The antagonists, the Extensors of the Fingers, relax. The Extensors of the Wrist work as synergists to fix or move the wrist into full extension so that the power of the Flexors of the Fingers, which can also flex this joint, is not diverted to this purpose, but increased as the extended wrist joint acts as a fulcrum for their action.

The appropriate impulses for contraction or relaxation are conveyed to the muscles concerned in any particular movement, from the Central Nervous System. As it is movements, and not individual muscles or even muscle groups, which are represented in the cerebral cortex, the importance of concentrating on the movement rather than on the contraction of a specific muscle or muscle group in re-education cannot be over-emphasised. Furthermore, as the movements which are represented are those to which the patient is accustomed, i.e. natural movements, these are of prime importance.

Two-joint Muscles

Most groups of muscles include at least one which extends across more than one joint. These muscles are most effective in moving one joint when they are stretched over the other, as under these conditions the latter joint is used as a fulcrum and the stretching of the muscle acts as an additional stimulus to contraction.

EXAMPLE. To work the Hamstrings as Flexors of the Knee, the hip joint must flex or be flexed by synergic action; alternatively, to work the Hamstrings as Extensors of the Hip, the knee must extend or be extended during the movement of hip extension.

GROUP MOVEMENT OF JOINTS

Most natural movements involve the use of a series of joints controlled by the integrated action of many muscle groups. The control of these movements may be voluntary and conscious, but in many instances it is unconscious and reflex in character and controlled from the basal ganglia or reflex centres in the spinal cord. The basic patterns seem to be those of thrust, withdrawal, swing and strike.

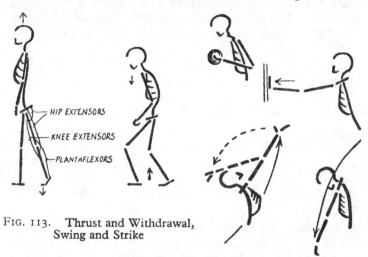

FIG. 113. Thrust and Withdrawal, Swing and Strike

EXAMPLE. In walking, plantaflexion of the ankle joint and extension in the knee and hip result progressively in response to firm pressure on the ball of the foot, but should there be pain in the foot as the result of injury or ill-fitting shoes, a flexion reaction is often imperfectly inhibited to produce a sagging posture and a limping gait.

MUSCULAR WEAKNESS AND PARALYSIS

Weakness or paralysis in any muscle or group of muscles not only results in loss of movement or stability of a particular joint, but creates a state of muscular imbalance which affects all the groups concerned in the production of co-ordinated movement. If the weakened muscles are to recover their full function, they must be protected while they are ineffective and encouraged by re-education, until they are able finally to take their place once more as effective members of the teams of muscles, which work together to perform natural and skilled movements.

Causes of Weakness or Paralysis

As contraction is the only means by which muscle power can be maintained or increased, any lesion or habit which prevents or limits contraction will result in muscle wasting.   Complete loss of ability to contract is known as paralysis, partial loss as paresis, or a muscle may be merely weak or sub-normal.

Lesions affecting the Anterior Horn Cells

Destruction of the Anterior Horn Cells results in permanent in-activity of the motor unit, i.e. flaccid paralysis.   Damage to these cells, short of their destruction, may increase their threshold to such an extent that they remain dormant.

Lesions affecting the Motor Pathways

Interference with the passage of impulses along motor pathways causes paralysis.   Spastic paralysis results from upper motor neurone lesions and flaccid paralysis from lower motor neurone lesions.

Lesions affecting the Muscle Tissue

Degeneration of the muscle tissue results in loss of strength which is usually progressive, i.e. muscular dystrophy.   Ischaemia causes structural changes, i.e. Volkmann's ischaemic contracture, and extensive scar tissue may replace contractile tissue as the result of deep flesh injuries.

Disuse of Normal Nerve and Muscle Tissue

Loss of strength and wasting from disuse is by no means uncommon. A patient may not use his muscles—

a. because he cannot; as contraction is inhibited by pain or protective spasm of antagonistic muscles.

b. because he does not need to; joints fixed by splintage are stable and unable to move, therefore there is no necessity for the patient to contract his muscles unless he is compelled to by strong resistance offered to other strong muscles in the same series or by his own voluntary effort.   Static muscle work is essential to maintain circulation, muscle power and the movement of tendons passing over the temporarily immobilised joints, which are essential for recovery of function when splintage is removed.

c. because he will not; some patients resist all efforts to make them do sufficient muscular contraction to prevent disuse atrophy.

Some Constitutional Diseases

A marked degree of muscle wasting, which cannot be put down entirely to disuse, occurs in some diseases, notably in rheumatoid arthritis.

Functional

There is no organic cause, but the muscles do not function, although they may be made to contract by electrical stimulation of the nerve or by methods of facilitation.

THE PREVENTION OF MUSCLE WASTING

In Flaccid Paralysis

Muscles deprived of their motor nerve supply are limp, hypotonic and unable to contract. Rapid wasting takes place and cannot be prevented, although it is thought that it can be arrested by improving the blood supply to the area by stimulation of the muscle fibres by electrical means. Although little can be done to prevent wasting in these cases measures are taken to keep both the muscles and the joint structures in as good a condition as possible in preparation for a return to normal function.

Principles of Treatment during Flaccid Paralysis

1. *The Affected Muscles must be protected from prolonged Overstretching by adequate Support and Splintage*

Normal muscles protect themselves from overstretching by a reflex contraction, but those suffering from flaccid paralysis are unable to do so, as they are incapable of contraction; consequently, they may become stretched beyond their physiological limit and injured by the force of gravity or the unopposed action of healthy antagonistic muscles.

EXAMPLE. A lesion affecting the Anterior Tibial Nerve results in a dropped foot, as gravity and the unopposed action of the Calf Muscles plantaflex the foot. To prevent injury to the Anterior Tibial Muscles a splint or toe-spring must be worn until their power of contraction is sufficient to restore muscle balance.

2. *The Circulation to the Area must be maintained to ensure Adequate Nutrition to the Paralysed Muscles by Active Exercise for Other Normal Muscles in the Area, Contrast Baths etc.*

Paralysis leads to coldness and blueness of the area, indicating poor circulation. The arterial blood flow to muscles is much increased during active work to supply the oxygen and nutrition essential for repair and, at the same time, the local venous return is assisted by the intermittent pressure exerted on the vessels, by the contracting muscles, and by the movement of joints.

3. *The Range of Movement in Joints Immobilised by the Paralysis and the Extensibility of the Affected Muscles must be Maintained by Passive Movements*

The fibrous tissue which constitutes the sheaths of muscles, ligaments of joints and fascia, undergo adaptive shortening if subjected to prolonged immobilisation.   One full-range movement at frequent intervals is sufficient to prevent this and, in practice, two full-range passive movements performed twice daily are found to be adequate.

Where muscles work over more than one joint they must be stretched over these joints at the same time.   Example — wrist and finger flexors: wrist and fingers must be fully extended in one movement.

4. *Remembrance of the Pattern of Movement must be stimulated and kept alive by Passive Movement while Active Movement is impossible*

Movement is associated in the brain with numerous sensory impulses from the joints, muscles, skin and eyes.   In the absence of voluntary movement, stimulation of these sensory impulses by passive movement may remind the brain of the pattern of movement, in preparation for the time when the motor pathway will once more be intact. In this way co-ordinated movement, made possible again by the return of power to the affected muscles, is remembered and does not require to be re-learnt or re-developed.

The passive movements used for this purpose must obviously follow the natural pattern of movement with regard to the group movement of joints.

5. *The Strength and Use of Normal Muscles in the Area must be maintained by Resisted Exercise*

Unless the limb is flail (all muscles paralysed) all possible activity is encouraged.   Thus wasting from disuse is prevented and circulation to the part is improved.

EXAMPLE.   A man with Anterior Tibial paralysis is able to walk about provided he wears a toe-spring, and the advantage of his being able to work is obvious.

In Spastic Paralysis

Muscles which receive a motor nerve supply only by means of a spinal reflex, since they are cut off from the higher centres by a lesion affecting the upper motor neurone, are tense, hypertonic and incapable of voluntary contraction or relaxation.   This condition is known as spastic paralysis and wasting is not marked.

When a limb or segment of the body is 'locked' in spasm circulation is impeded and muscle and joint contractures may develop over a period of time.   The aim of treatment is to initiate movement to maintain normal joint range and muscle extensibility and at the same time improve the circulation. While the limb remains immobile any potential for voluntary control is masked by the spasm. Reflex movement initiated by means of Proprioceptive Neuromuscular Facilitation techniques, i.e. the stretch stimulus coupled with a command for voluntary effort, develop any voluntary control which remains and may lead to a permanent reduction in spasm. Controlled sustained passive stretching also inhibits spasm sufficiently to permit movement. Active or passive mobilization may be preceded by massage or packing with ice to reduce spasm and make movement easier.

In Primary Lesions of the Muscle Tissue

In this case loss of power cannot be arrested, although a temporary improvement often follows light exercise in cases which have not previously received treatment. This is probably the result of making the best use of fibres which still function.

In Disuse Atrophy

Provided there is no constitutional disease, e.g. Rheumatoid Disease, muscle atrophy from disuse can be prevented or controlled by strong and frequent contraction against resistance as wasting occurs because an insufficient demand is made to elicit a strong enough contraction. Exercise must be carried out within the limits of the disability but with skill and imagination this can be organised. Any type of active work is suitable provided the right muscles are activated sufficiently to maintain or improve their normal strength and endurance. Exercises with manual resistance is advisable in the early stages to make sure that the contraction is pain-free and satisfactory and to give the physiotherapist the opportunity to assess the patient's capacity for activity and to give instruction in those activities he must practise on his own. It is important that the patient should fully understand and appreciate the need for his own effort to ensure his co-operation in carrying out a régime of *free exercise*, the slogan for which is, 'Five minutes in every hour'. If his co-operation is doubtful or his ability to exert voluntary effort is reduced he will require constant supervision or individual treatment. Whenever possible the patient should continue with his normal work, when this is impossible other *occupational activities* suited to his abilities can be substituted. Suitable *games and sports* of a competitive nature supply a demand for activity but need careful supervision and control to avoid development of 'trick' movement, e.g. development of a faulty pattern of walking in order to move rapidly.

The wasting of muscles in Rheumatoid Disease is not entirely due to disuse. Isometric muscle work *in the pain-free range* helps to prevent atrophy and often leads to increased pain-free movement which can be used for functional activities.

THE INITIATION OF MUSCULAR CONTRACTION
(Early Re-education)

Denervated muscles are incapable of contraction except by direct stimulation of the muscle fibres by suitable electrical means.

Innervated muscles contract in response to a demand for activity provided the demand is sufficient. As contraction is the only means by which muscles regain their normal function it is essential that a response is obtained as soon as possible from muscles affected by paralysis.

The lesion causing paralysis and the inactivity which follows both increase the threshold of excitability of the anterior horn cells (A.H.C.). Once the acute phase of the lesion has passed reactivation of the motor unit is possible except when there has been permanent damage, e.g. death of the cell or lack of continuity of its axon. The A.H.C. is much more difficult to stimulate, when its threshold is increased therefore it fails to react to the normal level of stimulation, in which case the patient's maximal voluntary effort of contraction is insufficient to gain a response. An increase in the demand is required and supplied by stimulation of sensory receptors, i.e. proprioceptors and exteroceptors, which discharge impulses to the A.H.C.s to increase central excitation and lower the threshold of the cells. With a lower threshold the A.H.C.s are more easily stimulated and the arrival of repeated stimuli reduces the threshold still more and facilitates the passage of impulses along all the nervous pathways used. When stimulated the A.H.C.s discharge impulses to the muscle fibres which respond by contracting. A single discharge of impulses results in a muscle twitch but discharges repeated sufficiently frequently lead to summation and a sustained contraction.

Measures Used to Obtain Initiation of Contraction

1. *Warmth.* The area affected must be warm, as moderate warmth improves the quality of the contraction. Any method designed to improve the circulation in the area is effective; active exercise of unaffected muscles against strong resistance is the method of choice.

2. *Stabilisation.* Stabilisation of the bones of origin of the affected muscles and of joints distal to those over which these muscles work, improves their efficiency. Whenever possible stabilisation should be achieved by isometric contraction of strong synergic muscles working against maximal resistance as their effort re-inforces that of the muscles in question, e.g. for initiating elbow flexors the shoulder and wrist are stabilised by their flexors working against resistance applied by the physiotherapist's hands.

3. *Grip or Manual Contact.* The physiotherapist's hands give

pressure only *in the direction of the movement,* to direct the patient's effort and give sensory stimulation.

4. *Stretch.* Stimulation of the muscle spindles elicits reflex contraction of that muscle provided the reflex arc is intact. Sharp but controlled stretching of the affected muscle at the limit of its extended range is followed *immediately* by the patient's maximum effort of contraction thus:

NOW (Stretch)—PULL! (Let it move)

The muscles must be stretched in all their components of action and the more accurate the stretch the greater its effect for producing a contraction. Prolonged stretching or failure to allow the muscle to shorten inhibits the contraction.

The command for voluntary effort must be brief, forceful and timed to coincide with the stretch reflex. The stretch reflex is applied several times in quick succession and then repeated after a short rest for as long as a satisfactory response is obtained.

Some muscles do not respond to the stretch reflex applied from the lengthened range as well as others, e.g. triceps. Once the ability to initiate contraction is established muscle strengthening continues until normal function is restored.

5. *Irradiation.*

(*i*) The use of resistance to functional movements of the opposite limbs which normally produces fixator action on the other side can assist initiation of contraction in the affected muscle. For example, resistance to the extension–abduction pattern of one arm results in extension and abduction of the other arm to prevent the body rolling towards the moving arm.

(*ii*) The use of resistance to strong groups which normally work with the affected muscle also encourages contraction of that muscle. For example, the eating pattern involves flexion of the shoulder, elbow, wrist and fingers. Therefore, strong resistance given to the shoulder, wrist and fingers flexors will stimulate the flexors of the elbow to contract.

STRENGTHENING METHODS
(Re-education)

The art of training or strengthening muscles lies in creating the conditions under which they are called upon to work to full capacity against an ever-increasing resistance. Increase in strength and hypertrophy occur in response to an increase in intra-muscular tension set up by the factors which oppose their contraction. It is, therefore, essential that these opposing factors, which constitute the resistance, must be increased as the strength of the muscles improves.

An increase in resistance which is too rapid results in overloading, which prevents contraction and may damage the muscles. Underloading will not increase strength, but may be sufficient to prevent wasting of muscles.

At the beginning of treatment, assessment of the strength of the muscles is essential. A suitable resistance is then selected, which includes consideration of the poundage of the resisting force, the leverage, the speed, and the duration of the movement. As treatment continues, progression of one or all of these factors in made as muscle strength develops. Account must be taken of *all* work the muscles in question are called upon to do, whether it be Exercises in the Physiotherapy Department, Occupational Therapy, Specific Home Exercises, Work, or the ordinary activities of everyday life.

Re-education may be regarded as a continuous process which begins, while the muscles are still paralysed, in the form of an attempted initiation of contraction, and extends until maximum function is achieved.

The exact stage in this re-education process at which any particular muscle group begins is determined by the findings at the assessment made when treatment begins.

TREATMENT TO INCREASE MUSCULAR STRENGTH AND FUNCTION

Once the power of contraction has been regained, the muscles are strengthened progressively until maximum function is obtained. Passive movements, support, and artificial methods of assisting the circulation are discontinued gradually and are replaced by active exercise.

Principles of Treatment to Increase Strength and Function

1. *The Affected Muscles must be Strengthened Progressively by Resisted Exercises, which are Specific for the Group to which the Muscles belong*

a. *Range.* The range of movement is increased.

b. *Type of Muscle Work.* Concentric, eccentric and static muscle work are elicited.

c. *Resistance.* The resistance is increased by:

(*i*) increasing the poundage of the resistance;

(*ii*) increasing the leverage of the resistance.

d. *Speed.* Increase or decrease in the speed of movement is a progression for concentric work. Decrease in speed is a progression for eccentric work. Lengthening of the contraction period is a progression for static holding.

e. *Duration.* Increase in the number of times an exercise is performed or decrease in the rest period between each series of exercises, or a combination of both according to circumstances, makes more work for the muscles.

2. *Full Function of the Affected Muscles as Members of the Teams of Muscles which Work to produce Skilled and Co-ordinated Movement, must be restored by Free Activities, Natural and Skilled Movements*

Progression of these exercises follows on lines similar to those stated above for resisted exercises. Pendular movements requiring relatively little power are used at first to assist in the restoration of muscle balance, progressing to slow sustained or rapid movements requiring more power. Small-range movements in which many joints must be controlled are the most highly skilled.

Types of Exercises used to strengthen Muscles and restore Function

All active exercises maintain or increase muscle strength providing intra-muscular tension is increased sufficiently by the demands of the resisting forces. Weak muscles are provided with work suitable to their capacity by the use of Assisted-Resisted, Free, or Resisted Exercises, while Objective, Recreational or Occupational Activities ensure their return to functional use.

It cannot be over-emphasised that the choice of a particular exercise does not necessarily ensure the desired effect: it is the manner and speed with which the exercise is performed which determines the effect it produces. In general, strengthening exercises are slow and precise.

Assisted-Resisted Exercises

These are rarely used to strengthen muscles except in cases of marked weakness when strength is insufficient to complete the range of movement.

Free Exercises

Free exercises are valuable as they can be practised at regular and frequent intervals and at home. Careful selection of the starting positions and accurate teaching ensure the use of the muscles in question and grade the exercise to match their capacity for work.

Resisted Exercises

These exercises create the tension in muscles essential for increase in power and hypertrophy. Emphasis on the activity of the affected group restores the balance of muscle strength rapidly and so prevents trick movement and strain elsewhere.

Proprioceptive neuromuscular facilitation is most effective in this context. Repeated contractions, slow reversals and rhythmic stabilisations are all suitable techniques.

Activities

These are essential to ensure integrated action of muscle groups in the production of movement. They also restore confidence and general health.

Assessment of Progress

Re-assessment of the patient's abilities is made at frequent intervals to guide progression of activities and estimate progress.

16

TECHNIQUE OF STRENGTHENING MUSCLES

THE MUSCLES OF THE FOOT

THE action of the foot muscles is to stabilise it to support the body weight, and to provide the power essential for its use as a lever to propel the body forwards.

THE INTRINSIC MUSCLES

Lack of power in these muscles produces a dropped transverse arch, buckling of the toes, and Hallux Valgus. To restore the state of muscle balance, the weak muscles must be exercised to produce two movements.

(*i*) *Flexion of the Metatarsophalangeal Joint, combined with Extension of the Interphalangeal Joints.*

This restores the position of the transverse arch and straightens the toes by using the Interossei, Lumbricals, Adductor Hallucis, Flexors Hallucis and Minimi Brevis, and so balances the action of the Long Flexors (and Flexor Digitorum Brevis) which buckle the toes when their action is unopposed.

(*ii*) *Toe Abduction and Adduction.*

The Dorsal Interossei, Abductor Hallucis and Abductor Minimi Digiti part the toes from the mid-line of the foot and extend them. The Plantar Interossei and Adductor Hallucis draw the toes together and flex them.

Flexor Digitorum Brevis and Flexor Accessorius are associated with the Long Flexors, and help to arch the sole of the foot so that the skin is wrinkled. Extensor Digitorum Brevis works only with the Long Extensor of the toes.

Assisted Exercise for the Intrinsic Muscles. As many people are far from foot conscious, it is often necessary to use manual assistance to give the patient the feeling of the movement, or faradic stimulation to help in 'finding' the muscles, and so convince him of his ability to contract them.

Examples of Free Exercises for the Intrinsic Muscles. At first these are non-weight-bearing progressing to weight-bearing. Any exercise which produces buckling of the toes, i.e. extension at the metatarso-phalangeal joints with flexion at the interphalangeal joints, must be avoided. The balanced action of the Intrinsic Muscles with that of

183

the Long Flexors, as in the push off from the toes in walking, is taught and practised until the normal reflex is re-established.

a. *sitting (Toes resting on a book); Toe flexion and extension at the metatarsophalangeal joint with pressure on the balls of the Toe* (see Ex. (g), Para. 3, p. 141).

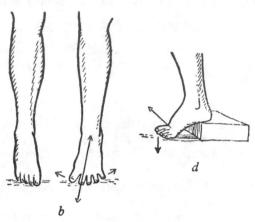

FIG. 114

b. *sitting; Toe spreading.*

c. *sitting; Foot arching.*

d. *standing (Heel raised and supported); same movement as* (a) *to train push off from Toes.*

Resisted Exercise for the Intrinsic Muscles. The movements can be localised and resisted manually by the physiotherapist.

Activities. The use of the muscles in walking, jumping and running must be trained and practised. A mirror is of great value until the patient becomes foot conscious and able to appreciate the feel of the movement.

THE DORSIFLEXORS

Full-range contraction of these muscles is only possible with the knee bent, as tension of the Calf Muscles limits the range when the knee is straight.

Assisted Exercise for the Dorsiflexors. From *side lying, with the knee bent,* assistance can be given with the hands. If a sitting position is used the knee must again be bent, and a suitable grasp for the physiotherapist is round the heel, so that the foot rests on her forearm, while the other hand fixes the lower leg and palpates the muscles during contraction.

Mechanical assistance can be arranged with a pulley and weight.

Examples of Free Exercises for the Dorsiflexors. Full-range work is made possible by bending the knee, but as the power of the muscles increases, the opposition created by tension of the Calf Muscles when the knee is extended leads to a stronger contraction. This combination of movements is used as the leg swings forward in walking.

    a. *sitting leg crossed; one Foot dorsiflexion and slow plantaflexion* (see Fig. 86a, p. 140).

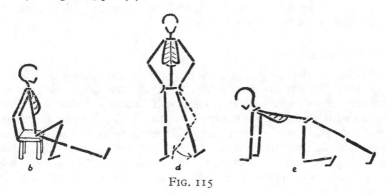

FIG. 115

    b. *inclined long sitting; Leg flexion and Ankle dorsiflexion.*
    c. *long sitting; Ankle dorsiflexion, alternately.*
    d. *half standing; Heel placing.* This exercise can be done in any direction with or without hopping on the other foot (Jig or Reel).
    e. *prone kneeling; one Foot dorsiflexion,* with or without Leg movement.

Examples of Resisted Exercise for the Dorsiflexors. Manual resistance can be given. The action of Extensor Hallucis can be emphasised by resistance applied on the dorsum of the big toe, that

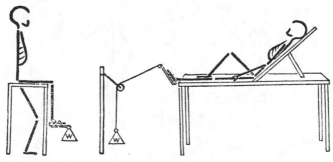

FIG. 116

of Extensor Digitorum Longus (and Brevis) by resistance on the dorsum of the toes. Tibialis Anterior contracts most strongly when dorsiflexion and inversion are resisted. Resistance can also be arranged by using weights, pulley and weight, and springs. An elongated sole, firmly and comfortably attached to the patient's shoe, provides additional leverage for the resistance, and a suitable means of attachment.

Activities. Walking, walking uphill and climbing, bicycling (with pedal straps), walking on all fours, and long jump are all activities in which these muscles are used.

THE PLANTAFLEXORS

These muscles are powerful as they propel the body forwards and help to stabilise the foot and ankle. With the exception of Soleus they all work across more than one joint, and because of this, the Long Flexors of the toes are most capable in this capacity when the metatarsophalangeal joint is extended. Gastrocnemius is most efficient when the knee is extended, while the function of Soleus is mainly postural to steady the leg on the foot. Tibialis Anterior is primarily an invertor, and supports the longitudinal arch of the foot, but it can assist dorsiflexion.

Assisted Exercise for the Plantaflexors. With the patient in side lying, manual assistance is given by the physiotherapist.

Examples of Free Exercises for the Plantaflexors (Fig. 117)
Non-weight-bearing

    a. *long sitting* }*(Heels free); Toe pointing, alternately.*
       or half standing
    b. *prone lying (Feet over end of plinth); Toe pointing, alternately.*
    c. *sitting; Heel raising.*

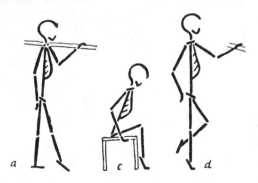

FIG. 117

Weight-bearing

    d. *half standing; one Heel raising* (Fig. 117).

    e. *reach grasp high standing; Heel raising and slowly lowering.*

    f. *standing; 'Bob' jump, hopping or dancing steps.*

Resisted Exercise for the Plantaflexors. Manual resistance can be offered to the muscles with the patient in positions such as *long sitting* or *prone lying (with knees bent)*, care being taken to see that resistance is given on a sufficient area of the sole to avoid straining the intertarsal joints and plantar structures. The action of the Long Flexors can be localised by fixing the ankle joint in dorsiflexion and resisting under the toes.

Mechanical and auto-resistance is given by a treadle machine or it can be arranged thus—

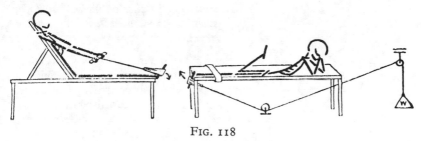

FIG. 118

Activities. Suitable activities include walking, running, jumping, balance walk sideways or up an incline, cycling and rowing.

THE INVERTORS

These muscles rotate the foot inwards, chiefly at the transverse tarsal and subtaloid joints, and maintain the longitudinal arch of the foot, in addition to assisting movements of the ankle joint.

Assisted Exercise for the Invertors. With the patient in *long sitting* or *half lying*, the physiotherapist gives manual assistance by fixing with one hand above the ankle and the other grasping round the heel with the sole of the foot resting on the forearm. Movement then occurs round a vertical axis and gravity is eliminated. Alternatively, a swing board can be used by the patient, the slope of the board on which the foot rests being altered by pulling on the ropes.

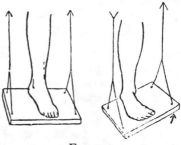

FIG. 119

Examples of Free Exercises for the Invertors
Non-weight-bearing
   a. *sitting; inner border raising.*
   b. *long sitting; turn soles of Feet to face each other.*
   c. *sitting; brush stockings, or sand, into pile between Feet* (lower leg must be kept vertical).
   d. *sitting; pick up beanbag between Feet, or with one Foot, and pass it to opposite Hand.*

Weight-bearing
   e. *standing; brace longitudinal arch.* The ball of the great toe must remain on the ground; the movement is assisted by rotating the leg laterally so that the patellae look outwards.

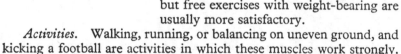

   f. *standing; balance on inclined surface, such as see-saw rocker, or inclined form.*

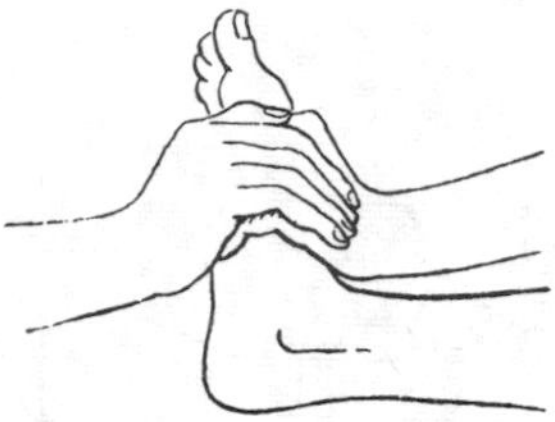

FIG. 120

Resisted Exercise for the Invertors. Manual resistance can be given with a clasp grasp with the patient in *half lying.* Mechanical resistance can also be arranged, but free exercises with weight-bearing are usually more satisfactory.

Activities. Walking, running, or balancing on uneven ground, and kicking a football are activities in which these muscles work strongly.

THE EVERTORS

In the non-weight-bearing position Peroneus Longus and Brevis evert the foot and assist plantaflexion, while Peroneus Tertius, if present, assists eversion and dorsiflexion. In the weight-bearing position Peroneus Longus depresses the ball of the great toe, and enables the foot to remain plantagrade while the medial arch is maintained by the invertors.

Assisted Exercise for the Evertors. These are performed in a manner similar to that used for the invertors.

Examples of Free Exercises for the Evertors
Non-weight-bearing
   a. *sitting; outer border raising.*
   b. *sitting; brushing movement outwards.*

Weight-bearing
   c. *standing; pressing ball of great toe to ground and raising outer border of Foot.*

d. *standing, or Toe standing; balance on surface which slopes downwards and medialwards.*

Resisted Exercise for the Evertors. Resistance can be given by manual pressure on the lateral side of the foot. Weight resistance can be arranged in *side lying*.

Activities. Walking on uneven ground and tiptoe walking.

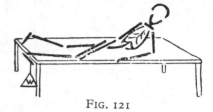

FIG. 121

The action of all the previous muscles groups are combined in exercises such as Foot rolling, or by the use of a balance board. Emphasis can then be placed on any particular group or muscle (Fig. 122).

THE KNEE EXTENSORS

The Quadriceps Muscles extend the knee joint and are of prime importance in maintaining its stability. The texture of these muscles is coarse and they waste rapidly if they are not used. In addition to its function as an extensor of the knee, Rectus Femoris assists flexion of the hip joint and the action of Vastus Medialis is essential for the production of the last few degrees of knee extension and for the medial rotation of the femur on the tibia which constitutes the 'screw home', or locking movement at the completion of this movement.

Assisted Exercise for the Knee Extensors. A suitable position for the patient is *side lying* with the leg supported or suspended in the horizontal position to eliminate the effect of gravity on the joint. The thigh is fixed with the hip in extension, to remove tension from the

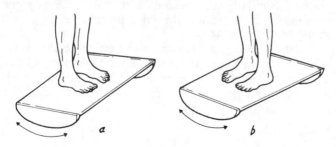

FIG. 122

Hamstrings and obtain the advantage of slight tension on the Rectus Femoris as it passes across the front of the hip. Manual resistance in the stronger part of the range of movement is added as soon as possible to increase the quality of the contraction.

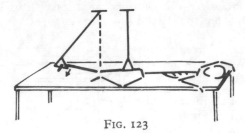

FIG. 123

Examples of Free Exercise for the Knee Extensors
Non-weight-bearing

a. *lying; static Quadriceps contraction (or setting).*

Three methods which may be used to obtain this contraction are:

(*i*) The contraction is taught on the unaffected leg and is seen and felt by the patient, who then attempts a similar contraction on the other leg.

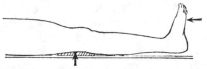

FIG. 124.   Quadriceps Contraction

(ii) *In lying* one hand gives compression on the sole of the foot and resists plantaflexion strongly while the other is placed under the back of the knee joint.   A command to hold the knee down and straight against resistance is given at the same time as all joints of the leg are approximated.   Similarly in *standing* with the knee straight and weight-bearing pressure behind the knee in an attempt to bend it stimulates extension (Fig. 124).

(*iii*) The physiotherapist puts one hand on the muscles and the other under the patient's heel; the patient is then asked to feel the pressure on the heel and attempt to relieve it by lifting the leg.   No movement takes place, but the muscles are thrown into a state of strong contraction.

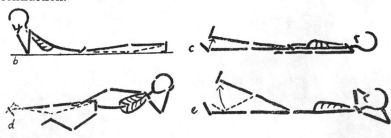

FIG. 125

Quadriceps contractions are reinforced by strong dorsiflexion of the ankle joint and inversion of the foot.   When effusion is present only non-weight-bearing exercises are used and only a small range of flexion, if any, is allowed.

b. *prone lying (Feet dorsiflexed); Knee extension* (Fig. 125).
c. *lying; Quadriceps contractions followed by one straight Leg lifting and lowering, slowly.*   The leg must not be lifted too high because increasing tension on the Hamstrings will force it to bend.
d. *side lying; one Hip and Knee bending and stretching.*
e. *lying; one Hip and Knee bending, Knee stretching and leg lowering.*
f. *high sitting; Knee stretching.*
g *lying (with Hips lifted); Hip and Knee bending and stretching.* This is only suitable for the young and agile.

Partial Weight-bearing
h. *prone kneeling; Knee stretching*
i. *heave grasp standing; Knee bending and stretching.*   Part of the weight is taken on the arms throughout.

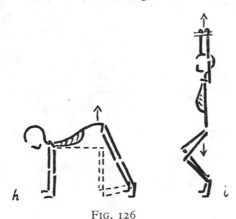

FIG. 126

Weight-bearing

    j. *Back against standing; Knee bending and stretching.*

    k. *fallout standing; push off to standing.*

    l. *standing; step up and down.*

    m. *Toe standing; 'bob' or 'stride' jump.*

    n. *Toe standing; step and hop, with bent or straight Knee.*

    Examples of Resisted Exercise for the Knee Extensors.   Manual resistance can be given in a variety of positions including *half lying, high sitting* and *prone lying.*   The natural thrusting movement of the leg as a whole is resisted in *lying* or *side lying* with pressure on the sole of the foot and on the hamstrings.

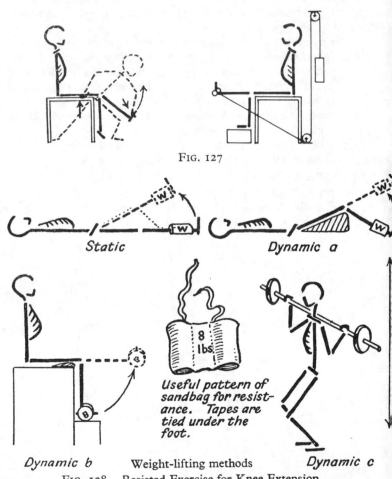

Fig. 127

Static   Dynamic a

Useful pattern of sandbag for resistance. Tapes are tied under the foot.

Dynamic b   Weight-lifting methods   *Dynamic c*

Fig. 128   Resisted Exercise for Knee Extension

The patient may resist his own knee extension by the use of the weight or pressure of the contralateral limb when the ankles are crossed (see p. 53) or weights and pulleys may be arranged in a variety of ways (see p. 56). Springs are useful in some positions or a medicine ball may be held between the feet or thrown by them during knee extension from *high sitting*.

Progressive Resistance Exercises (see p. 54) are often used to increase the power and endurance of the Knee Extensors. Methods of applying these exercises vary considerably but in every case it appears that the selection of the starting position and the rate of progression are important factors to be considered at each successive stage of treatment. A precise but flexible routine must be designed to meet the capabilities of the individual patient and his efforts must be carefully observed. Some suggestions as to suitable positions and methods are as follows:

(*i*) Static Weight Lifting. Static muscle work is used while effusion is present or when the condition of the joint contraindicates movement. From *half crook lying* or *inclined lying* the muscles are first contracted to take the strain of the resisting force, the leg is then lifted with the knee fully extended until it is in line with the thigh of the crooked leg and then lowered to the floor and relaxed before the procedure is repeated. An endurance programme is usually most suitable, working on the basis of a 10 R.M. with increase in repetitions to the maximum of 100 before re-assessment. It is not suitable to give a heavy resistance in this position because with a long lever too great a resistance may be given to the hip flexor and abdominal muscles.

(*ii*) Dynamic Weight Lifting A. From *crook lying* (*with the thigh firmly supported*) the lower leg is fully extended and then lowered to the floor. Exercise in this position provides a useful intermediate stage between that of static work and the method by which the de Lorme boot is lifted in *high sitting*, as the latter position imposes considerable strain on the anterior structures of the joint when the leg is bent to a right angle. Contraction of the muscles involving movement of a joint is normally used only when effusion has subsided but in many cases the presence of chronic or minimal swelling may be ignored unless it is increased by exercise. A power programme is usually introduced at this stage.

(*iii*) Dynamic Weight Lifting B. From *high sitting*, with a small pillow under the popliteal space, the knee is fully extended to lift the de Lorme boot and then lowered. The movement must be smooth and controlled throughout; the boot may rest on a support between each lift or only between each group of repetitions.

(*iv*) Dynamic Weight Lifting C. The bar-bell is held supported across the back of the shoulders while the knees are fully bent and stretched for the required number of repetitions. The back is held erect throughout the movement. If the calf muscles are shortened a small lift under the heels may be provided. This method provides strong work for the Knee Extensors within the framework of the normal thrusting pattern of movement of the lower limbs and it must therefore be regarded as very satisfactory.

Examples of Activities to use the Knee Extensors. These are very numerous. In non-weight-bearing positions such as *high sitting* and *crook sitting* beanbags and balls can be balanced on the feet and thrown by a rapid extension of one or both knees. Bicycling, breast-stroke swimming, rope climbing and rowing with a sliding seat all give good exercise to these muscles.

During weight-bearing, walking up and down hills or stairs, running, jumping, skipping, lifting heavy weights using the knees, and balance walking with knee bending and stretching, while a weight is carried in the hands, are examples. Care must be taken to ensure rhythmical and even movement and to see that full advantage is taken of the extensor thrust.

THE KNEE FLEXORS

The Hamstrings (Biceps Femoris, Semitendinosus and Semimembranosus) are the most important Flexors of the Knee, and, as they also extend the hip, they can be strengthened by producing this movement when the knee is extended. Assistance in flexing the knee is given

FIG. 129

to the Hamstrings by Sartorius, Gracilis and Popliteus, and when the foot is on the ground Gastrocnemius and Plantaris also help.

Assisted Exercise for the Knee Flexors. In *side lying* the leg is supported or suspended in the horizontal position with the hip joint flexed, the thigh is then fixed and knee flexion is assisted manually.

A re-education board slightly inclined can also be used, provided the frictional resistance it offers is sufficient to prevent knee flexion occurring passively. Manual resistance to the movement is added as soon as possible in the strongest part of the range of movement to increase the quality of the contraction.

Examples of Free Exercises to work the Knee Flexors (Fig. 130)

    a. *side lying; one Hip and Knee bending.*
    b. *hanging; Knee bending.*
    c. *standing; one Hip and Knee bending.*

d. *prone lying; Knee bending and stretching slowly.*

e. *crouch position; crouch 'Bunny' jump, or Feet changing by leaping.*

Resisted Exercise for the Knee Flexors. *Side lying*, with the leg supported and the hip flexed, and *prone lying* are convenient positions for manual resistance. Total flexion of the leg is resisted with one hand

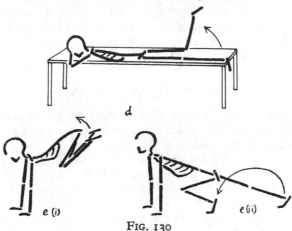

FIG. 130

on the sole of the foot and the other above the knee. A weight resistance on the foot can be applied in *half standing* or *prone lying*, in the latter case the muscles only work in their outer range.

Spring or weight and pulleys can be used in *side lying* with the leg supported, *prone or crook half lying*.

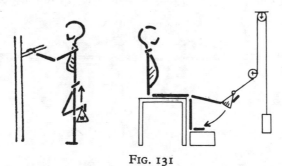

FIG. 131

Activities. These muscles are used in walking and running, and in any upward jump in which the feet are lifted high with the knees bent, as for example squat vaults and forward jump over a rope.

THE MUSCLES ROUND THE HIP JOINT

In many conditions producing pain in this joint, the latter is held in a position of flexion, adduction and lateral rotation. It is, therefore, often essential to exercise the Hip Extensors, Abductors and Medial Rotators to counteract the tendency to deformity. In mid-thigh amputations, when the Hamstrings and some of the Adductors are cut, the remaining Extensors and Adductors must be hypertrophied to restore the balance of muscle power which is essential for the correct usage of an artificial limb.

THE HIP EXTENSORS

Acting from above, these muscles extend the flexed hip until the leg is in line with the body and then about 15° beyond this, until movement is stopped by the tension of the Flexors and the ilio-femoral ligament. When they work with reversed origin and insertion, the pelvis is tilted backwards on the femoral heads, as in raising the trunk from the stooping position. Gluteus Maximus is regarded as the true antagonist of the Flexors; it is assisted by the Hamstrings whenever strong resistance is offered, the latter being most effective when the knee is straight. The inner range of contracting is emphasised to correct lack of full extension in walking.

Assisted Exercise for the Hip Extensors. *Side lying* is the neutral position from which to work these muscles. Manual assistance is the most effective with or without the limb supported in suspension, in water, or on a re-education board. In each case the pelvis can be relatively well fixed by positioning the other leg in full flexion.

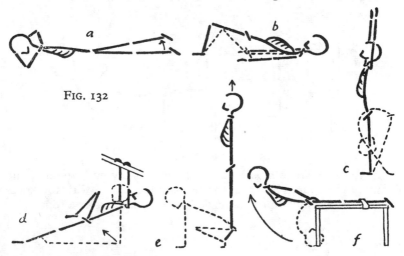

Fig. 132

Examples of Free Exercises for the Hip Extensors
   a. *prone lying or standing; one Leg lifting.*
   b. *crook lying; Gluteal contraction, and Pelvis lifting.*
   c. *relaxed stoop stride standing; Trunk raising.*
   d. *stretch grasp long sitting; Hip raising to fall hanging.*
   e. *crouch; change to standing (or upward jump).*
   f. *Leg prone lying; Trunk raising.*

Resisted Exercise for the Hip Extensors. Resistance to these muscles can be offered in a number of ways according to the range of work required.

For manual resistance, when the leg is moved *prone lying* or *side lying* are convenient positions for the patient. Resistance is given on the sole of the foot which is plantaflexed and over the hamstrings. Movement of the trunk is resisted from *stoop high ride* or *stoop stride sitting.*

A simple and effective method of giving weight resistance is from *stoop standing (with Trunk support)* with a weight attached to the foot, a medicine ball held between the feet or manually and one or both legs can be used.

Spring or weight and pulley resistance can also be arranged in many ways, for example, from *lying* the leg is extended against a spring resistance, or a weight and pulley circuit resists extension of the leg as a whole, during a thrusting movement, or of the hip only, from *sitting.*

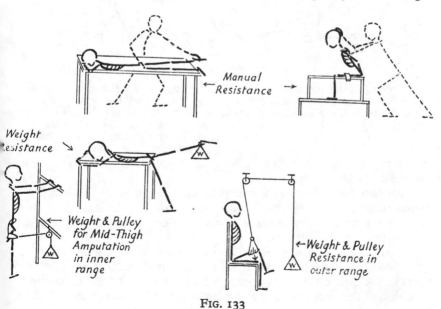

FIG. 133

Activities which involve Work for the Hip Extensors. These are numerous also and include walking, running, especially uphill, jumping and many other forms of athletics, putting the weight, skipping, swimming, ballroom dancing, lifting, pushing and rowing.

THE HIP FLEXORS

The Hip Flexors are Psoas Major and Iliacus, assisted by Pectineus Rectus Femoris (long head) and Sartorius, the latter being most effective when both the hip and the knee are flexed simultaneously. The Adductor Muscles can also assist flexion when strong resistance is offered.

The work of these muscles is associated with that of the Lumbar Flexors. When both legs are flexed on the trunk, the action of Psoas and Iliacus tends to extend the lumbar spine and tilt the pelvis forward as the result of imperfect fixation of their origins, therefore to increase their efficiency the Flexors of the Lumbar Spine work strongly to stabilise the lumbar spine and the pelvis. As flexion of the hip joints continues tension of the Hamstrings tilts the pelvis backwards and flexes the lumbar spine.

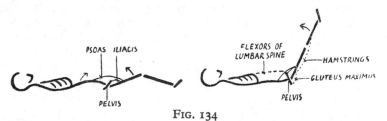

FIG. 134

Arching of the lumbar spine due to failure to fix the origins of Psoas and Iliacus at the beginning of hip flexion.

Fixation of the origins of Psoas and Iliacus by the action of the straight Abdominal Muscles and by tension of the Hamstrings. The latter is greater when the knees are straight.

When only one hip is flexed, the pelvis is stabilised by the Extensors of the other Hip.

Movement of the pelvis and trunk on the thighs, as in changing from *lying* to *sitting*, works these muscles strongly, the lumbar spine arches at the beginning of the movement unless it is controlled by the use of the Lumbar Flexors.

Assisted Exercise for the Hip Flexors. Side lying or lying are suitable positions from which to assist the movement manually, the lumbar region and pelvic tilt being controlled by extension of the other hip. Flexion of the knee of the moving leg at the same time as that of the hip makes inner range work possible and the movement then follows the natural pattern.   Self-assistance can also be given when the patient clasps his hands under the thigh.   Resistance in the stronger part of the range is added as soon as possible.

Examples of Free Exercise for the Hip Flexors

    a. *Leg lift lying; one or both Hip and Knee bending.*
    b. *lying or crook lying; change to crook sitting.*
    c. *prone kneeling; one Hip and Knee bending (to put Head on Knee).*
    d. *standing; one Hip and Knee bending (to pass beanbag under thigh).*
    e. *hanging; one or both Hip and Knee bending upward.*
    f. *long sitting; Leg lifting (to roll football below Knees).*

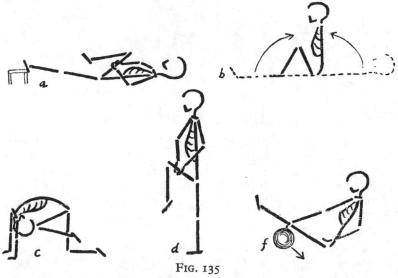

FIG. 135

Resisted Exercise for the Hip Flexors.   Strong resistance to hip flexion is offered by gravity in the upright position especially when the knee is straight, as the muscles work at a considerable mechanical disadvantage and against the growing tension of the Hamstrings as flexion increases.

Manual resistance is given with one hand on the dorsum of the foot, which is fully dorsiflexed and over the Quadriceps.   The knee can either flex as the movement progresses or remain extended.

Mechanical resistance can be arranged by attaching a weight or other resistance to the foot from *half lying, lying* or *half sitting.*   Weight and pulleys are used to resist a total flexion pattern of the leg.

Activities.   Running with high knee bending, long and forward jump over a rope, 'Double Through' skipping, climbing, somersaults and squat vaults work the Hip Flexors strongly in conjunction with the Abdominal Muscles.

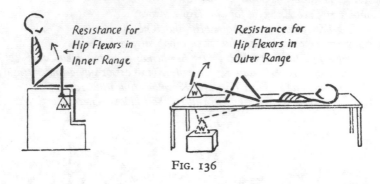

FIG. 136

THE HIP ABDUCTORS

Working from their origin on the hip bones, these muscles (Gluteus Medius, Minimus and Tensor Fascia Lata) abduct each leg to about 30°.   Emphasis on the action of the Tensor Fascia Lata is obtained by abducting the leg with flexion of the hip and the action of Gluteus Medius is emphasised when the leg is extended to the limit of its range.

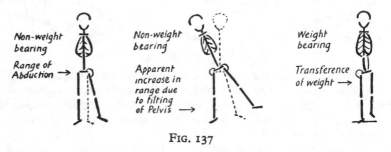

FIG. 137

When one leg is fixed and the other abducted, an apparent increase in range of the abducted leg is produced by lateral tilting of the pelvis at the hip joint of the fixed leg by the Abductors of that Hip joint working with reversed origin and insertion.   To transfer the whole weight of the body on to one leg as in walking, the Abductors of the Hip of the standing leg work with reversed origin and insertion to tilt the pelvis

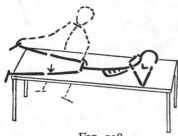

FIG. 138

laterally, while the trunk is kept up-right by the Lumbar Side Flexors on the opposite side.

Assisted Exercise for the Hip Abductors. Support or suspension of the moving leg in the horizontal position counter-balances the effect of gravity. Both legs can be moved simultaneously in the *prone* or *supine position* (*Leg parting*) when one leg is moved, the other leg fully abducted to fix the pelvis and limit the movement to that hip joint.

Manual assistance is given in *lying, half lying* or *side lying.*

Examples of Free Exercise for the Hip Abductors
  a. *lying, prone lying or hanging; Leg parting.*
  b. *lying or high half standing; Leg shortening and lengthening.*
  c. *half standing; one Leg lifting sideways.*
  d. *side falling; one Leg lifting.*
  e. *half yard grasp high half standing; change to star position.*

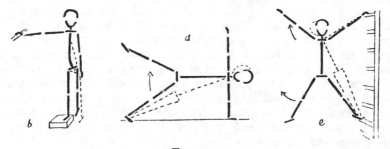

FIG. 139

Resisted Exercise for the Hip Abductors. As the small degree of abduction required to produce a lateral tilt of the pelvis on the standing leg during transference of weight is of major importance, the pattern of this movement must be emphasised. Manual or mechanical resistance to *Leg shortening,* in order to work the Abductors of the Hip of the stationary leg, is easily arranged by fixing one foot and resisting the movement on the other. Note that the muscles of the hip on the side of the fixed foot work with the Lumbar Side Flexors on the opposite side, chiefly Quadratus Lumborum.

Resistance to the movement of the leg on the pelvis is given in *prone* or *supine lying* with the leg in suspension, the resistance being arranged horizontally. Weight resistance is given in *half standing,* or in *side lying* with either a long or a short lever.

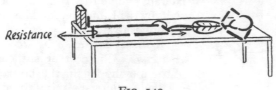

FIG. 140

Activities. Breast-stroke swimming, overarm bowling at cricket, leapfrog, walking and running exercise these muscles.

THE HIP ADDUCTORS

These muscles (Adductores Magnus, Longus and Brevis, assisted by Pectineus and Gracilis) form a powerful group; they are frequently subject to adaptive shortening but are comparatively rarely weakened in relation to the opposing group, except as the result of mid-thigh amputation. Their action is thought to be associated with that of the Muscles of the Pelvic Floor.

Assisted Exercise for the Hip Adductors. When both hips are adducted simultaneously from the non-weight-bearing positions the pelvis is fixed, but it is remarkably difficult to control substitution of a lateral tilt and side flexion of the lumbar spine when only one leg is moved. *Lying*, with the spine fully flexed to the side opposite to that of the moving leg, is suggested as a means of localising the movement to the hip joint, and it also permits a wide range of pure adduction. Inner range work with the hip in extension is usually limited by contact with the other leg, but when the hip is flexed a wider range is obtained by crossing the thighs.

Manual assistance can be given for one or both legs with gravity counter-balanced in *lying* or *prone lying*, with or without the limbs being supported by suspension or water. In *lying* a re-education board under the leg can be used. Resistance is added in the strongest part of the range as soon as possible.

Examples of Free Exercise for the Hip Adductors
a. *stride lying or stride long sitting; Leg crossing.*
b. *sitting; Leg crossing.*
c. *Leg lift lying or reverse hanging; Leg parting and closing.*
d. *Leg lift lying or hanging; grasp and hold sandbag or ball between Feet or Knees.*
e. *low wing Foot support sideways standing; push off with Foot on floor to take weight on supported Foot.*

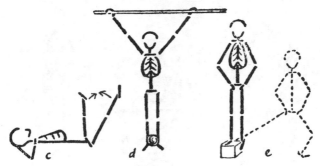

FIG. 141

Resisted Exercise for the Hip Adductors.   Manual resistance can be given at either the foot or knee.   Resistance by springs or weights and

FIG. 142

pulleys, is applied in such positions as *lying, prone lying, side lying* or *reach grasp high half standing.*

Activities.   Horse riding, breast-stroke swimming, rope climbing, roller skating and ski-ing work the muscles strongly.

THE MEDIAL ROTATORS OF THE HIP

Medial rotation of the hip is performed by the same muscles which abduct the femur, i.e. Tensor Fascia Lata, Gluteus Medius and Minimus.   Therefore a pattern of movement in which the muscles work to abduct with medial rotation is the most effective for strengthening these muscles.

Assisted Exercise for the Medial Rotators of the Hip.   Assistance is given manually with the knees and hips bent or straight, the grasps being the same as those used for the performance of the passive movement (Chapter 14, p. 146).

Examples of Free Exercise for the Medial Rotators of the Hip

The leg can be moved on the pelvis or the pelvis on the leg.

a. *sitting; swing or place the Feet apart, keeping the Knees together.*

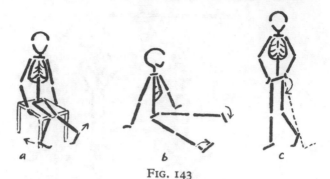

FIG. 143

b. *stride lying or stride long sitting; Leg rolling inwards* (Fig. 143b).
c. *half standing; one Knee rolling inwards* (Fig. 143c).
d. *Knees bent prone lying; Feet pressing apart.*
e. *half standing; Pelvis and Trunk turning towards the standing Leg.*

Resisted Exercise for the Medial Rotators of the Hip. From *high sitting* manual resistance is given on the lateral side of the foot and on the inner side of the knee joint, or from *lying* with the knee held in full extension the inward rolling movement is resisted by the hands placed over the adductor muscles.

Activities. Kicking, as in soccer, golf, and all movements which involve turning towards the stationary leg, use the muscles strongly. Medial rotation of the hip is a component of the movement required for the push off in walking and running.

THE LATERAL ROTATORS OF THE HIP

Lateral rotation is a powerful movement which is produced by many muscles (Obturators Internus and Externus, Quadratus Femoris, Gemelli Superior and Inferior, assisted by Piriformis, Gluteus Maximus, Sartorius and the Adductors).

Assisted Exercise for the Lateral Rotators of the Hip. Manual assistance is given in a manner similar to that used for the performance of the passive movement.

Examples of Free Exercise for the Lateral Rotators of the Hip

a. *cross sitting; press lateral side of Knee to ground.*
b. *stride lying or stride long sitting; Leg rolling outward.*
c. *half standing; Leg rotation to point Toe sideways.*
d. *Toe standing; Hip and Knee bending, parting Knees as far as possible.*

e. *stride prone lying; with Ankles dorsiflexed, press Heels inwards till medial border of Foot rests on floor.*

Resisted Exercise for the Lateral Rotators of the Hip. As the Adductors are also lateral rotators these two movements should be combined to strengthen these muscles. From *high sitting* the thigh is held in adduction by resistance while the movement is resisted by a hand placed on the medial side of the foot. In *lying* resistance to the outward rolling of the leg can be given on the lateral side of the thigh.

Activities. These muscles are used strongly during many movements in ballet dancing, Scots dancing and fencing.

THE MUSCLES OF THE PELVIC FLOOR

The Levatores Ani and Coccygei together form a pelvic diaphragm or muscular floor of the pelvis. The Levatores Ani constrict the lower end of the rectum (or 'back passage') and the vagina in the female, and support the pelvic viscera with the assistance of the Coccygei, which draw the coccyx forwards. The urethra (or 'front passage') is constricted by the Sphincter Urethrae.

Contraction of these muscles takes place in response to the pressure exerted on them by the downward thrust of the viscera, and the latter is increased by an increase in the intra-abdominal pressure. Their action also appears to be associated with that of the Hip Extensors and Adductors. Weakness or overstretching often leads to incontinence or prolapse which is most distressing to the patient.

Method of Teaching Contraction. Faradic stimulation may be necessary to teach the patient to appreciate the feeling of contraction, otherwise instruction to 'Draw up' the 'back passage' or 'front passage' is usually understood. This can be done as a localised movement or in conjunction with exercise for the Hip Extensors or Adductors. The patient may also be recommended to try stopping and starting the flow of urine during micturition.

Assistance is given to the muscles by positioning designed to reduce the effect of the downward thrust of the pelvic viscera, e.g. *crook lying with Pelvis lifted, lying,* or *prone lying.* Progression is made by using the inclined and finally the erect positions for exercises and maintenance of control.

Examples of Exercises in which the Muscles of the Pelvic Floor Work

a. *crook lying (with Pelvis lifted); brace Buttocks, press Knees together, and pull up between Legs.*

b. *Leg lift lying (Heels supported and Legs crossed); Hip raising and adduction with Pelvic Floor contraction.*

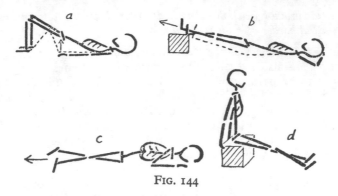

FIG. 144

c. *side lying* (*Legs bent*); *Leg stretching and adduction with Pelvic Floor contraction.*

d. *inclined long sitting* (*Ankles crossed*); *brace Buttocks, press Knees together and contract Pelvic Floor.*

e. *standing Legs crossed; Heel raising with Pelvic Floor contraction.*

Resisted Exercises for the Adductors of the Hip, particularly those which also use the Hip Extensors, are used, e.g. *crook lying; Knee closing* (*with Pelvis lifting*) *and outdrawing* (*with Pelvis lowering*).

As control improves the contractions of the pelvic floor are maintained during general trunk and leg exercises and the patient is trained to brace the muscles before any activity which raises the intra-abdominal pressure, such as coughing, sneezing, laughing or lifting heavy weights.

THE MUSCLES OF THE TRUNK

The anterior and posterior muscles of the trunk, the Back and Abdominal Muscles, flex and extend the spine and combine to produce side flexion and rotation.

They may work to produce movement with their lower attachment on the pelvis fixed; with their upper attachment on the thorax fixed; or with both attachments free to move. When they work with both attachments fixed a static or postural contraction results, the balanced contraction of the muscles being responsible for the active posture of the trunk and the support of the abdominal viscera.

THE EXTENSORS OF THE SPINE

The Sacrospinalis Muscles are the principal extensors of the thoracic and lumbar spines. They can be assisted by Quadratus Lumborum in the lumbar region and by many of the deep muscles of the back; the latter, however, probably work mainly in a postural capacity. The muscles which extend the head-neck are closely related

to those which extend the spine as a whole.   Other muscles which
work in conjunction with the Extensors of the Spine are the Retractors
and Depressors of the Scapulae and the Extensors of the Hip.

Extension is free in the cervical and lumbar region of the spine and
very limited in the thoracic region.   The effective action of the muscles
can be emphasised in one region only, they may work as a whole from
a fixed point at their lower or upper attachment, or with both attachments free to move.

Assisted Exercise for the Extensors of the Spine.   Gravity is counterbalanced in *side lying* and the action of the muscles may be assisted by
hand.   Owing to the weight of the part to be moved it is convenient to
suspend the body from the waist downwards prior to movement.   The
physiotherapist places one knee in the patient's back to fix at the axis
of movement and uses her hands to assist the action of the muscles.
As a progression, the support of a plinth with a polished surface may
be used, or small movements of extension may be attempted against

FIG. 145

tension springs when the body is suspended in the supine position.
In *prone lying* with the arms clasped behind the back and the feet fixed
the patient's efforts can be assisted by horizontal traction on the arms.
His effort is reinforced by strong extension of his head and neck at the
beginning of the movement.

Examples of Free Exercise for the Extensors of the Spine

a. *prone lying; Trunk raising.*

This exercise can be progressed and modified in numerous ways,
for example:

(*i*) One or both legs can be lifted.

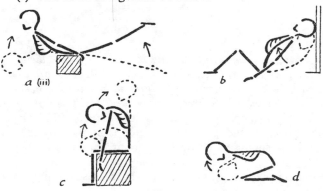

FIG. 146

(*ii*) The leverage of the trunk can be increased by elevating the arms to *bend, yard, Head rest* or *stretch positions*.

(*iii*) The hips may be supported on a form.

(*iv*) The raised position may be held while a ball is bowled or thrown to a partner (relax between each catch and throw).

(*v*) The ankles may be grasped when the knees are bent.

b. *crook lying, crook half lying, relaxed crook sitting, stretch crook sitting, or standing; Back arching* (Fig. 146).

   c. *relaxed stride sitting, or relaxed stride standing; Trunk raising vertebra by vertebra.*

   d. *relaxed stoop kneel sitting; Trunk raising to the horizontal.*

   e. *prone kneeling or half yard grasp standing; one Arm and Leg lifting.*

   f. *hanging; Leg lifting backward.*

Resisted Exercise for the Extensors of the Spine. Resistance can be given from *prone lying*, the physiotherapist placing one hand on the occiput with her other forearm fixing the thighs. From *sitting* (Fig. 143(*c*)) resistance can be given on the head or on the arms which are lifted with elevation as the movement progresses.

Weight resistance is simple and effective, for example:

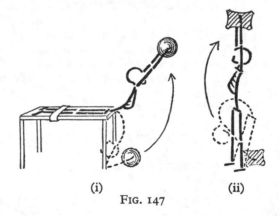

(i)   (ii)

FIG. 147

(*i*) *relaxed Leg prone lying; Trunk raising to lift a medicine ball.*

(*ii*) *relaxed stoop stride standing; Trunk raising to lift a sandbag above Head and lower it to the ground between the Feet.*

(*iii*) *prone lying with Feet fixed; Trunk raising (lifting sandbag placed between Shoulders) or Leg lifting (with sandbag between Feet).*

Spring or weight and pulley resistance is applied by means of a halter round the shoulders or by the patient holding the rope in the hands.

Activities. Rowing, tug-of-war, crawl-stroke swimming, arch and tunnel ball and all forms of lifting are some of the activities in which these muscles work.

THE FLEXORS OF THE SPINE

With the exception of the Transverus Abdominis, whose only function is to support and compress the abdominal viscera, all the Abdominal Muscles work to produce flexion of the spine.   The Recti are the chief muscles responsible, but they are assisted by the Obliqui Internus and Externus.   Gluteus Maximus produces flexion of the lumbar spine indirectly by tilting the pelvis backwards when it works with reversed origin and insertion.

Assisted Exercise for the Flexors of the Spine. *Crook half lying* is a suitable position for assisting concentric and eccentric work for these muscles.   The patient lifts the head and draws the shoulders forward, help being given by horizontal traction on the arms and, if necessary, support behind the head.   A

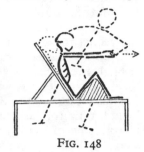

FIG. 148

wider range of movement is obtained by placing a small pillow behind the waist.   In *side lying* the head and shoulders or the pelvis can be moved with the physiotherapist's assistance.

Examples of Free Exercise for the Flexors of the Spine

   a. *crook lying, sitting, prone kneeling or standing; Pelvis tilting backward.*
   b. *prone kneeling; Back humping and hollowing, slowly.*

FIG. 149

c. *lying; Head and Shoulder raising to look at Feet.*

d. *relaxed crook sitting; change to lying (rounding Back) and raise.*

e. *Head rest crook sitting (Feet fixed); Back arching and raising.*

f. *lying; Hip and Leg lifting, to touch wall or floor behind Head (avoid accidental somersault).*

These muscles work strongly statically as fixators for the Hip Flexors and in many shoulder exercises, to prevent hollowing of the back, and when the head is lifted from *lying* they can be felt to tense. Compression of the abdominal viscera which involves relatively static work for the muscles is achieved by accenting the expiratory phase of breathing, when all the Abdominal Muscles (including Transversus) contract as the antagonistic muscle, the Diaphragm, is relaxed.

Resisted Exercise for the Flexors of the Spine. These muscles work strongly in association with the Hip Flexors, therefore resisted exercises for these muscles can be used to achieve concentric and eccentric work for the Flexors of the Spine. The movement must be continued to include tilting of the pelvis and flexion of the lumbar spine. Resistance to rounding of the back from *lying* (*Feet fixed*) can be offered by a weight held on the chest or with the arms extended. Manual resistance can be given from sitting on the forehead (with the head and neck locking in full flexion) and/or on the front of one or both shoulders. In this movement it is important to make sure that the direction of the resistance is *upwards* otherwise flexion of the hips will be the only movement resisted.

Gravity is usually a sufficiently strong resistance when the muscles are worked in their outer range, but a weight held on the chest or in

FIG. 150

extended arms increases the load in *lying; change to long sitting* and in *lying (Head and Shoulders unsupported); Back arching slowly and raising.*

Activities. Examples of these are long jumping, hurdling, somersaults, squat vaults, and climbing.

THE SIDE FLEXORS

The Back and Abdominal Muscles of one side work together to produce side flexion. The chief muscles concerned are the Sacrospinalis, Quadratus Lumborum, Rectus Abdominis and the Internal and External Obliques.   When the arms are fixed and the pelvis is free to move, Latissimus Dorsi, working with reversed origin and insertion, can produce the movement by lifting the pelvis upwards and forwards.   Strengthening and hypertrophy of the latter are of major importance in the rehabilitation of those who have sustained injury to the spinal cord.

Assisted Exercise for the Side Flexors.   Prone lying with the trunk suspended over the end of the plinth is suitable for movement of the upper part of the body in the neutral position (see p. 152), (Fig. 101c). For movement of the lower part of the body *heave grasp lying* with the pelvis and legs suspended is often used, particularly when work is required for Latissimus Dorsi.   A plinth with a polished surface may be substituted for suspension or the body may be floated in a re-education pool.   Manual assistance and control of the movement is given in every case.

Note.   In Fig. 151 the axis of movement is over the moving joint and the plane of pelvic movement is horizontal.   If the axis is moved

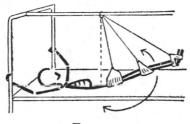

FIG. 151

towards the feet, a pendular swing results, increasing the difficulty at the limit of side flexion provided movement is at a speed slower than that of the natural swing of the pendulum.   During a pendular swing some rotation of the pelvis accompanies the movement of side flexion.

Examples of Free Exercise for the Side Flexors.   This movement is free in the lumbar region and limited in the thoracic region.   Sometimes it is necessary to limit the action of the muscles to one region only, as for instance in unilateral exercise for partially mobile scoliosis. To promote the thoracic movement, exercises involving the arms or those with the lumbar region fixed in flexion are preferable.   For lumbar movement, exercises for the legs are most effective and movement of the whole spine is freest in weightless exercises in extension.

1. Mainly for the Thoracic Region
   a. *inclined prone kneeling; low Dog crawl.*
   b. *bend stoop stride sitting; one Arm stretching upwards with one Arm stretching downwards (to limit of movement).*
   c. *under bend stoop stride sitting; Trunk side bending, localising movement with fists.*
2. Mainly for the Lumbar Region
   d. *reach grasp standing; one Leg shortening.*
   e. *hanging; Leg lifting sideways.*
   f. *standing; one Leg lifting sideways or swinging sideways with hopping*
3. For the Whole Spine
   g. *yard Foot support sideways standing; Trunk side bending, with opposite Arm swinging overhead.*
   h. *Forehead support prone lying; Trunk raising followed by Trunk side bending.*

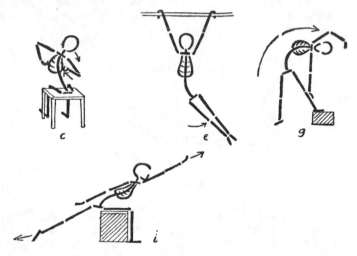

FIG. 152

4. Bending to Opposite Side in the Two Regions
   i. *bend fallout sitting; one Arm stretching upwards and other Arm downwards with lateral rotation of the latter.*

The lumbar region is bent to the side of the sitting leg and the thoracic to the side of the arm which is upward.

Resisted Exercise for the Side Flexors. In the upright position a weight held or lifted in one hand is a simple method of resistance, a vertical throw of a medicine ball above the head provides strong work for the muscles.

Activities.   Most movements of lifting and reaching up with one arm work these muscles.   Overarm bowling, window cleaning and climbing a rope are examples.   In walking, running, and creeping, movement/ of the pelvis involves side flexion, although the range of movement is small.

THE TRUNK ROTATORS

The Back and Abdominal Muscles combine to produce rotation, which takes place mainly in the lower thoracic region.   The fibres of the muscles concerned lie obliquely, i.e. the trunk rotators to the right lie in the direction of an oblique line running downwards and to the right anteriorly (right Internal Oblique, left External Oblique) and downwards and to the left posteriorly (left Rotatores, right Multifidus).

Assisted Exercise for the Trunk Rotators.   Rotation is assisted manually in the *sitting* position by horizontal pressure on the front of one shoulder and on the back of the other.   From *lying*, the patient can be helped to rotate and roll over on to one side, or into the *prone* position. To do this the physiotherapist stands on the side of the bed towards which the patient turns and the upper arm and leg are folded across the body and the pelvis is rolled on to one side with the help of one of the physiotherapist's hands on the sacrum, then her other hand brings the shoulders into line, with pressure on the scapula.

Examples of Free Exercises for the Trunk Rotators

 a. *yard crook lying; Pelvis and Leg rolling from side to side.*   The leverage is increased by stretching one or both Knees and lifting the Legs.

 b. *ride sitting; Trunk rotation to alternate sides with loose Arm swinging.*

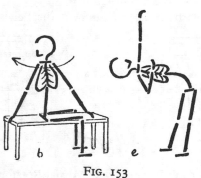

FIG. 153

 c. *prone kneeling; Trunk rotation with one Arm reaching upwards to receive a beanbag and then pass it back to partner under the Trunk.*

d. *ring grasp cross or ride sitting (with partner); Trunk rotation while one Arm bends as the other stretches.*

e. *stoop stride standing or yard Legs crossed standing; Trunk rotation with loose Arm swinging.*

f. *cross or ride sitting; Trunk rotation to pass ball to physiotherapist, who stands behind.*

Resisted Exercise for the Trunk Rotators.   Trunk rotation in *close sitting* is resisted manually with pressure on the shoulders.   Weights held in the hand can be added in *prone kneeling; Trunk rotation* (as in

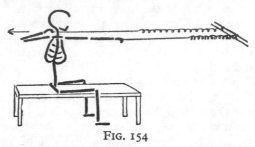

FIG. 154

Free Exercise 'c').   Spring or weights and pulleys are arranged horizontally with the patient in *reach grasp ride sitting.*

As breathing is impeded in the turn position, frequent rests may be necessary, or the exercises can be performed with breathing (expiration with turning and inspiration in the neutral position).

Activities.   Examples of these are sawing, running, archery, tennis, golf, overarm throwing, punching.

THE PELVIS ROTATORS

The pelvis can be rotated while the legs and shoulders remain stationary.

When the whole body is in alignment the Pelvis Rotators to the

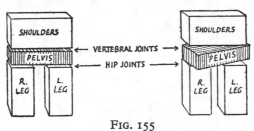

FIG. 155

left are the right Trunk Rotators, the Medial Rotators of the left Leg, and the Lateral Rotators of the right Leg, all working with reversed origin and insertion.

THE ELEVATORS OF THE SHOULDER GIRDLE

Elevation of the shoulder girdle frequently accompanies elevation of the arm but it may occur independently without rotation of the scapula as in shoulder shrugging. The muscles responsible for this movement, Trapezius (upper fibres) and Levator Scapulae, also steady the scapula during movements of the shoulder, maintain the postural level of the shoulders and (working with reversed origin and insertion) draw the head backwards. If the muscles work on one side only the head is bent to that side.

Assisted Exercise for the Shoulder Elevators. The work of these muscles in shoulder shrugging is reduced when the body is in the horizontal position as gravity is neutralised, e.g. in *crook lying* and *prone kneeling*. Manual assistance to the movement or to the maintenance of a higher postural level may be given by pressure under the elbows when the arms are folded.

Examples of Free Exercises for the Shoulder Elevators

    a. *crook lying, prone kneeling or sitting; Shoulder shrugging.*
    b. *crook lying or prone kneeling; Head side bending* (with or without Shoulder shrugging).
    c. *stride standing or sitting: any Arm movement above the horizontal* (including ball throwing).

In training a new postural level of the shoulder girdle it is essential for the patient to appreciate the 'feeling' of the new level. The use of a mirror may be helpful at first but this has the disadvantage of encouraging the patient to use the sense of sight as a substitute for kinaesthetic sense and therefore should be discontinued as soon as the patient can 'feel' the new position.

Resisted Exercise for the Shoulder Elevators. The physiotherapist's hands or sandbags resting on the patient's shoulders, or weights held in his hands, resist the shrugging action of the muscles. Spring or weight and pulley circuits can also be used. Resistance to elevation of the arms is given by lifting a medicine ball above the head.

The muscles antagonistic to the Elevators are the Serratus Anterior (lower fibres) and Pectoralis Minor, which work as Depressors when the movement is not performed by gravity. Latissimus Dorsi, however, is mainly responsible for downward pressure of the arms and shoulder girdle when resistance to the movement is given on the arms.

THE PROTRACTORS OF THE SCAPULAE

(Muscles which move the Scapulae forwards round the Chest wall)

Serratus Anterior and Pectoralis Minor move the scapulae forwards round the chest wall so that the glenoid cavity looks approximately forwards.   Flexion of the gleno-humeral joint is usually associated with the movement, as in forward pushing or punching.   The vertebral border of the scapula is held in apposition to the chest wall by Serratus Anterior with the assistance of Latissimus Dorsi.

Examples of Free Exercise for the Protractors of the Scapulae

   a. *Back support sitting; Shoulder drawing forward to round the upper Back and to place each Hand behind the opposite Shoulder* (avoid stooping).
   b. *prone kneeling; crawling.*
   c. *reach support standing (Hands on wall); Trunk falling forwards from Ankles and push off with Hands to regain balance.*
   d. *prone falling; Arm bending and stretching* ('press ups').

Resisted Exercise for the Protractors of the Scapulae.   Any forward thrusting movement of the arms against resistance stimulates these muscles.   Positions in which the hand is fixed and the arms extend to move the trunk are suitable, e.g. *Forearm support prone kneeling; Arm extension* in which resistance is given manually over the scapulae; lifting a weight vertically upwards from the chest, or by springs or weights and pulleys in *Back lean sitting* can also be used.

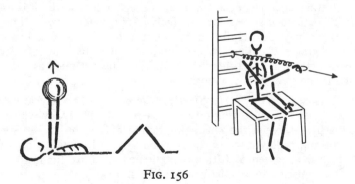

FIG. 156

Activities.   Punch-ball, boxing, digging, sawing, bowls, and forward throwing of a ball all work these muscles strongly.

THE RETRACTORS OF THE SCAPULAE

These muscles (Rhomboid Major and Minor, Trapezius, middle fibres) approximate the vertebral borders of the scapulae, bracing back the shoulders and steadying the scapulae during movements of the arms. They frequently work with the Extensors and Lateral Rotators of the Shoulders and the Extensors of the Spine but they can be activated independently.

Assisted Exercise for the Retractors of the Scapulae. The arm is used to lever the scapula round the chest wall when assisting the action of these muscles.

The physiotherapist uses one hand to palpate the scapula and to press it against the chest wall while her other hand grasps the patient's upper arm which is flexed and abducted into the plane of the scapula. *Prone lying* at the side of the plinth is the starting position of choice, as the trunk is fixed without pressure on the scapula.

Examples of Free Exercise for the Retractors of the Scapula

    a. *sitting; Arm rotation laterally with deep breathing and Scapula retraction.*

    b. *relaxed crook sitting; Back arching.*

    c. *across bend sitting; Elbow pulling backwards.*

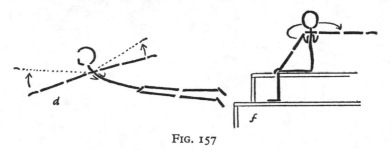

FIG. 157

    d. *yard prone lying; Head and Shoulder and Arm raising.*

    e. *fall hanging; Arm bending.*

    f. *high ride sitting; Trunk turning with one Arm pressing backward.*

Resisted Exercise for the Retractors of the Scapulae. The action of the muscles can be localised fairly well when they work against manual or mechanical traction given on the arm in the plane of the scapula. Any form of resistance offered to pulling movements or lifting from stooping, with or without trunk rotation, can be employed.

Activities. This group of muscles is used in breast-stroke swimming, rowing, tug-of-war. The use of a rake or saw (backward movement)

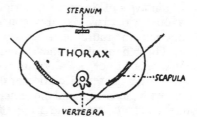

FIG. 158. Horizontal Section of Thorax to show Plane of the Scapula

is an example of how the Retractors help to steady the scapula and maintain the poise of the shoulders during a wide variety of skilled occupational movements in which the arms are used.

ROTATION OF THE SCAPULA

Lateral or forward rotation of the scapula (so that the glenoid cavity looks upwards) is accompanied by scapula protraction and is inseparable from movement at the gleno-humeral joint during elevation of the arm.   The chief muscles concerned are Serratus Anterior and Trapezius (upper and lower fibres).

Medial or backward rotation, which is the reverse movement, is produced by the Levator Scapulae and the Rhomboids, assisted in their outer range by Pectoralis Minor.

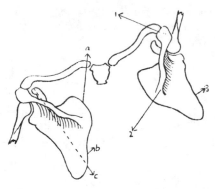

FIG. 159.   Rotation of the Scapula

Medial Rotators	Lateral Rotators
a. Levator Scapulae	1. Trapezius (upper fibres)
b. Rhomboids	2. Trapezius (lower fibres)
c. Pectoralis Minor	3. Serratus Anterior

Paralysis of Serratus Anterior is not uncommon and re-education as power returns requires consideration, because of the variety of functions the muscle performs.

The actions of the muscle are—(1) Protraction of the scapula with Pectoralis Minor, usually during pushing or thrusting movements of the arm; (2) Lateral Rotation of the scapula with Trapezius, in association with gleno-humeral movement to elevate the arm; (3) Stabilisation of the scapula, to fix the origin of Deltoid, to keep the scapula against the chest wall and to prevent medial rotation when weights are carried in front of the body; (4) Elevation of the ribs in inspiration when the arms are fixed; in this case it works with reversed origin and insertion.

The muscle may work as a fixator (3) at an early stage of recovery, but this is difficult to assess, therefore re-education of Protraction and Lateral Rotation are attempted.

RE-EDUCATION OF SCAPULAR FUNCTION

Re-education of scapular function is of prime importance in all conditions affecting the shoulder joint as the direction in which the glenoid cavity faces profoundly influences movement at the gleno-humeral joint. Loss of function in the arm leads to inefficiency of scapular muscles, and the scapula may have been immobilised either in elevation and protraction *without rotation*, e.g. by the use of a sling following an arm injury, or in a position of depression and retraction as the result of the weight of a paralysed arm, e.g. in hemiplegia.

Normally when the arm is lifted upwards and across the face the scapula moves upwards and forwards with lateral rotation so that the glenoid cavity faces forwards and upwards and the inferior angle moves towards the axillary line. As the arm moves downwards and backwards the opposite movement takes place, as in extending the arm to support the body. Similarly as the arm moves upwards and outwards, as in preparation for serving at tennis, the scapula moves upwards and backwards with lateral rotation, and conversely, during the striking or chopping movement, it moves downwards, forwards and rotates medially. Movements of the scapula can be initiated and its position stabilised manually in *side lying* or *forearm support lying* by placing one hand on the lateral angle and the other on the axillary or vertebral border according to the direction of the movement to be resisted. Maintenance of any position which involves taking weight on the arms (hands, forearms or elbows) stimulates the scapular muscles and these should be practised as soon as possible, e.g. *forearm support prone* or *side lying* or *prone kneeling*.

THE SHOULDER FLEXORS

Pectoralis Major (clavicular portion) and Deltoid (anterior fibres) are the chief muscles concerned in flexing the gleno-humeral joint. Their action is reinforced by assistance from the sternocostal portion of Pectoralis Major and by Biceps when the arm is drawn into line with the body from the fully extended position. The Shoulder Flexors work with the Scapula Protractors and the Elbow Extensors to produce the group movement of joints which results in a forward thrust of the arm.

Assisted Exercise for the Shoulder Flexors. The muscles can be worked with the arm in abduction or adduction. Assistance is given manually, with the same grasps which are used for the passive movements, the shoulder girdle being fixed to localise the movement.

Side lying with the arm adducted and supported horizontally in axial suspension counterbalances gravity, and the movement can be free or assisted or resisted by the physiotherapist. Flexion of the elbow with extension of the shoulder and vice versa follows the natural pattern of movement and prevents an aimless swing of the arm. Auto-assistance with a rope and pulley may be arranged in *sitting* or *half lying* with the pulley overhead.

Examples of Free Exercise for the Shoulder Flexors. Exercises already suggested for the Protractors of the Scapula are suitable for these muscles also. In addition the following are useful:—

a. *half bend side lying; one Shoulder flexion.*
b. *crook lying; alternate Arm lifting upwards and downwards.*

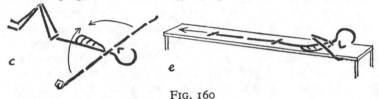

FIG. 160

c. *yard crook lying; Arm lifting to the vertical (to pass beanbag from one Hand to the other).*
d. *bend sitting; Arm stretching forwards.*
e. *bend grasp prone lying (on form); Arm stretching to push body backwards along the form ('Reverse Seals').*

Resisted Exercise for the Shoulder Flexors. Lifting of weights held in the hands in a forward direction is a simple method of resistance. *Crook lying* with the moving arm free over the side of the plinth, *walk standing* or *sitting* on a chair, are suitable starting positions. Spring or weight and pulleys can be used to resist the forward thrust of the arm.

Activities. These are very numerous and include many household chores, such as scrubbing, polishing, washing, ironing, and hanging

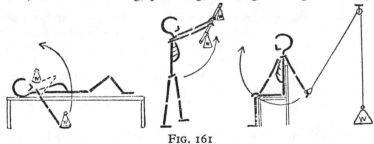

FIG. 161

out clothes, and using a hand sewing-machine; garden jobs, such as digging, hoeing, and hedge clipping; recreations, such as weight lifting, throwing a ball over- or underarm or serving at tennis; work involving planing, sawing, stoking or painting.

THE SHOULDER EXTENSORS

The muscles which extend the shoulder are Deltoid (posterior fibres), Teres Major, Latissimus Dorsi and Pectoralis Major (sterno-costal portion).   The first two muscles are primarily responsible for the inner range, when the arm is drawn backwards from the plane of the trunk.   Latissimus Dorsi and Pectoralis Major, on the other hand, are powerful extensors from the fully flexed position until the arm is drawn into line with the trunk, as in chopping movements or in pulling the body upwards on the arms from hanging.   With the exception of Pectoralis Major, the muscles also work strongly to achieve the final elevation of the arm.

Assisted Exercise for the Shoulder Extensors.   Side lying with the arm suspended in slings or supported on a re-education board eliminates gravity for early re-education.   Flexion of the elbow as the muscles approach the inner range of contraction shortens the leverage in the weakest part of the range and follows the natural pattern of movement. Extension in abduction can be used to work Deltoid and Teres Major, the patient *sitting* with the arm supported horizontally.   In this position the pull of Pectoralis Major is antagonistic to the movement, and Latissimus Dorsi works at a distinct disadvantage owing to the obliquity of its pull.

Examples of Free Exercise for the Shoulder Extensors

   a. *prone lying (on plinth with one Arm over side); one Arm lift* b *and lower.*
   b. *stoop stride standing; alternate Arm swinging forward and backward.*
   c. *yard or stretch prone lying; Arm lifting.*

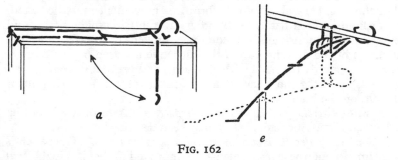

FIG. 162

   d. *stretch prone lying (forms); Arm bending to draw body along* (*'Seals'*).

e. *under grasp fall hanging (bar or rings); Arm bending, to raise Chest to bar.*

f. *climbing wall-bars or ladder using the Arms, or rope climbing.*

Resisted Exercise for the Shoulder Extensors. The physiotherapist resists extension with one hand placed behind the elbow as the patient

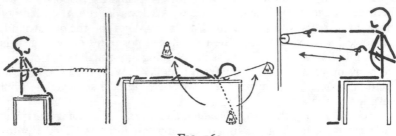

FIG. 163

draws the arm downwards and backwards. Weights, springs and self-resistance can be arranged.

Activities. The muscles work during any form of climbing in which the arms play a part, in chopping and pulling movements and in crawl-stroke swimming.

THE SHOULDER ABDUCTORS

Abduction is initiated by Supraspinatus and continued by Deltoid. Provided the shoulder girdle is free to move, lateral rotation of the scapula invariably accompanies movement at the gleno-humeral joint. To localise the work of the Shoulder Abductors, the shoulder girdle must be fixed, and in these circumstances abduction is possible to about 80°. Some lateral rotation of the humerus is essential to permit abduction, and the ability to perform this movement must be tested.

Deltoid is often paralysed by injury to the Circumflex nerve, and lesions of the Supraspinatus tendon may prevent or interfere with the initiation of the movement and the subsequent action of this muscle, which is to steady the head of the humerus and prevent it from gliding upwards in the glenoid cavity as the result of the upward pull of Deltoid on the bone.

Assisted Exercise for the Shoulder Abductors. A method of assisting the action of the Abductors has already been described on p. 158.

Examples of Free Exercise for the Shoulder Abductors. The patient's performance of these movements is improved if he is taught that lateral rotation at the shoulder joint precedes abduction, i.e. *turn* and lift.

a. *bend crook lying; Shoulder abduction.*
b. *side lying; one Arm lifting and slowly lowering.*
c. *side towards wall standing; creep one Arm up the wall.*
d. *bend sitting; Arm stretching sideways and upwards.*
e. *sitting; Arm lifting sideways and upwards to throw or pass ball from Hand to Hand.*
f. *yard stride standing; Arm swinging across body and sideways, upward.*

The muscles work strongly, and mainly statically, in any exercise in which the arm is held abducted, e.g.—*Arm circling in small range to spin a hoop round the Wrist or one Finger.*

Resisted Exercise for the Shoulder Abductors. Manual resistance is given by resisting the scapular muscles by pressure on the shoulder

FIG. 164

(over the origin of Deltoid), movement is then pivoted at the shoulder joint and resisted by the other hand.

Weights held in the hands are lifted sideways upwards and slowly lowered; this should be done bilaterally to avoid transference of the movement to the spine (side flexion). Weight and pulley, and spring resistance can be applied to either the upper arm or through the hands.

Activities. These muscles work during overarm bowling in cricket, skipping with a rope, 'Butterfly' breast-stroke swimming, and lifting and carrying a bucket in one hand.

THE SHOULDER ADDUCTORS

In the erect position the movement of adduction is usually performed by gravity or controlled by the Shoulder Abductors. As the Shoulder Adductors (Pectoralis Major, Latissimus Dorsi, Teres Major and Coraco-brachialis) all work in some other capacity to produce movement in the shoulder joint, strengthening of this movement, as such, is rarely required.   However, the muscles must be activated in their capacity as Adductors to maintain the pattern of movement in cases of general weakness and instability of the shoulder joint.

ROTATION OF THE SHOULDER JOINT

Rotation at the gleno-humeral joint is essential in all movements in which the arm is lifted above shoulder level or when the hand is put into a side pocket or behind the back; it is therefore of the greatest importance in many functional activities.   Both medial and lateral rotation are frequently limited in shoulder lesions and must be given special attention as partial rotation normally precedes all angular movements used in functional activities.

THE LATERAL ROTATORS OF THE SHOULDER JOINT

Infraspinatus, Teres Minor, and Deltoid (posterior fibres) work to rotate the gleno-humeral joint laterally.   The movement is of considerable importance as it is essential for elevation of the arm through abduction (in the coronal plane).

Assisted Exercise for the Lateral Rotators of the Shoulder Joint. Assistance to the action of the muscles is given with the patient's elbow bent to a right angle and the arm either adducted or abducted, the range of movement being greater in the former position.   With one hand the physiotherapist grasps just above the elbow giving traction on the humerus, and this hand acts as a pivot for the movement of the patient's forearm as this is grasped and carried outwards from across the body when the humerus is in the adducted position.   Alternatively, support of the arm in slings may be used.   See Fig. 105, p. 158.

Examples of Free Exercise for the Lateral Rotators of the Shoulder Joint
  a. *sitting (Elbows bent and tucked in); wide clapping movements in the horizontal plane, with emphasis on Hand parting.*
  b. *crook lying or sitting; clasp Hands behind Head.*
  c. *stride standing (grasp stick in both Hands); Arm lifting and Elbow bending, to put stick behind Shoulders.*
  d. *standing; pass beanbag over Shoulder with one Hand (Lateral rotation) to other Hand behind Waist (Medial Rotation).*
  e. *Head rest relaxed crook sitting; Head and Trunk raising with Arm parting, 'cover the Face, then show the Face'.*
  f. *sitting; Arm rotation (medial and lateral alternately) during Arm lifting sideways upwards and lowering.*

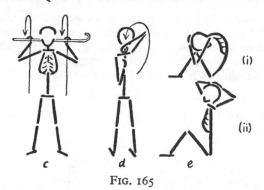

FIG. 165

Resisted Exercise for the Lateral Rotators of the Shoulder Joint. Manual resistance is given in a manner similar to that used for assistance. In *side lying*, with the arm adducted and stabilised by the physiotherapist or by the patient's other hand, a weight is lifted in the hand from the plinth until the forearm is vertical.

Resistance with the arm abducted and the elbow bent is given manually on the hand or wrist.

THE MEDIAL ROTATORS OF THE SHOULDER JOINT

Pectoralis Major, Latissimus Dorsi, and Deltoid (anterior fibres) rotate the humerus medially and are assisted by Subscapularis in the adducted position. Inner range work for the muscles is required to put the hand behind the back.

THE ELBOW FLEXORS

Biceps, Brachialis and Brachioradialis are the prime movers in elbow flexion. The action of the Biceps is most effective in the outer range when it has supinated the forearm and with the shoulder extended. Brachialis continues the movement in the middle and inner ranges and Brachioradialis helps when the forearm is in the mid-prone position. Pronator Teres and the other muscles attached to the medial epicondyle help when strong resistance is applied to the movement.

Assisted Exercise for the Elbow Flexors. The physiotherapist can give assistance to the muscles with the patient's arm in adduction or abduction. To localise the movement, she fixes the upper arm with one hand and helps to flex the forearm with the other, directing the patient's hand towards his mouth. On returning to the extended position allowance must be made for the carrying angle (Fig. 167).

Gravity is counterbalanced by supporting or suspending the arm in the horizontal position, with the patient in *side lying* or *sitting*.   To obtain the maximum efficiency of Biceps, movement of the elbow should be preceded or accompanied by extension of the shoulder, as in the natural withdrawal movement of the arm.

Examples of Free Exercise for the Elbow Flexors

    a. *sitting; Arm bending and stretching (accent on bending).*

FIG. 166

    b. *sitting; Arm swinging sideways and upwards with bending, to tap Shoulders.*
    c. *standing; catch a light ball in the Hands.*
    d. *half reach walk standing; Elbow bending and stretching with Shoulder extension and flexion (as if to draw a circle).*
    e. *hanging or fall hanging; Arm bending.*

Resisted Exercise for the Elbow Flexors.   In treating weakness resulting from traumatic injury only free weightless exercises are used until

FIG. 167

all danger of myositis ossificans has passed, or resistance exercises are ordered by the doctor in charge of the case.

For manual resistance the patient is in *lying*, or *half lying*, with the upper arm supported on the plinth and fixed by one of the physiotherapist's hands, the movement being resisted by her other hand which is grasped by the patient.

Lifting a weight held in the hand provides a simple and measurable form of resistance, and weights and pulleys or springs can also be employed in the final stages.

Activities.   These muscles work strongly in all lifting movements.

THE ELBOW EXTENSORS

Triceps, assisted by Anconeus, extends the elbow. In giving assistance or resistance to these muscles allowance must be made for the carrying angle.

Assisted Exercises for the Elbow Extensors.   These are arranged in a manner similar to that already described for the Elbow Flexors, but in this case, when movement is not localised to the elbow joint, it is combined with shoulder flexion, as it then most nearly approaches the natural thrusting movement.

Examples of Free Exercise for the Elbow Extensors. Pushing, thrusting and flinging movements, during which the upper arm is held horizontally or vertically, bring the muscles into action.

  a. *prone kneeling; Arm bending and stretching.*
  b. *bend crook lying; Arm stretching vertically upwards.*
  c. *prone lying or sitting with Arm supported on a table; Arm reaching forwards to touch or retrieve some object.*
  d. *walk standing; punching movement freely or against punch-ball.*
  e. *prone falling; Arm bending and stretching.*

Resisted Exercise for the Elbow Extensors. Manual resistance is given to elbow extension with pronation; the elbow is supported by pressure on the triceps.

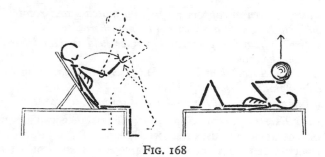

FIG. 168

Weights lifted vertically in the hands when the body is in *crook lying*, or *standing*, provide work for the muscles. Weights and pulleys or springs can be arranged to give resistance to elbow extension in a manner similar to that shown in Fig. 42, p. 57.

Activities. Overarm throwing, punching, sawing, scrubbing and polishing movements all involve the use of these muscles.

THE SUPINATORS

Supinator is the chief muscle involved in supinating the forearm. When the elbow is flexed it is powerfully assisted by Biceps Brachii, and Brachioradialis also helps in the outer range of the movement.

Assisted Exercise for the Supinators. Manual assistance is the most usual method. With the patient's elbow flexed to a right angle to eliminate the possibility of shoulder movement, the physiotherapist fixes the lower end of the humerus with one hand and with her other hand she either grasps round the patient's wrist or takes a handshake grasp with her first and second fingers extended across its anterior aspect to stabilise it. Slight traction is given in the long axis of the forearm and the patient is instructed to turn his palm upwards as the physiotherapist gives assistance.

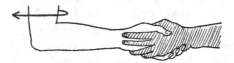

FIG. 169.   Modified Handshake Grasp for assisting
or resisting Supination

Self-assistance is sometimes useful, the patient clasping his fingers in front of him with the palms downwards and elbows bent, then rotating both forearms until the palms face upwards.

Examples of Free Exercise for the Supinators

    a. *sitting, Forearm supported; pick up matches and rotate Forearm on little Finger to hand them to physiotherapist.*

    b. *sitting, Forearm supported; tap ruler held in Hand from side to side on the table.*

    c. *standing, upper Arm held to Side; screwing movement as to turn door-handle or use screwdriver.*

    d. *sitting; pick up ball from table and throw it upwards.*

Resisted Exercise for the Supinators. Resistance can be given by the physiotherapist who uses the same grasp as for assistance. Additional leverage can be gained if she grasps the ends of a stick and

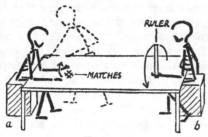

FIG. 170

resists the efforts of the patient to rotate.   See Fig. 108, left, p. 163, for diagram of free movement.

A Wrist Pronator and Supinator Machine may be used if available. This consists of a handle which rotates on a horizontal axis, the resistance offered being adjustable by means of a screw.   With the elbow flexed and the forearm in line with the axis of rotation, the patient grasps the handle of the machine and supinates to rotate it.

Activities.   These muscles work when a spoon is used to carry food to the mouth and to bring the palm of the hand in contact with the face.   All activities which involve screwing movements can be practised; sewing and plaiting 'under' are useful movements especially for women.

THE PRONATORS

Pronator Teres and Pronator Quadratus are the muscles mainly responsible for pronation.   They are assisted by Palmaris Longus and Flexor Carpi Radialis and by Brachioradialis in the outer range of movement.

Work for this group is provided by methods similar to those used to work the Supinators, but the movement takes place in the reverse direction as, for example, in unscrewing.

THE MUSCLES OF THE HAND

THE WRIST EXTENSORS

The wrist is extended by Extensor Carpi Radialis Longus, Extensor Carpi Radialis Brevis and Extensor Carpi Ulnaris assisted by the long Extensors of the fingers.   The muscles work strongly as synergists during the action of gripping when the wrist is extended to increase the leverage of the long Flexors of the Fingers.

Assisted Exercise for the Wrist Extensors.   For manual assistance the physiotherapist fixes the patient's forearm with one hand and grasps round the metacarpal bones with her other hand, so that her fingers lie in the palm and her thumb across the back of the patient's hand. The patient is instructed to allow the fingers to bend during the movement of wrist extension to relax the tension of the long Flexors and to follow the natural pattern of the gripping movement. The effect of gravity is counterbalanced when the forearm and ulnar border of the hand rest on a horizontal surface such as a polished table top or a spring may be incorporated in a 'lively' splint.

Examples of Free Exercise for the Wrist Extensors. The natural movement of gripping forms the basis of all free exercises in which these muscles work, and the sensory stimuli received from the hand when an object is grasped are of great importance. When the muscles are weak it is an advantage to perform the movement with both hands simultaneously and, if possible, with the forearms and hands submerged in warm water.

a. *sitting (Forearm and ulnar border of Hand supported); Wrist extension as the Hand grasps a rubber or wool ball.*

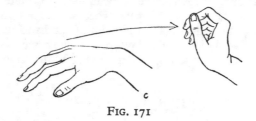

FIG. 171

b. *sitting (anterior aspect of Forearm supported, Hand relaxed over edge of table); Wrist extension to make a fist and grasp some light object.*

c. *sitting (Forearm and Finger-tips supported on table); Wrist extension to make staccato tapping movements of Fingers on table.*

d. *sitting; grasp and squeeze a tennis ball.*

Resisted Exercise for the Wrist Extensors. Manual resistance can be offered with the same grasp as for assistance. Other forms of resistance are applied with the patient grasping a stirrup handle and pulling the wrist into extension, or by grasping round and rotating a thick rod (about 2 inches in diameter) which is prevented from rotating freely by the physiotherapist or by a mechanical device, as in the case of the Wrist Roll Machine.

THE WRIST FLEXORS

Flexor Carpi Radialis, Flexor Carpi Ulnaris and Palmaris Longus flex the wrist with the assistance of Flexor Digitorum Sublimus and

Flexor Pollicis Longus. These muscles can be exercised in a manner similar to that used for the Wrist Extensors, but the movement is

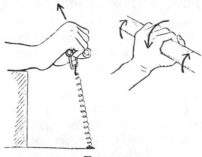

FIG. 172

reversed and it must be remembered that the fingers must be allowed to extend during the movement to avoid limitation of the range.

THE ULNAR AND RADIAL FLEXORS

Flexor and Extensor Muscles combine to produce ulnar and radial flexion or deviation. The Ulnar Flexors are Flexor Carpi Ulnaris and Extensor Carpi Ulnaris, and the Radial Flexors are Flexor Carpi Radialis and Extensor Carpi Radialis Longus and Brevis. Strengthening of all these muscles has already been considered when they work in the capacity of Wrist Flexors and Extensors, but ulnar and radial

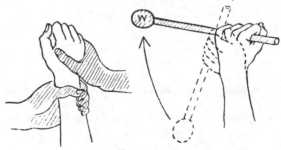

FIG. 173

flexion provide an alternative method of working them and another pattern of co-ordination.

Exercise is carried out with the wrist in mid-position, the hand being in line with the forearm, the position of which is adjusted as required to allow the movement to be performed with gravity eliminated or resisting. Assistance or resistance are usually given manually but a weight or elastic recoil is sometimes useful.   Free Exercise can be performed with or without the resistance of gravity.

Muscles which move the Fingers and Thumb

The muscle groups which move or stabilise the fingers and thumb can be worked individually with suitable fixation of adjacent joints and with the physiotherapist's assistance, or resistance, given in the path of the movement.   Alternatively varying thicknesses of elastic may be used for assistance or resistance when it is attached to the fingers or thumb by loops or finger-stalls.   The functional and free use of the hand as a whole must never be omitted, as the memory of the complex patterns of co-ordinated movement involved in gripping objects and spreading the hand must be retained.

Examples of Free Exercise for the Hand

    a. *sitting; Finger and Thumb bending and stretching (use both Hands).*
    b. *sitting; Finger and Thumb parting and closing (use both Hands).*
    c. *sitting; Palm hollowing with Thumb and little Finger opposition.*
    d. *sitting; Palms on table; Finger raising.*

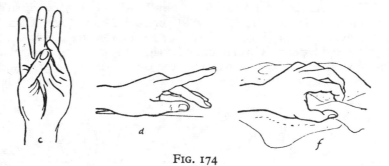

Fig. 174

    e. *sitting; throw, catch, squeeze and rotate balls of different sizes in the Hand.*
    f. *sitting (Palm facing downwards); collect and spread a towel, sheet of paper, rice or sand which lies on a table.*

Activities.   These are very numerous and include most everyday activities in which the hand is used, e.g. using a knife and fork, doing up and undoing buttons, tying shoelaces, opening and shutting doors, using scissors, needle, pen and typewriter.   Grasping and holding a variety of objects, such as shopping baskets and tools, and counting money must also be practised.   Games such as golf and tennis and playing musical instruments such as a piano and violin provide good exercise.

THE EXTENSORS OF THE HEAD AND NECK

These muscles work with the Extensors of the upper Back, they are the Rectus Capitis Major and Minor, Obliquus Superior, Semi-spinalis Capitis, Splenius Capitis and Trapezius (upper fibres). The action of the short muscles is responsible for movements at the atlanto-occipital and atlanto-axial joints. Movement in these distal joints should always precede that in the cervical spine when resistance is given to the head-neck.

Assisted Exercise for the Extensors of Head and Neck. Assistance can be given manually with the patient in *lying,* the head being supported in alignment with the trunk either by the physiotherapist's hand or with the help of sling suspension.

Examples of Free Exercise for the Extensors of the Head and Neck

    a. *sitting; Head dropping forward and raising to the vertical.*

    b. *prone lying or prone kneeling; Head dropping forward and raising.*

Resisted Exercise for the Extensors of the Head and Neck. This is given manually in *crook lying* or in *reach grasp stride sitting.* Prone lying or *Forearm support prone lying* is also a suitable starting position for the patient when strong resistance is required.

Spring or weight and pulley resistance can be arranged, but this must not be too strong. Any jarring movement likely to occur as the result of spring recoil as the head returns to the starting position must be avoided, the speed of this part of the movement

Fig. 175

must be controlled by the Extensor Muscles working eccentrically.

THE FLEXORS OF THE HEAD AND NECK

The Flexors of the Atlanto-occipital Joint are Longus Capitis, Rectus Capitis Anterior and Sternomastoid; Longus Cervicis, the Scaleni and Sternomastoid flex the cervical spine. These two movements can be isolated from each other to some extent.

Assistance for the muscles can be given with one or both of the physiotherapist's hands placed on the occiput with the patient in the *lying* position or a *low half lying.* Alternatively he can assist himself by using his own hands clasped behind the head.

Free exercises are also done from *lying,* the head being lifted and bent forwards till the chin touches the sterno-clavicular joint.

Resistance may be given manually, either on the forehead or under the chin. In the latter case pressure given inadvertently on the larynx must be avoided.

THE SIDE FLEXORS OF THE HEAD AND NECK

The Flexor and Extensor Muscles of one side only work to produce this movement. The Side Flexors are Rectus Capitis Lateralis, Semispinalis Capitis, Splenius Capitis, Sternomastoid and Trapezius (upper fibres).

Assisted Exercise for the Side Flexors of the Head and Neck. Lying with the shoulder girdle fixed is the most suitable position for assisting the action of these muscles. The physiotherapist sits behind the patient clasping her hands under the occiput or on the side of the head over the ears.

Examples of Free Exercise for the Side Flexors of the Head and Neck

a. *prone kneeling; Head side bending (to put ear on Shoulder).*
b. *Arms folded cross, crook or stride sitting; Head side bending.*
c. *side lying; Head raising and lowering.*

These movements can be combined with Trunk side flexion to the same side.

Resisted Exercise for the Side Flexors of the Head and Neck. Manual resistance is given from *low grasp lying* or *low grasp sitting*, a slight head traction preceding the movement.

FIG. 176

THE ROTATORS OF THE HEAD AND NECK

The muscles forming this group are the Obliqus Capitis Inferior, Rectus Capitis Posterior Major, Splenius Capitis of the side towards which the movement takes place and Sternomastoid of the opposite side. Assistance and Resistance to the muscles are given from the same starting positions and with the same grasps that are used for the Head and Neck Side Flexors.

Examples of Free Exercises for the Rotators of the Head and Neck

a. *half low grasp sitting; Head turning with one Arm lifting sideways.*
b. *prone kneeling; Head turning.*
c. *sitting or cross sitting; Trunk bending and turning with Head turning to put ear towards opposite Knee.*

Head rotation often accompanies movements involving Trunk rotation.

THE STERNOMASTOID MUSCLE

The Sternomastoid Muscle of one side bends the head to the same side and rotates it to the opposite side.   These movements may be

FIG. 177.   Grasp for resisting the action of
the Right Sternomastoid Muscle

performed consecutively and a convenient grasp for resistance by the physiotherapist is one in which one of her hands is placed across the vertex of the patient's head while the other hand is cupped under the chin so that the fingers extend above the tempero-mandibular joint. Resistance is given to side flexion with the fingers of the upper hand and to rotation with the fingers of the lower hand.

PART V

17

NEUROMUSCULAR CO-ORDINATION
CO-ORDINATED MOVEMENT

CO-ORDINATED movement, which is smooth, accurate and purposeful, is brought about by the integrated action of many muscles, superimposed upon a basis of efficient postural activity. The muscles concerned are grouped together as prime movers, antagonists, synergists and fixators, according to the particular function they are called upon to perform.

GROUP ACTION OF MUSCLES

The contraction of the prime movers results in the movement of a joint, while the reciprocal relaxation of the opposing group, the antagonists, controls their action without impeding it. Other muscles may work as synergists, either to alter the direction of the pull of the prime movers, or, where the latter pass across more than one joint, to stabilise the joint in which movement is not required. Efficiency is still further ensured by muscular fixation of the bone, or bones, from which the prime movers take origin (or alternatively, into which they are inserted, should they work with reversed origin and insertion). These fixator muscles may be in the immediate vicinity of the movement, but when strong resistance is offered, muscles all over the body are frequently involved.

NERVOUS CONTROL

The Motor Pathways. The action of each muscle group is determined by the afferent impulses which reach it by the motor pathways.

The Cerebral Cortex. Voluntary movement is usually, if not invariably, initiated in response to some sensory stimulus. It is now thought that an initiation centre exists in the brain stem which alerts the cerebral cortex, which then is responsible for planning the pattern of movement. This plan is based on memories of patterns used on previous occasions.

The Cerebellum. The cerebellum is a receiving station of information which reaches it by the afferent pathways conveying impulses of

236

kinaesthetic sensation from the periphery and from other parts of the brain including the cerebral cortex and the vestibular nucleus. In the light of this information the delicate adjustments, which ensure harmonious inter-action of the various groups of muscles concerned in the pattern of movement, are made and conveyed to the anterior horn cells by either the extra-pyramidal tracts or other descending pathways of the spinal cord.

Kinaesthetic Sensation. The afferent impulses of kinaesthetic sensation arise from proprioceptors situated in muscles, tendons and joints and they record contraction or stretching of muscle and the knowledge of movement and position of the limbs. Some of these impulses reach the level of consciousness but many end in the spinal cord and cerebellum.

INCO-ORDINATION

Interference with the function of any one of the factors which contribute to the production of a co-ordinated movement will result in jerky, arhythmic or inaccurate movement, which is said to be inco-ordinated, as the harmonious working together of the muscles is disturbed. The type of inco-ordination, and the exercises designed to help in overcoming it, vary according to the location of the lesion which causes it. Four main types usually benefit from suitable exercise therapy.

Causation

1. Inco-ordination associated with weakness or flaccidity of a particular muscle group.

In this case, either some lesion of the lower motor neurones prevents the appropriate impulses from reaching the muscles, or the condition of the muscles modifies their normal reaction to these impulses.

2. Inco-ordination associated with spasticity of the muscles.

Lesions affecting the motor area of the cerebral cortex, or the upper motor neurones, result in spasticity of the muscles, therefore, even when some appropriate impulses are able to reach them, the condition of the muscles is such that their response to them is abnormal.

3. Inco-ordination resulting from cerebellar lesions.

This is generally known as cerebellar 'ataxia', the prefix 'a' meaning 'without' and the Greek word 'taxis' meaning 'order'. There is marked hypotonicity of the muscles, which tire easily, and inadequate fixator action, not only of the muscles directly concerned with the group action, but of the body generally. Movement is irregular and swaying, with a marked intention tremor.

4. Inco-ordination resulting from loss of kinaesthetic sensation.

'Sensory ataxia', or in the case of tabes dorsalis, 'tabetic ataxia', describes this type. Without using his eyes to gain the information, the patient with this condition is completely unaware of the position of the body in space, or of the position of the joints. The muscles are hypotonic and tire easily, but they are unaware of this as the sensation of fatigue is not recorded.

Involuntary movements, sometimes associated with these conditions, or a state of abnormal general tension superimposed on an otherwise normal pattern of group action, may interfere with movement and reduce its efficiency.

RE-EDUCATION

Co-ordinated movement is natural to the body, which tends to remain still if only inco-ordinated movement is possible. It is therefore of major importance to interest and encourage patients suffering from inco-ordination to persevere in making the effort to overcome it. This requires infinite patience and persistence on the part of the physiotherapist, especially if and when the condition is associated with mental deterioration. Each patient requires individual attention as the problems of no two are identical, resistance often steadies and makes the movement possible, but as progress is made, group work is a valuable adjunct to individual treatment.

The Use of Alternative Nervous Pathways

It is rare that all the available nervous pathways, by which the impulses essential for co-ordinated movement travel, are blocked, and the purpose of re-education is to encourage the use of those which remain, or to develop alternative routes.

As an analogy it may be helpful to consider a pathway worn through an acre or so of bracken or some other type of undergrowth. It is easy enough to walk through it when the pathway is used constantly and is well worn. If, however, the pathway is blocked, an alternative route can be used, but the going will be difficult at first though it will become progressively easier each time it is used, provided the same alternative route is used on each occasion. In this way a new pathway is eventually established.

The Condition of the Muscles

As a preliminary to re-educating the movement, the condition of the muscles requires attention as they are the effector organs concerned. They must be prepared to receive the co-ordinating impulses so that their reaction to them is as normal as possible, by an attempt to relax those which are spastic or tense, and to strengthen those which are weak. It is probable also that in all long-standing cases in which inco-ordination is a feature, some degree of disuse atrophy is present owing to the disinclination to move.

Principles of Re-education

Weakness or Flaccidity of a Particular Muscle Group. This differs from the other conditions in that the inevitable inco-ordination which results is usually only transitory. Inco-ordinated movement is not tolerated by the body if it can be avoided, and in this case it is able to avoid it by altering the pattern of the movement in such a way that the function of the affected muscles is transferred to other groups. This substitution of an alternative pattern is the basis of 'trick' movement, which is often functionally effective, but always wasteful of energy.

Treatment is designed to correct imbalances by emphasis on the activity of weak or ineffective muscles and to restore the normal integrated action of muscles in the performance of patterns of functional movement. The latter is achieved most successfully by slow reversals techniques with normal timing (see p. 87).

Spasticity of Muscles. The spasticity of the muscles modifies their reaction to the stimuli they receive as they cannot, or can only with difficulty, relax and so allow movement to occur. There is marked reluctance to attempt movement, while in those which are achieved, the essential rhythm which is characteristic of efficient movement is lost. Treatment is designed to promote relaxation, to stimulate effort, to give confidence in the ability to move and to train rhythm. Relaxation methods have already been described (see Chapter 6, 'Relaxation'). Active exercises based on everyday movements help to make the patient as independent as possible and give him confidence. Those which involve the use of the more proximal joints and are large and basic in character are used first. All exercises are performed rhythmically to aid relaxation and reduce fatigue, assistance being given when necessary but only after, and as long as, the effort is made to do them independently. Rhythmic counting, music, or the rhythm of a bouncing ball are used to regulate the speed of the movement, as the effort to keep in time helps to interest the patient and demands his full attention. Training in accuracy and the finer and highly co-ordinated movements, such as those of the hand, is deferred until basic movements and rhythm are established.

Cerebellar Ataxia. Loss of the function of the cerebellum, which is a co-ordinating centre, results in loss of the co-ordinating impulses which are normally discharged from it. The muscles become hypotonic and postural fixation is disturbed, consequently balance is difficult and movements are irregular, swaying and inaccurate.

Any improvement which results from treatment by exercises is probably due to an increased use of the pathways which remain, or it is thought possible that the cerebrum may be able to compensate to some extent for the loss of cerebellar function.

The aim of treatment is to restore stability of the trunk and proximal joints to provide a stable background for movement. When muscular weakness is severe, strengthening methods must be used first but the main emphasis in treatment is given to holdings (isometric contraction) which are done in any and every part of the range. Holdings are maintained as long as possible and their strength and endurance is increased by resistance to increase the demand on the Neuromuscular Mechanism and help to develop new nervous pathways for the impulses required. Movement should be limited to functional activities or to a limited number of resisted movements in patterns closely allied to those of functional movements.

Loss of the Kinaesthetic Sense. Information as to the whereabouts of the body in space, the position of the joints and the tension in muscles, forms an essential part of the data upon which neuromuscular co-ordination is based. Lesions causing loss of this information result in hypotonicity of the muscles and inco-ordinated movement. Substitution of the sense of sight to compensate for the loss of the kinaesthetic sense forms the basis of re-education, and by maintaining relatively normal body movements it may be possible to bring into use some undamaged but hitherto redundant nervous pathways capable of conveying the impulses of kinaesthetic sensation.

Exercises based on Frenkel's principles are used to train smooth movement and precision, with emphasis on the ultimate aim of helping the patient to carry out the normal activities of everyday life.

FRENKEL'S EXERCISES

Dr. H. S. Frenkel was Medical Superintendent of the Sanatorium 'Freihof' in Switzerland towards the end of the last century. He made a special study of tabes dorsalis and devised a method of treating the ataxia, which is a prominent symptom of the disease, by means of systematic and graduated exercises. Since then his methods have been used to treat the inco-ordination which results from many other diseases, e.g. disseminated sclerosis.

He aimed at establishing voluntary control of movement by the use of any part of the sensory mechanism which remained intact, notably sight, sound and touch, to compensate for the loss of kinaesthetic sensation. The process of learning this alternative method of control is similar to that required to learn any new exercise, the essentials being—

a. Concentration of the attention.
b. Precision.
c. Repetition.

The ultimate aim is to establish control of movement so that the patient is able and confident in his ability to carry out those activities which are essential for independence in everyday life.

Technique

1. The patient is positioned and suitably clothed so that he can see the limbs throughout the exercise.

2. A concise explanation and demonstration of the exercise is given before movement is attempted, to give the patient a clear mental picture of it.

3. The patient must give his full attention to the performance of the exercise to make the movement smooth and accurate.

4. The speed of movement is dictated by the physiotherapist by means of rhythmic counting, movement of her hand, or the use of suitable music.

5. The range of movement is indicated by marking the spot on which the foot or hand is to be placed.

6. The exercise must be repeated many times until it is perfect and easy. It is then discarded and a more difficult one is substituted.

7. As these exercises are very tiring at first, frequent rest periods must be allowed. The patient retains little or no ability to recognise fatigue, but it is usually indicated by a deterioration in the quality of the movement, or by a rise in the pulse rate.

Progression

Progression is made by altering the speed, range and complexity of the exercise. Fairly quick movements require less control than slow ones. Later, alteration in the speed of consecutive movements, and interruptions which involve stopping and starting to command, are introduced. Wide range and primitive movements, in which large joints are used, gradually give way to those involving the use of small joints, limited range and a more frequent alteration of direction. Finally simple movements are built up into sequences to form specific actions which require the use and control of a number of joints and more than one limb, e.g. walking.

According to the degree of disability, re-education exercises start in *lying* with the head propped up and with the limbs fully supported and progress is made to exercises in *sitting*, and then in *standing*.

Examples of Frenkel's Exercises

Exercise for the legs in *lying*.

a. *lying (Head raised); Hip abduction and adduction.*
The leg is fully supported throughout on the smooth surface of a plinth or on a re-education board.

b. *lying (Head raised); one Hip and Knee flexion and extension.*
The heel is supported throughout and slides on the plinth to a position indicated by the physiotherapist.

c. *lying (Head raised); one Leg raising to place Heel on specified mark.*
The mark may be made on the plinth, on the patient's other foot or shin, or the heel may be placed in the palm of the physiotherapist's hand.

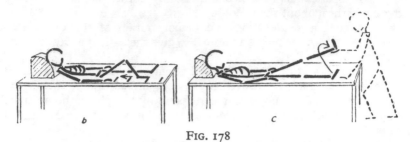

FIG. 178

d. *lying (Head raised); Hip and Knee flexion and extension, abduction and adduction.*
The legs may work alternately or in opposition to each other. Stopping and starting during the course of the movement may be introduced to increase the control required to perform any of these exercises.

Exercise for the legs in *sitting.*
e. *sitting; one Leg stretching, to slide Heel to a position indicated by a mark on the floor.*
f. *sitting; alternate Leg stretching and lifting to place Heel or Toe on specified mark.*
g. *stride sitting; change to standing and then sit down again.*
The feet are drawn back and the trunk inclined forwards from the hips to get the centre of gravity over the base.   The patient then extends the legs and draws himself up with the help of his hands grasping the wall-bars or other suitable apparatus.

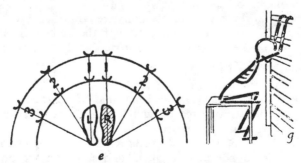

FIG. 179.   e, Plan to show suitable marking on floor

Exercise for the legs in *standing*.

h. *stride standing; transference of weight from Foot to Foot.*

i. *stride standing; walking sideways placing Feet on marks on the floor.*

Some support may be necessary, but the patient must be able to see his feet.

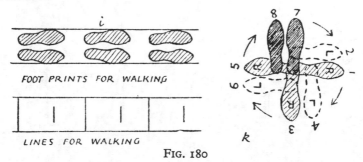

FOOT PRINTS FOR WALKING

LINES FOR WALKING

k

FIG. 180

j. *standing; walking placing Feet on marks.*

The length of the stride can be varied by the physiotherapist according to the patient's capacity.

k. *standing; turn round.*

Patients find this difficult and are helped by marks on the floor.

l. *standing; walking and changing direction to avoid obstacles.*

Group work is of great value as control improves, as it teaches the patient to concentrate on his own efforts without being distracted by those of other people. In walking, he gains confidence and becomes accustomed to moving about with others, to altering direction and stopping if he wishes, to avoid bumping into them. The ability to climb stairs and to step on and off a kerb helps him to independence.

Exercises for the arms.

m. *sitting (one Arm supported on a table or in slings); Shoulder flexion or extension to place Hand on a specified mark.*

n. *sitting; one Arm stretching, to thread it through a small hoop or ring.*

o. *sitting; picking up objects and putting them down on specified marks.*

Diversional activities such as plaiting, building with toy bricks, or drawing on a blackboard, lead to more useful movements such as using a knife and fork, doing up buttons and doing the hair.

EXERCISES TO PROMOTE MOVEMENT AND RHYTHM

All exercises are repeated continuously to a rhythmic count, or to suitable music.

a. *sitting; one Hip flexion and adduction (to cross one Thigh over the other), the movement is then reversed and repeated.*

b. *half lying; one Leg abduction to bring Knee to side of plinth, followed by one Knee bending to put Foot on floor, the movement is then reversed and repeated.*

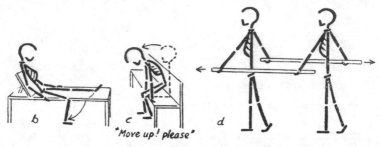

"Move up! please"

FIG. 181

c. *sitting; lean forward and take weight on Feet (as if to stand), then sit down again.* Later this can be done progressing along the seat as if moving up to make room for someone else to sit.

d. *standing; Arm swing forwards and backwards (with partner, holding two sticks).*

e. *standing or walking; bounce and catch, or throw and catch a ball.*

Marching to music, ballroom dancing or swimming, if possible, should be encouraged.

18

POSTURE

POSTURE is the attitude assumed by the body either with support during muscular inactivity, or by means of the co-ordinated action of many muscles working to maintain stability or to form an essential basis which is being adapted constantly to the movement which is superimposed upon it.

INACTIVE POSTURES

These are attitudes adopted for resting or sleeping, and they are most suitable for this purpose when all the essential muscular activity required to maintain life is reduced to a minimum. Those postures which make minimal demands upon the muscles responsible for the maintenance of essential body functions, such as respiration and circulation, are preferable. The postures or positions used for training general relaxation fulfil these conditions by allowing freedom for respiratory movement and the least possible work for the heart muscle.

ACTIVE POSTURES

The integrated action of many muscles is required to maintain active postures, which may be either static or dynamic.

Static Postures. A constant pattern of posture is maintained by the inter-action of groups of muscles which work more or less statically to stabilise the joints, and in opposition to gravity or other forces. In the erect postures they preserve a state of equilibrium.

Dynamic Postures. This type of active posture is required to form an efficient basis for movement. The pattern of the posture is constantly modified and adjusted to meet the changing circumstances which arise as the result of movement.

THE POSTURAL MECHANISM

The Muscles

The intensity and distribution of the muscle work which is required for both static and dynamic postures varies considerably with the pattern of the posture, and the physical characteristics of the individual who assumes it. The groups of muscles most frequently employed are those which are used to maintain the erect position of the body, by working to counteract the effects of gravity. They are consequently known as the anti-gravity muscles and their action with regard to joints is usually that of extension.

These anti-gravity muscles present certain structural characteristics which enable them to perform their function with efficiency and the minimum of effort.   The form of the muscles is multi-pennate and fan-shaped, an arrangement which signifies powerful action as opposed to the ability to produce a wide range of movement at high speed. Many of the constituent fibres are 'red', indicating their capability of sustained contraction without fatigue, due to their low metabolic rate of action (Chapter 15, p. 167).

Nervous Control

Postures are maintained or adapted as a result of neuromuscular co-ordination, the appropriate muscles being innervated by means of a very complex reflex mechanism.

The Postural Reflexes. A reflex is, by definition, an efferent response to an afferent stimulus.   The efferent response in this instance is a motor one, the anti-gravity muscles being the principal effector

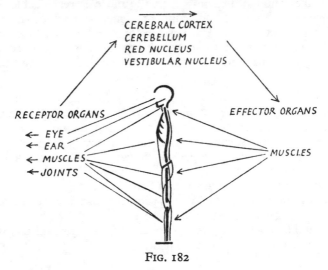

FIG. 182

organs.   Afferent stimuli arise from a variety of sources all over the body, the most important receptors being situated in the muscles themselves, the eyes and the ears.

(*i*) *The Muscles.* Neuromuscular and neurotendinous spindles within the muscles record changing tension.   Increased tension causes stimulation and results in a reflex contraction of the muscle, and so appears to be a manifestation of the myotatic, or stretch, reflex.

(*ii*) *The Eyes.* Visual sensation records any alteration in the position of the body with regard to its surroundings, and the eyes form one of the receptors for the 'righting' reflexes which enable the head and body to restore themselves to the erect position from other less usual attitudes.

(*iii*) *The Ears.* Stimulation of the receptors of the vestibular nerve results from the movement of fluid contained in the semicircular canals of the internal ear. Each canal lies in a different plane, which is at right angles to both the others, and any movement of the head disturbs the fluid they contain, and thus knowledge of the movement and the direction in which it takes place are recorded.

(*iv*) *Joint Structures.* In the weight-bearing position approximation of bones stimulates receptors in joint structures and elicits reflex reactions to maintain the position.

Skin sensation also plays a part, especially that of the soles of the feet, when the body is in standing positions.

Impulses from all these receptors are conveyed and co-ordinated in the Central Nervous System, the chief centres involved being the cerebral cortex, the cerebellum, the red nucleus and the vestibular nucleus.

A very elementary summary of the chief components of the complex series of reflexes which together constitute the Postural Reflex is given in the diagram opposite. Details will be found in any Physiology textbook.

THE PATTERN OF POSTURE

Patterns of posture, both static and dynamic, are gradually built up by the integration of the many reflexes which together make up the Postural Reflex. Some of these component reflexes are inborn and some are conditioned, being developed as the result of constant repetition of postures maintained by voluntary control.

Good Posture

Posture is said to be good when it fulfils the purpose for which it is used with maximum efficiency and minimum effort.

As the physical characteristics of no two people are identical, the precise pattern of good posture must vary with the individual. It is possible, however, to generalise to some extent. For example, in the erect postures the alignment of specific parts of the body usually leads to perfect balance of one segment upon another, a state which can be maintained with the minimum of muscular effort and which is aesthetically pleasing to the eye.

As dynamic postures involve constant readjustment to maintain the efficiency of the postural background throughout the progress of the movement, they are much more difficult to assess. In many activities, however, the same alignment of the various segments of the body which is satisfactory in the erect static postures forms the basis from which these adjustments are made; for example, in walking or sitting and writing. In the erect positions the plane of this alignment is vertical, but in many dynamic postures it is inclined or even horizontal, in which case the effect of gravity on the various body segments is altered and the muscle work required to maintain the alignment is adjusted accordingly.

Development of Good Posture

Efficient posture develops quite naturally, provided the essential mechanisms for its maintenance and adjustment are intact and healthy.

The chief factors which predispose to the health and development of the muscles and the postural reflex are—

(*i*) a stable psychological background,

(*ii*) good hygienic conditions,

(*iii*) opportunity for plenty of natural free movement.

Emotion and mental attitude have a profound effect upon the nervous system as a whole, and this is reflected in the posture of the individual. Joy, happiness and confidence are stimulating and are reflected by an alert posture in which positions of extension predominate. Conversely unhappiness, conflict and a feeling of inferiority have just the opposite effect and result in postures in which positions of flexion are most conspicuous.

This connection between mental and physical attitudes has always been recognised and used in dancing and on the stage. It is certain that the mental attitude affects the physical, either temporarily or permanently. Is it not possible that this can also happen in reverse? In other words, cannot a physical attitude adopted consciously affect the mental attitude?

Good hygienic conditions, particularly with regard to nutrition and sleep, are essential for a healthy nervous system and for the growth and development of bones and muscles. In addition, the opportunity for plenty of natural free movements also encourages the harmonious development of the skeletal muscles. Activities which are much enjoyed by the normal healthy child at play, for example, running, jumping, and climbing, are those in which movements of active extension predominate.

Poor Posture

Posture is poor when it is inefficient, that is, when it fails to serve the purpose for which it was designed, or if an unnecessary amount of muscular effort is used to maintain it.

Faulty alignment of the body segments in the erect positions may lead to the necessity for additional muscle work to maintain balance. On the other hand, efficient compensation may take place, in which case no additional muscular effort is required, but the attendant ligamentous strain or cramping of thoracic movement are disadvantages which can-

not be ignored.   In addition, postures which involve a marked increase
in any or all of the curves of the spine are aesthetically displeasing, clothes
do not fit these subjects well and this may in itself have an unwelcome
psychological reaction.

The purpose of dynamic posture is to serve as an efficient and
adaptable background to movement.   Posture patterns which do not
fulfil this function impede and reduce the efficiency of the movement

FIG. 183.   Good and Faulty Alignment in *standing* and *running*

and therefore must be considered poor, e.g. standing square to the net
while making a forehand drive at tennis.

Tension in muscles other than those required to act either to produce movement or to maintain posture hinders the efficiency of both
and wastes energy.

Factors which predispose to Poor Posture

The causes of poor posture are often very obscure, and, even if they
are known, are difficult to remove.

The factors which most often contribute to the establishment of an
inefficient postural pattern are the mental attitude of the patient and
poor hygienic conditions.   General debility after a constitutional ill-
ness and prolonged fatigue are also contributory causes, as they reduce
the efficiency of the nervous system as a whole.

Local factors such as localised pain, muscular weakness, occupational stresses, or localised tension which serves no useful purpose, lead
to muscular disbalance and alter the postural pattern, but do not necessarily reduce its efficiency under the circumstances.   If, however, this
altered pattern of posture is continued after the cause for it is removed,
it must be regarded as a postural defect.

A faulty idea of what constitutes good posture may also lead to the
establishment of an inefficient pattern by repeated voluntary effort.

Principles of Re-education

The measures which can be taken by the physiotherapist to combat poor posture and to train another and more efficient postural pattern depend largely on the cause. The success of any physical treatment invariably depends on her ability to gain the co-operation of the patient.

Postures which are the result of an unsatisfactory mental attitude and poor hygienic conditions can only be remedied permanently by an alteration in the habitual mental attitude and by improvement of the hygienic conditions, and these are measures with which the physiotherapist herself is not often able, or competent, to deal. Postural defects rarely lead to marked structural changes; if they are prolonged, however, muscles and ligaments do adapt their length to the habitual position maintained by the joints, and this may lead to some limitation of the normal joint range. This limitation, if present, may make it impossible for the patient to assume a good position at some future date when the attitude and conditions have improved. Relaxation, mobility exercises and a repeated presentation of a satisfactory postural pattern will prepare the way for improvement. During this period of instruction a cheerful atmosphere, a spirit of enjoyment and judicious praise may build up the desire of the patient to re-establish a more satisfactory postural pattern by voluntary effort.

When general debility and fatigue are the cause, these must obviously be treated first. Training in relaxation to avoid unnecessary tension and assistance in remembering the feeling of a satisfactory alignment of the body are helpful meanwhile.

Local conditions which result in the alteration of postural pattern, and which can be removed, should receive suitable attention. Pain is alleviated by appropriate means, muscular weakness cured by specific exercise to restore the balance of muscle power, localised tension removed by relaxation methods. Occupational strains can sometimes be relieved by analysis of the movements required and substitution of a new pattern which is more satisfactory mechanically. While these local methods of treatment are in progress, a good pattern of posture must be constantly presented to the patient, so that it is remembered and will therefore be re-established when the local cause of alteration has been removed.

A faulty idea of correct posture can be cured by inducing the patient to accept a new and satisfactory pattern and then by teaching him how to assume it and make it habitual by repeated voluntary effort.

Technique of Re-education

The atmosphere in which instruction is given to the patient is of the greatest importance in postural re-education, and the physiotherapist

can do much to gain co-operation by her manner and approach.   The
patient must be made to feel that the acquisition of good posture is
worth while, and that any efforts he makes to attain it will be noticed
and appreciated, while his difficulties and shortcomings will be understood.   Individual instruction is essential as no two patients have
identical difficulties, but they have also much in common to learn and,
for this, group instruction is valuable.   The inclusion of group activities in any programme of re-education is conducive to an atmosphere
of enjoyment and the patient is usually stimulated by working with
others.

Relaxation

The ability to relax is an important factor in re-education, as some
degree of useless and unnecessary tension is nearly always associated
with poor posture.   To begin with, general relaxation with the body
in horizontal positions reduces muscular tension and gives a feeling of
alignment.   Voluntary relaxation of specific muscle groups can then
be taught and practised so that the patient learns to recognise tension
and is able to relax at will, if and when it develops during the maintenance of either static or dynamic postures.

Because of the excessive use of the arms in front of the body and
the necessity to lean forwards which many occupations demand, as in
washing clothes or writing at a desk, these tensions usually occur in
muscles round the shoulder girdle and in the neck extensors.   Local
and voluntary relaxation of these groups can be taught in *lying* and the
erect positions, first by the contrast method and later by learning to
recognise a state of tension and then 'letting go'.

Examples of Relaxation Methods

    a. *crook lying, lying or prone lying; general relaxation.*
    b. *crook lying; relax Shoulders to supporting surface, with expiration.*
    c. *Forehead support prone lying; Head raising and lowering with*
       relaxation.
    d. *sitting; Shoulder shrugging and retraction followed by relaxation.*
Physiological relaxation can also be used in the treatment of occupation-
induced tensions (see p. 68).

Mobility

The maintenance of normal mobility is essential to enable a wide
variety of postures to be assumed.   Abnormal mobility, however, is a
liability rather than an asset, as additional muscular effort is required
to control it, and in some cases it may be a contributory factor in the
development of poor posture.

Normal mobility is maintained by general free exercises which are
rhythmical in character and include full-range movement of all joints.

Emphasis is laid on full extension as this is the movement which is most liable to limitation, except in the case of the lumbar spine and the shoulder joints, where flexion and lateral rotation respectively are more likely to be limited.   If joint stiffness has developed, specific mobility measures for the joint affected are used to make sure that the loss of range in one joint is not masked by a compensatory increase in the mobility of the adjacent joints.   For example, stiff shoulders which will not permit full elevation of the arm are readily compensated by hyperextension in the lumbar spine.

Exercises and agilities which increase the respiratory excursions are of great importance and should on no account be omitted, and those which involve hanging positions give good alignment of the body and are much enjoyed by children.

Muscle Power

General muscular weakness is rarely if ever the root cause of poor posture, but the opportunity for free movement and harmonious muscular development helps to maintain their tone and efficiency, and so to withstand any strain which may be imposed by occupational stresses. The use of the anti-gravity muscles is of special importance as these are the groups which are most frequently called upon to act in a postural capacity.

If and when joint stiffness is present, exercise for the muscles which have been stretched are essential to ensure relaxation of their antagonists and to restore muscular balance.   For example, work for the upper Back Extensors and Scapula Retractors is required during re-education of a stooping posture (see Chapter 15, 'Muscle Strength', p. 167).

Presentation of a Good Posture

There is no one method of teaching any one patient to assume and experience the feeling of good posture.   The method and the technique selected for a particular patient must depend on the patient and the physiotherapist, but one thing appears to be essential and that is that the physiotherapist must have faith in the method she adopts.

Those who have habitual poor posture often feel uncomfortable and unnatural in any position other than the one to which they have become accustomed.   This is not surprising, but emphasises the importance of convincing the patient that good posture 'looks' right, and will prove efficient in the long run.   In other words, the physiotherapist must 'sell' the pattern of good posture.

A mirror, posture recorder or photographs may be useful for this purpose, so that the image can be compared with pictures of experts which demonstrate a good general pattern of alignment.   Video-tapes may also be used.   This is particularly impressive in training dynamic posture in activities such as tennis, diving and lifting where faulty posture can have such a marked effect on the efficiency of the movement.

Training of static postures in the erect position is basic, partly because most people, with the exception of very small children, are compelled to spend most of their waking hours in upright positions which are relatively static, for example, standing and sitting. Even in walking the alignment of the trunk remains more or less the same, and incidentally the ability to remain still without undue effort, when the occasion demands it, is a habit well worth acquiring.

In the erect postures, the control of each segment of the body in relation to the rest is by no means a simple thing to learn. The position of the whole is profoundly influenced by the position of the head, of the pelvic tilt, and by the state of comfort and position of the feet. Different authorities stress the importance of one or other of these factors but in fact they are all important and any one may prove to be the dominant factor.

Establishment of a new and satisfactory pattern of posture is accelerated by strong and prolonged holding against maximal resistance in a satisfactory pattern of posture. This resistance is applied manually in directions which are at first known to the patient with a dynamic command to 'HOLD!' to focus his attention. Later resistance is applied in quick succession from a variety of directions unknown to the patient.

The Head

An upward thrust of the vertex in the erect positions may be sufficient to achieve satisfactory alignment of the whole body, provided no unnecessary tension is allowed to develop elsewhere. To prevent

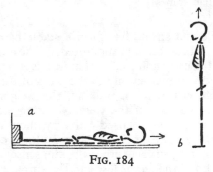

FIG. 184

tension in the initial stages this thrust may be practised in the horizontal and inclined positions, e.g.

a. *crook lying or lying with Feet support; Body lengthening*
b. *half lying, sitting or standing; Head stretching upwards.*

The Pelvic Tilt

Voluntary control of the pelvic tilt teaches the patient to recognise any deviation from the normal, and trains him to be able to adjust and correct it at will. In *crook lying* the trunk is supported in a position of alignment and the pelvis is free to move in an antero-posterior direction, therefore this position is selected to start with. Contraction of the Hip Extensors, as if to lift the hips off the floor, and of the straight Abdominal Muscles, tilts the pelvis backwards and the reverse movement is achieved by the hollowing of the lumbar spine.

Once the ability to adjust the pelvic tilt has been learnt it can be performed in a variety of positions which include *sitting* and *standing*, and it can be controlled at the angle of tilt required.

   c. *crook lying; Gluteal and Abdominal contraction* (to flatten lower Back to floor), *followed by relaxation, then hollowing of Back.*

   d. *low wing sitting; Pelvis tilting and adjustment.*

   e. *low wing standing; Pelvis tilting and adjustment.*

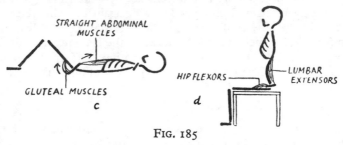

FIG. 185

The movement may be felt and appreciated by placing the hands over the anterior superior iliac spines.

The Feet

Painless, mobile and strong feet form a stable base on which the weight of the body is balanced and supported. The arches are braced, and the weight of the body adjusted so that it falls through the summit of the arch and is distributed evenly to the areas of the feet which are designed for weight-bearing. In walking, the weight is transferred progressively from one part of the weight-bearing area to the next. Bracing of the arches can be practised with or without weight-bearing, but in every case the weight-bearing areas must be in contact with the floor or other supporting surface, otherwise the sensory stimulation of pressure on the soles of the feet is lost and the surfaces are unlikely to remain on the same plane.

   f. *sitting; bracing of the longitudinal arch and pressing the Toes to the floor.* (All weight-bearing areas must be kept in contact with the floor.)

g. *standing (Feet turned forwards and slightly apart); Hip rotation outwards* (to make patellae look laterally).

The Complete Picture

Where the complete pattern of good posture does not emerge as the result of the adjustment of any one of the areas which have been already mentioned, it must be built up gradually and progressively from complete relaxation.   A state of balanced tension and much concentration is required at first, but the effort and tension are progressively reduced by repetition.   Every new poise or movement requires effort at first, but this is reduced as the pattern on which it is based is simplified and becomes more efficient and the passage of the co-ordinating impulses on the neuromuscular pathways is facilitated.   Provided there is sufficient repetition and precision, the new and satisfactory pattern of posture becomes habitual and therefore no longer requires voluntary control, as it is maintained by a conditional reflex which is part of the postural reflex.

19

WALKING AIDS

There are a number of aids available to assist people who have difficulty in walking or who cannot walk independently without one. These external aids are crutches, sticks and frames. Braces and splints which can be used to assist walking are not described in this book.

CRUTCHES

There are three basic types of crutches and they are used to reduce weight-bearing on one or both legs, or to give additional support where balance is impaired and strength is inadequate.

1. Axillary Crutches

They are made of wood with an axillary pad, a hand piece and a rubber ferrule. The position of the hand piece and the total length are usually adjustable (**Fig. 186**).

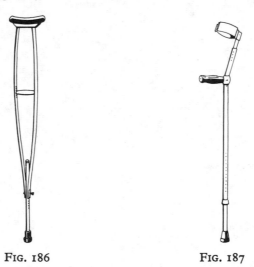

FIG. 186   FIG. 187

The axillary pad should rest against the chest wall approximately 5 cm.

below the apex of the axilla and the hand grip should be adjusted to allow the elbow to be slightly flexed when weight is not being taken. Weight is transmitted down the arm to the hand piece. The elbow is extended. On no account should weight be taken through the axillary pad as this could lead to a neuropraxia of the Radial Nerve or Brachial Plexus.

Measurement of length. There is a variety of ways of measuring the patient for crutches. It is usually carried out with the patient in lying.

a. With shoes off — measure from the apex of the axilla to the lower margin of the medial malleolus. This is an easy measurement and is reasonably reliable.

b. With shoes on — 5 cm vertically down from the apex of the axilla to a point 20 cm lateral to the heel of the shoe. This tends to be less accurate than the first method.

The measurement from the auxillary pad to the hand grip should be taken with the elbow slightly flexed (approximately 15°) from a point 5 cm below the apex of the axilla to the ulnar styloid. Once the patient is standing with the support of the crutches, the physiotherapist must the correct way to use the crutches and to see that they do not allow the axillary pad to press into the axilla.

2. Elbow Crutches

They are made of metal and have a metal or plastic forearm band. They are usually adjustable in length by means of a press clip or metal button and have a rubber ferrule (Fig. 187). These crutches are particularly suitable for patients with good balance and strong arms. Weight is transmitted in exactly the same way as for axillary crutches.

Measurement of length. The measurement is usually taken with the patient in the lying position with the shoes on. The elbow is slightly flexed (approximately 15°) and the measurement is taken from the ulnar styloid to a point 20 cm lateral to the heel of the shoe. Once the patient is standing with the support, the length must be checked.

3. Gutter Crutches. (*Adjustable arthritic crutches; forearm support crutches*)

They are made of metal with a padded forearm support and strap, an adjustable hand piece and a rubber ferrule (Fig. 188).

These are used for patients with Rheumatoid Disease, who require some form of support but cannot take weight through hands, wrists and elbows because of deformity and/or pain. The crutch is adjustable in length in the same way as the elbow crutch. It should also be adjustable in the length of forearm support and in the angle of the hand piece to allow for deformities.

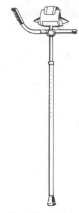

FIG. 188

Measurement of length

(a) If the patient is able to stand, it is better to assess the required length in this position from elbow to the floor.

(b) Measurement can be carried out with the patient lying with shoes on, and is taken from the point of the flexed elbow to 20 cm lateral to the heel.

A patient with Rheumatoid Disease may allow the hips and knees to flex in the weight-bearing position because of muscle weakness and/or pain, but with gutter crutches for support he may be able to obtain more extension. This must be taken into account in any adjustment.

Preparation for Crutch Walking
a. Arms

The power of the extensors and adductors of the shoulder and the extensors of the elbow must be assessed and if necessary strengthened before the patient starts walking. The hand grip must also be tested to see that the patient has sufficient power and mobility to grasp the hand piece. The results of this assessment will determine the type of crutch chosen.

b. Legs

(*i*) *Non-weight-bearing*. The mobility and strength of the unaffected leg should be assessed, paying particular attention to the hip abductors and extensors, the knee extensors and the plantar flexors of the ankle. These muscles must be sufficiently strong to take weight. The patient is taught hip-hitching on the non-weight-bearing side if it is required.

(*ii*) *Partial weight-bearing*. The mobility and strength of both legs should be assessed and muscles strengthened where necessary.

c. Balance

Sitting and standing balance must be tested and trained if necessary.

Demonstration

The physiotherapist should demonstrate the appropriate crutch walking to the patient, emphasising the important points.

Crutch Walking

The physiotherapist should have an assistant when the patient is to stand and walk for the first time. This person may be another physiotherapist, a nurse, another health care worker or a relative. The physiotherapist must instruct the assistant on how to support the patient to the upright position and then how to transfer the patient on to the crutches.

(i) *Non-weight-bearing*. The patient should always stand with a triangular base, i.e. crutches either in front or behind the weight-bearing leg (Fig. 189).

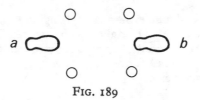

Fig. 189

To walk, the patient first moves the crutches a little further forward (Fig. 190a), takes weight down through the crutches and lifts the foot forward to a position just behind the line of the crutches (Fig. 190b). Once this is mastered the patient may progress to lifting the foot forward to a position just in front of the line of the crutches (Fig. 190c).

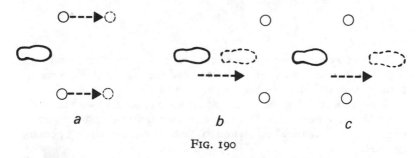

Fig. 190

It is important in certain cases for the patient to progress to 'shadow walking', where the affected leg is moved in sequence simulating walking but taking no weight.

(*ii*). *Partial weight-bearing*.   There are two methods of partial weight-bearing.

a. This is a progression from shadow walking, where no weight is taken through the affected leg, to permit a gradual increase of weight to be taken.   The crutches and the affected leg are taken forward and put down together.   Weight is then taken through the crutches and the affected leg while the unaffected leg is brought through (Fig. 191a and b).

FIG. 191

b. This method simulates normal walking and more weight is taken through the affected leg.   The right crutch is moved forward followed by the left leg, then the left crutch is moved forward followed by the right leg (Figs. 192a and b).   This can be progressed to moving the right crutch with left leg and vice versa.

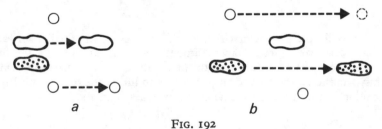

FIG. 192

Sticks

Sticks may be either of wood or metal with curved or straight hand pieces.   The metal ones are adjustable and therefore suitable for assessment purposes.   The wooden ones are cut to the required length.

Measurement.   The measurement can usually be taken with the patient in the standing position.   The elbow is slightly flexed and the measurement is taken from the ulnar styloid to the floor approximately 15 cm from the heel.

Use of sticks.   The patient may use two sticks in the same way as the methods described for partial weight-bearing walking with crutches. Sticks allow more weight to be taken through the leg than do crutches. One stick may be used on the unaffected side so that the stick and the affected leg are placed forward together, taking some of the weight through the stick.

Tripod or Quadrapod (Figs. 193a and b)

FIG. 193

Metal sticks with three- or four-pronged bases give a more stable support than a stick.

Frames

FIG. 194

The commonest type is the lightweight frame with four feet which may be adjustable in height (Fig. 194). The patient lifts the frame forward, then leans on it and takes two steps (Figs. 195a and b). The patient should take even steps, keeping the frame well forward. A bag can be attached to the front of the frame to carry small items.

a   *b*

FIG. 195

Ataxic patients who are too unsteady to lift a frame forward may be able to use a rollator frame which can be pushed (Fig. 196) or a reciprocal frame where each side moves independently (Fig. 197).

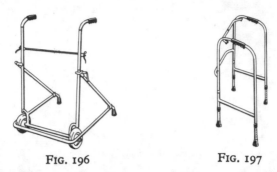

FIG. 196   FIG. 197

Safety. The physiotherapist must check the safety of all walking aids not only when giving them to a patient, but regularly throughout a treatment programme. The patient must be taught to inspect his walking aids and know where to obtain replacement parts. Ferrules, which are made of rubber or plastic, should be rough to give a high co-efficient of friction. The general structure including screws, metal clips, press buttons, hand grips and axillary pads must all be in good condition.

PART VI

20

INDIVIDUAL, GROUP AND MASS TREATMENT BY EXERCISES

THE physiotherapist must give her undivided attention to a patient when passive movement is given, but active exercise can often be taught or supervised either individually or with others.

INDIVIDUAL EXERCISE

As each patient's problem differs in some respects from that of others individual treatment is essential to obtain and accelerate his rehabilitation by correcting specific imbalances of muscle strength, limitation of joint range and establishing co-ordination. The physiotherapist must know and check her patient's abilities with regard to functional activities and work with him to gain independence by training self-care in the circumstances in which he lives whenever this is possible, e.g. in the ward, home or workshop.

As too much individual attention leads to the patient relying on the presence of the physiotherapist as a stimulus to activity, he must be encouraged and given the opportunity to practise on his own.

GROUP EXERCISE

Group exercise provides the opportunity for the patient to practise activities he 'can do' to build up his endurance and increase the speed of his performance. Working with other patients stimulates his effort and helps to give him confidence in his own abilities while his performance is guided and controlled by the physiotherapist.

At the outset it is essential to distinguish Group Exercise from Mass Exercise. The latter is performed by a large number of people to a formal word of command, or a rhythm dictated by an instructor, and little or no assistance or correction can be given to the individual. In contrast, where a small number of people work together in Group Exercise there is concentration on the needs of the individual while the stimulation which results from working with others is utilised.

A small number of patients, preferably never exceeding six or eight are grouped together because they have some common disability which will benefit from exercises which are similar in character.   While there is common ground with regard to the exercises there is also room for modification in range, effort and speed of movement, so that they can be adapted to suit the individual needs of each member of the group and thus produce the maximum effect.   Because of the common ground, the pattern of each exercise can be taught to the whole group simultaneously; time is then allowed for free practice of the whole or part of the exercise, during which each patient performs the movement according to his own capacity and in his own rhythm, being helped, resisted, encouraged and corrected by the physiotherapist according to his individual need.

The Value of Group Exercise

1. The patient learns to take a measure of responsibility for his own exercise, and so is helped towards adequate home practice.   Patients treated individually for too long come to rely on the presence and assistance of the physiotherapist and are conditioned to feel that these are essential.   In a group, the amount of attention given to the individual patient decreases in proportion to the number in the group, and yet a measure of help, supervision and encouragement is available when required.

2. The patient learns to work with others and no longer considers himself set apart from his fellow-men because of his disability.   Help is at hand if he needs it, meanwhile he learns to take his place with other members of the community.

3. The patient is given confidence in the treatment and is therefore stimulated to further effort, as progress on the part of other members of the group does not pass unnoticed.

4. The patient is given confidence in his ability to hold his own with others when the group performs some exercises in unison.

5. Effort is stimulated by some activities which call for a mild form of competition.   True competition can only take place on equal ground, therefore activities of this kind must be carefully controlled by the physiotherapist.

6. Patients are helped to forget their disability temporarily by Objective and Game-like Activities, which are only possible in Group Treatment.   This helps to promote natural movement, general activity and a cheerful outlook.   In small groups careful supervision can be given and help is at hand if required.

The value of Group Exercise must always be assessed from the point of view of the benefit to the patient.   From the physiotherapist's point of view much of her time is saved when several patients are treated simultaneously, but her effort must be very concentrated if maximum value from the treatment is to be obtained by all the patients in the group.

The Disadvantages of Group Treatment

These arise from the abuse or misunderstanding of the system. Faulty selection of patients, inadequate explanation to the patient, lack of, or inefficient, grading of groups, overcrowding of groups, and poor technique of instruction on the part of the physiotherapist, are the most common causes of failure to benefit the patient.

The Organisation of Group Exercise

As with any other form of exercise therapy the keynote of success is to give the patient the right exercises, at the right time, and in the right way. In other words, to match the exercises he is required to perform to his capacity to perform them.

Selection of Patients. Any patient who is capable of, and is expected to do, home exercise can be drafted into a suitable group once the basic instruction has been given and is understood. Group treatment cannot replace individual treatment; it is a progression from and an adjunct to it.

Grading of Groups. The patient must only be drafted to a group in which the exercises performed are suitable to his capacity, and he must be progressed from that group to another as his capacity increases.

Groups are formed according to the location and nature of the disability, the age group and sex of the patients, and are graded according to the nature and strength of the exercises performed.

For example, a convenient method of grading Leg Exercises for Men is as follows—

(*i*) *Leg C.* (Traumatic Injuries; for non-weight-bearing exercise.)

(*ii*) *Leg B.* (Traumatic Injuries; for partial weight-bearing exercise.)

(*iii*) *Leg A.* (Traumatic Injuries; for full weight-bearing exercises and activities leading to final rehabilitation.)

The members of these groups are most likely to be fairly young men who could expect to achieve full rehabilitation, e.g. before and after menisectomy.

(*iv*) *Leg X.* (Non-traumatic Conditions, for non-weight-bearing exercise.)

The majority of members of this group would in all probability be elderly and would therefore require exercise at a slower rhythm.

(*v*) *Weight Lifting and Pulleys.* Patients needing repetitive resisted exercise for various parts of the body can work simultaneously under the direction of one physiotherapist who checks the magnitude of the weight and its application for each in turn. She can stimulate the patient's effort verbally and supervise their performance.

This list of groups is by no means exhaustive and is only intended as an example of a satisfactory arrangement for a large department in which a wide variety of conditions are treated.   It is an advantage for progressive groups to exercise simultaneously, as this facilitates the movement of patients from one group to another without the necessity of altering the time of the appointment for the treatment.   Re-grading must be made at frequent intervals.   This requires skilled assessment by the physiotherapist and determines the success of this method of giving treatment.

Explanation to the Patient.   Before joining a group the patient must be given preliminary instruction in some of the exercises and an explanation of their purpose with regard to his disability.   His confidence must be gained so that he feels he can report progress or any further symptoms which may arise.   It is sometimes advisable to let a patient watch a group at work, or to allow him to take part in some of the exercises with the help of the physiotherapist with whom he has had individual treatment, before he is finally expected to work as a member of the group.

The Number of Patients in a Group.   The number of patients who can be successfully treated in a group depends to some extent on the nature of their disability and how much help or resistance each will require, and also on the ability of the physiotherapist to see and give this attention when it is needed.   Overcrowding results in a form of mass exercise as the number of patients in the group makes it impossible for the physiotherapist to give adequate individual attention.   The ability to look after several patients at one and the same time only comes with experience.

The Technique of Instruction.   The technique of conducting Group Exercises is basically the same as that required to teach and supervise individual exercise.   The ability to see where help and encouragement are required in the case of several people is merely an extension of the ability required to give it to one, and it comes with practice and experience.

Some have a natural flair for this type of work and their personality gets across without much attention to technique; still, every skill has its technique, a knowledge of which will improve performance, and even without much natural ability, a very adequate standard can be reached by studying this technique and by experience in applying it.

MASS EXERCISE

This method is only suitable for giving general exercise.   Because of the large number who take part, it is impossible for the instructor to give much more than general encouragement and correction during the presentation of the exercises.   Frequently, but not necessarily, the exercises are done in unison to a formal command or a rhythm dictated by the instructor, in which case the identity of the individual is submerged to produce a uniform pattern of movement, as for example in army drill or exercises arranged for demonstration purposes.

Introduced at the right time and used in conjunction with individual or group treatment this method of giving exercise often plays a part in the whole scheme of rehabilitation, as the circulation and general exercise tolerance are improved, and the discipline of working with others is stimulating.   For many cases, however, it is unsuitable as it does not cater for the specialised needs of the individual.

RECREATIONAL ACTIVITIES AND SPORTS

These often provide a challenge to the patient which he cannot easily resist as can be seen when a football is left on the floor of a Department where men are coming for treatment!   Basic patterns of functional movement are used in many of these activities and, as skill and effort are needed to succeed or excel, they make a valuable contribution to rehabilitation.

The physiotherapist should have a working knowledge of as many suitable activities as possible so that she can direct the patient's interest to those within his capabilities.   Swimming and ball games are particularly useful but adequate supervision in the early stages is required to prevent accidents and unnecessary frustration.   Supervision must be as informal as possible and, whenever it is practical, the physiotherapist should join in the activity.

Some patients with considerable residual disability find much satisfaction in continuing to practise competitive sporting activities after their rehabilitation is virtually completed, e.g. archery for paraplegics. Activities of this kind can be a social asset and should be encouraged.

21

SCHEMES OF EXERCISES

FOLLOWING the assessment of patients, the aims are determined for the individual or group. The therapist then plans a set of exercises designed for the initial aims. These can be progressed or altered depending on their effect on the patient or group.

The exercises may be either general or specific according to the nature of the patient's condition and the aims of treatment.

GENERAL EXERCISES

These provide activity for the whole body, although they can be adapted to lay emphasis on exercise for a particular area if this is required. They are used in the treatment of general conditions, e.g. debility, rheumatoid arthritis, or as an adjunct to treatment given for a specific area whenever the nature of a localised lesion tends to reduce the normal efficiency of body movement generally.

The order in which the exercises are arranged is usually based on a definite plan which, however, need not be followed too rigidly, as any arrangement made must of necessity be extremely flexible to allow it to be adapted to the needs and condition of each patient.

Exercises which are easy and involve no great muscular effort come first to warm and prepare the body for the peak of effort which comes rather more than half-way through the set of exercises when the large muscles of the trunk work to move the heaviest parts of the body. The treatment session is completed by the inclusion of exercises which require no great muscular effort but considerable control and concentration.

By this arrangement plenty of variety of exercise is possible, as each part of the body is moved in turn and fatigue is prevented by ensuring that no one group of muscles is used in the same way in consecutive exercises.

Basic Plan for a Set of Exercises

1. *Respiratory Exercise.* This may be either a specific Breathing Exercise or some simple activity during which the patient gets out of breath with consequent increase in the respiratory excursions.

2. *Extremity Exercises.* These are easy and often well-known exercises to prepare the body for more strenuous activity. Either the Arm or Leg Exercise can come first according to which is most suitable to follow the Respiratory Exercise, or they may be combined.

3. *Head and Neck Exercise.* These are generally used to improve the posture of the head and are often more conveniently placed between the Trunk Exercises, as they provide relatively easy work in comparison with that required during movements which involve the trunk, and so prevent fatigue.

4. *Trunk Exercises.* Back and Abdominal Exercises, Trunk Side Bending and Rotation are all included in this group. They may be performed in any order which is convenient within the group.

5. *Extremity Exercises.* The Arm and Leg Exercises included at this stage differ from those at the beginning in that they require more control and concentration, possibly because of the difficulty of the starting position or of keeping the body in a state of equilibrium. A Balance Exercise is usually included in all tables designed for patients with poor posture or gait.

6. *Respiratory Exercise.* This is designed to have a quietening effect and is frequently followed or accompanied by correction of posture in the common positions and activities of everyday life, e.g. sitting, standing and walking.

Posture is checked or corrected before, during and after every exercise to ensure a satisfactory basis on which the movements made during the exercises are superimposed. When rest periods between exercises are necessary or desirable, these may take the form of relaxation in a suitable posture, e.g. *crook lying, crook half lying* or *Back lean standing*, or a change provided by a 'break' may be all that is required. A 'break' is some form of easy activity in which there is usually an element of competition and which is much enjoyed.

Changing Scheme

The physiotherapist must be ready to change exercises as the need arises. The patient may have achieved the aim of a particular exercise and it can be progressed or exchanged for a more difficult exercise. Alternatively, the exercise may have proved too difficult and may have to be changed for a simpler one, or it may not be a suitable choice for the particular patient. Too frequent changes often reduce the benefit to be gained by accurate knowledge and ample practice of the exercises. Changes which are too infrequent result in the exercises becoming unsuitable for the present condition of the patient and so impede progress and lead to boredom.

SPECIFIC EXERCISES

These are used in the treatment of local conditions when exercise for a specific area of the body is required, e.g. Colles fracture. When the local condition is such that it impedes the normal activities of the body as a whole, and when time permits, both specific and general exercises may be included in a treatment.

The arrangement of the exercises within a specific scheme can only be planned in broad outline, those which are strengthening and mobilising in effect being placed at the beginning, and those which train co-ordination and the functional use of the part predominating towards the end. An effort must be made to avoid using the same muscles strongly in consecutive exercises to avoid undue fatigue.

A satisfactory plan of the type of exercise and the timing of a half-hour period of treatment by group exercises is as follows:

(*i*) Assemble group, take register and assess condition of individual members of the group . . . . . 5 mins.
(*ii*) Subjective exercises which are strengthening or mobilising in effect during which the patient concentrates on precision of movement . . . . 10 ,,
(*iii*) Objective exercises and activities by means of which the functional use of the area being treated is tested and developed . . . . 10 ,,
(*iv*) Suggestion and practice of exercises suitable for home practice . . . . 5 ,,

PLANNING OF EXERCISES

Before choosing suitable exercises, the physiotherapist must know certain relevant facts about the patient or group of patients for whom it is to be designed.

From the doctor or the doctor's notes the following information about each patient is acquired:

1. Name
2. Age
3. Sex
4. Occupation
5. History
6. Present condition
7. Diagnosis
8. Treatment ordered, including Physical Treatment
9. Date of review by doctor.

From her own examination of the patient she observes and assesses:

10. The patient's capacity for exercise and his attitude to treatment
11. The number of treatment periods to be arranged each week.
12. The duration of each treatment period.

With this knowledge the physiotherapist is in a position to specify the precise aims of treatment and to select exercises suitable to fulfil these aims. When the exercises have been chosen, a careful check must be made to see that the aims of treatment have been fulfilled, that the effort required is well balanced and that the continuity and variety of the exercises is satisfactory. A record of the exercises, dated and written in correct terminology, is kept for use at subsequent treatments and for reference, together with notes indicating the patient's reaction and progress.

TREATMENT SESSION

The aims may require the inclusion of other techniques or skills such as electrotherapy, massage or passive manual mobilisation. The exercises must be related to the whole plan of treatment.

Patients may also be receiving treatment from other therapists, for example occupational therapists or speech therapists. In this case the physiotherapist should consider the total management of the patient and the place of physiotherapy treatment within this.

22

INSTRUCTING THE PATIENT

THE instruction which is given to a patient with regard to exercises must be presented to him in a manner which will gain his co-operation and ensure that he has a thorough understanding of what is required of him.

THE CO-OPERATION OF THE PATIENT

A brief explanation of the purpose of the exercises, given in simple terms which can be understood, goes a long way towards gaining the patient's confidence in the treatment, and the manner and department of the physiotherapist gives confidence in her ability to direct this treatment with efficiency. The calm and cheerful atmosphere created, once this confidence is established, supplies the background essential for either concentrated effort or maximal voluntary relaxation, and ensures the co-operation of the patient.

The co-operation of the patient is required for the performance of both passive movement and active exercise. During passive movements, except in cases of paralysis or when there is general anaesthesia, this co-operation takes the form of voluntary relaxation on the part of the patient while he permits his joints to be moved for him. It is relatively easy to persuade a patient to submit to any form of passive therapy provided it is pleasant and comfortable, but if pain or discomfort result, as they may, especially during some forced passive movements, a much greater degree of co-operation is required for him to permit the movement. In this case the patient must be convinced of the ultimate benefit of the treatment.

Voluntary effort on the part of the patient and an understanding of what is required of him are essential for the performance of active exercise and he must be stimulated and given every encouragement to make this effort. The design of the exercises and the manner in which they are presented are of the greatest importance in eliciting maximum effort.

THE TREATMENT ROOM

An atmosphere of efficiency is created by order and cleanliness in the treatment room, which should be light and well ventilated. In winter some form of heating is essential to enable the wearing of clothing suitable for exercise, while in summer some additional out-door space is an advantage for use in fine weather. When artificial lighting is required it should be adequate and well diffused, electric bulbs and shades being protected wherever activities involving the use of balls, beanbags or sticks are to be carried on. A clean floor with a non-slippery surface, such as close-grained unpolished wood or rubberised linoleum, is ideal. Sufficient space should be available to allow each patient to move freely without fear of collision with other patients or apparatus.

All portable apparatus, which will be required for the exercises, must be collected before they are begun so that it is at hand when needed and time is not wasted in fetching it during the period of treatment. Fittings such as wall-bars, horizontal bars and the like must be in good condition and inspection of these at frequent intervals by a competent authority is essential to ensure safety. When not in use, movable apparatus such as plinths, forms, stools and mattresses should be stacked neatly to make the most of the available free space. An adequate supply of small portable apparatus makes it possible for each patient to practise individually, and suitable containers for balls, bands, quoits, ropes, etc., should be provided and placed where both patients and physiotherapists know where to find them and to return them after use. A selection of brightly coloured beanbags, balls and bands are much appreciated by both children and adults, and when in use they give a colourful and cheerful appearance to the room.

Tidiness and an intelligent use of both space and apparatus do much to obtain the maximum value from the available facilities and to relieve apparent overcrowding.

Clothing

For the Patient. All garments which restrict movement or make it impossible for the physiotherapist to observe it accurately should be removed. It is not always easy to persuade patients to wear suitable clothing, but if a firm but reasonable stand is taken, from the first treatment, with every patient, the idea is soon accepted.

Generally speaking, it is advisable for men to strip to the waist for upper limb and trunk exercises, while for leg and strenuous trunk exercise the wearing of shorts instead of trousers is essential. Women should remove their dresses or blouses, and a petticoat or vest with adequate knickers, or shorts if available, are suitable for most exercises. Corsets and constricting belts, other than surgical belts which are only removed with the doctor's permission, must be taken off prior to trunk exercises. Constant vigilance on the part of the physiotherapist is necessary to ensure this, as women are even more loath to remove their corsets than the men are to remove their collars and ties! Rubber shoes may be required for activities where the floor is unsuitable for bare feet.   A bathing suit is very often a suitable garment for small children to wear for treatment except in very cold weather.

For the Physiotherapist. The physiotherapist must be neatly dressed in some suitable uniform which allows her sufficient freedom of movement.

PUNCTUALITY

Co-operation between the patient and the physiotherapist is necessary to see that treatments begin and end punctually, thus avoiding much uncertainty and waste of time.   This is particularly important in the case of group work for Out-Patients, when exercises must start at a prearranged time whether or not all members of the group are present.   Time is valuable to many who get an hour or so off work to come for treatment and those who arrive punctually should never be kept waiting.

POSITIONING OF PATIENT OR GROUPS

The essential condition in positioning a patient for exercise is that he shall have ample space in which to move freely, and it is usually desirable that he should have a clear view of the physiotherapist who is instructing him.   It is of equal importance that the physiotherapist should be able to see the patient from an angle which is suitable for assessing the efficiency of his movements.

Regular formations, such as lines, files and circles, may be used provided valuable time and energy are not wasted in achieving them, but it is often quicker and equally satisfactory to use the less formal method of merely asking the patient to 'find a space' and then checking that he has ample room for movement.   Physiotherapists who are unaccustomed to group work often find it easier to observe faulty movement when a regular formation is used, but a less formal arrangement has the advantage of emphasising the individual character of the exercise in which each patient attempts to improve his own performance without any suggestion of regimentation.

Whenever several groups are exercising in the same room at one and the same time it is advisable to arrange that each one faces in a different direction to avoid attention being distracted by the activities of other groups.

POSITIONING OF PHYSIOTHERAPIST

The position of the physiotherapist with regard to the group she is instructing is also of importance, especially where patients have sight, hearing or understanding difficulties.   When possible she should stand well back from the group, in front of it and slightly to one side, as in this position she can usually see and be seen by all without effort.

When space is limited a small platform on which she can stand, placed close to the group, is of great assistance. A position directly in front of a line or in the centre of a circle of patients is to be avoided. When a lateral view of an exercise is required to check the accuracy of the movement, the group can be turned to face in another direction or the physiotherapist can move round to the side.

The posture and movements of the physiotherapist do much to demonstrate her attitude towards both the patients and the treatment. Good posture, alert but well-controlled movements when these are required, and an absence of mannerisms give an impression of interest and efficiency.

It is advisable to sit or stand still when actually giving verbal instructions unless these are accompanied by a demonstration of the exercise. Restless or purposeless movements distract attention from what is being said as, for example, in the case of a speaker who walks to and fro continuously like a caged animal!

METHOD OF INSTRUCTION

Many exercises and most activities consist of a series of simple movements. For teaching purposes it is usually advisable to analyse the exercise and allow the patient to practise each of these simple movements before attempting to build them up into the sequence which constitutes the exercise as a whole. Otherwise attention becomes focused on the effort to remember the sequence rather than on the accurate performance of the constituent movements, e.g. transference of weight is perfected before the sequence of movements which constitute walking is attempted.

Instruction may be given verbally, by demonstration, or by the use of passive movement.

Verbal Instruction

Informal Explanation. The patient is told what to do in a few simple words, e.g.

Lift your arms sideways!

Try to *make* a fist!

Bend your leg *up*; *stretch* it *out*!

Economy of words is essential for clarity and a single instruction, which is carried out immediately, leaves the patient in no doubt as to what is required of him. Numerous instructions and lengthy explanations are confusing, as the first of them is generally forgotten by the time the exercise is due to start; likewise the constant repetition of unnecessary phrases such as 'I want you to' and 'Yes, that's right', are better omitted as they contribute little or nothing to the explanation.

Formal Commands. These are now rarely used, but they are a convenient method of starting an exercise which is well known. They specify the point in time at which the exercise is to begin, so that many patients can perform it in unison, or to a definite beat dictated by a musical accompaniment. A formal command is essential to achieve a fair start for most competitive games and activities.

Each command consists of three parts, (*i*) Preparatory or Descriptive, (*ii*) Pause, (*iii*) Executive word, e.g.

$$\left\{\begin{array}{l}\text{stride jump, with Arm lifting and lowering}\\ \text{On your marks}\end{array}\right\} \left\{\begin{array}{l}\cdots\cdots\cdots\cdots\\ \cdots\cdots\cdots\cdots\end{array}\right\} \left\{\begin{array}{l}begin!\\ go!\end{array}\right\}$$

(*i*)   (*ii*)   (*iii*)

Instruction by Demonstration

The use which is made of demonstration in the teaching of exercise is largely a matter of individual preference, some considering it an essential factor in presenting any exercise, others preferring to use it only when the occasion demands and as an adjunct to verbal explanation. Any demonstration given by the physiotherapist must be as perfect and as accurate as possible, so that the patient gets the correct mental picture of the exercise. Much valuable time may be wasted while the patient remains inactive watching a prolonged demonstration when he would be more profitably employed in an attempt to 'do' the exercise. It is often preferable for the physiotherapist to do the exercise with the patients in response to her own instructions, except when a rest period will be beneficial to them. It is interesting and very salutary to estimate, with the help of a stop-watch, the proportion of the treatment time during which exercise is actually performed by the patient in relation to that used exclusively by the physiotherapist in talking and demonstrating.

Instruction by Passive Movement

It is rarely necessary to use this method except for patients who are blind or deaf, or for those who have sustained long periods of inactivity during which the pattern of the movement, as recorded by the kinaesthetic sensation, has been forgotten.

Corrections

The need for corrections is inevitable, but they can be reduced to a minimum by clear, accurate instruction, and where possible it is always better to foresee a mistake and prevent it. Verbal corrections should invariably be constructive in character and they may be given while the exercise is in progress or during rest periods between bouts of activity. The patient's reaction to correction must be observed and suitable praise or encouragement given whenever a real effort is made to improve, e.g. *Lift your head higher*, or *That is better!* Unless some comment is made, patients often feel their efforts have passed unnoticed and they always appreciate being told how they are progressing.

For group work corrections may be general or individual.

General Corrections. These are given when several members of the group will benefit from them or to give a nervous or inattentive patient a chance to improve his performance without drawing the attention of the group to his mistake.

Individual Corrections. The patient is addressed by name before a verbal correction of this kind is given, or the physiotherapist can give manual help and guidance by standing beside a shy or nervous patient.

Patients often show a keen interest in observing, correcting and encouraging each other, and this is to be encouraged on suitable occasions, provided their efforts are carefully supervised

The Voice of the Physiotherapist

The physiotherapist's voice is of major importance in interpreting the nature, speed, rhythm and intensity of the exercises. Diction must be good so that every word can be heard clearly without strain, and a voice which is relatively low-pitched is an advantage as it is easily produced and pleasant to listen to. The volume should always be suited to the room and to the size of the audience and any tendency to shout, especially in group work, must be resisted.

Variation in pitch and volume, in the duration of words and the timing of sentences, makes it possible to interpret the precise nature of an infinite variety of activities and ensure emphasis where it is required. A voice which is flexible and varied commands attention from the listeners, and is never dull.

Every patient who has received instruction in active exercise should feel that he has benefited by, and enjoyed, the treatment. In addition, he should clearly understand that having gained a knowledge and experience of suitable exercises he is expected to co-operate in accelerating his own recovery by practice at home.

APPENDICES

I

DERIVED POSITIONS

THE position of the arms, legs or trunk may be altered in each of the fundamental positions to modify the effect of the positions, or of the exercises which are performed from them subsequently.

The purpose for which the modification is made may be:

1. To increase or decrease the size and stability of the base.
2. To raise or lower the centre of gravity.
3. To ensure maximum local or general relaxation.
4. To alter the position of the body in relation to gravity.
5. To provide control or fixation for a particular part of the body so that movement may be localised to a specific area.
6. To increase or decrease the muscle work required to maintain the position.
7. To increase or decrease the leverage.
8. To provide a convenient position from which a particular exercise is to be performed.

POSITIONS DERIVED FROM *STANDING*

By *Alteration of the Arms*

Only the description and static muscle work to hold the position of the arms is given below, that of the fundamental position to which this is added is not repeated (see Fundamental Positions, p. 32).

WING STANDING (wg. st.)

The hands rest on the crests of the ilia, the fingers, which are extended and adducted, being anterior and the thumbs posterior. The wrists are extended, forearms pronated, elbows flexed and shoulders abducted. The elbows point straight sideways.

Muscle Work. The Adductors of the Shoulder Joint and Extensors of the Elbows work slightly to press the hands to the trunk.

Effects and Uses. As the arms are held away from the trunk from the axilla to the iliac crests, the position allows the physiotherapist to grasp the patient round the shoulders during some trunk exercises. The fixed position of the arms prevents their swinging during trunk exercises. As this swing usually amplifies the movement and leaves the thorax free, the position should be avoided unless it serves some definite and useful purpose. It was at one time used extensively just to make the exercise appear tidy!

LOW WING STANDING (low wg. st.)

This is similar to the previous position, the fingers being placed across the front of the hip joints.

Effects and Uses. This is a position of control as the patient is able to feel with the hands the movement of flexion at the hip joint, tilting and lateral swing or any rotation of the pelvis, which may occur during the performance of an exercise.

BEND STANDING (bd. st.)

The shoulders are laterally rotated and adducted strongly, the elbows are flexed, the forearms are supinated with wrists and fingers flexed to rest above the lateral border of the acromion process.

Muscle Work

(*i*) The lateral Rotators and Adductors of the Shoulder work strongly.

(*ii*) The Retractors and Depressors of the Scapulae work strongly as fixators.

(*iii*) The Flexors of the Elbows and Supinators of the Forearm work to maintain the position of the forearms.

(*iv*) The Flexors of the Wrists and Fingers may work slightly.

Effects and Uses. The position is corrective for the position of the upper back, and the thorax is expanded. It may therefore be held during some trunk exercises to intensify their effect or used prior to arm stretching exercises. Full flexion of the elbow reduces the leverage for the Abductor Muscles of the Shoulder Joint, making it a suitable position from which to perform abduction movements when these muscles are weak.

REACH STANDING (rch. st,)

The shoulders are flexed and the elbows extended so that the arms are held parallel, shoulder width apart and at right angles to the body.

Muscle Work

(*i*) The Shoulder Flexors maintain the position against gravity.

(*ii*) The Transverse Back Muscles control the forward movement of the scapulae round the chest wall which is associated with shoulder flexion.

(*iii*) The Extensors of the Elbows, Radial Flexors of the Wrist and Extensors of the Fingers work slightly to keep the arms straight.

Effects and Uses. In the upright position the forward raising of the arms brings the centre of gravity of the body forwards and there is a natural tendency to over-compensate for this by extension of the lumbar spine. Control of the position of the scapulae by the Retractors and Depressors is essential to avoid restriction of inspiratory movements. The position is used prior to some arm and trunk exercises in the sagittal plane, and to assist balance during balance walking sideways. The hands may be supported on, or may grasp, some apparatus (*rch. gr. st.*) and this obviates the use of the Shoulder Flexor Muscles when the arms are used to control or steady the body for leg or head exercises.

YARD STANDING (yd. st.)

The arms are straight and elevated sideways to a horizontal position.

Muscle Work ,
(*i*) The Abductors, Extensors and Lateral Rotators of the Shoulder work Rotators of the Scapulae to stabilise the arms.

(*ii*) The Extensors of the Elbows, Wrists and Fingers work to hold the limbs in a straight line.

(*iii*) The tendency to elevate the shoulder girdle is controlled by the Scapulae Depressors.

Effects and Uses. The Abductors of the Shoulder work at a marked mechanical disadvantage as the length of the weight arm of the lever so greatly exceeds that of the power arm. The position is corrective for the posture of the upper back, facilitates body balance and is convenient for arm swinging exercises.

One arm only may be used ($\frac{1}{2}$ *yd. st.*), and when the hand grasps a support at a suitable height ($\frac{1}{2}$ *yd. gr. st.*) the body is steadied for leg and trunk exercises. Palms may be turned forwards (*yd. palms f. st.*) or upwards (*yd. palms u. st.*), the latter involving an additional lateral rotation at the shoulder joint with consequent further bracing of the upper Back Muscles.

STRETCH STANDING (str. st.)

The arms are fully elevated so that they are in line with the body, parallel to each other and with palms facing.

Muscle Work
(*i*) The Abductors, Extensors and Lateral Rotators of the Shoulder work strongly in conjunction with—

(*ii*) The Lateral Rotators of the Scapulae, to hold the arms in position.

(*iii*) The Extensors of the Elbows keep them straight.

(*iv*) The Wrists and Fingers are kept in alignment by interplay between the muscles working over the wrist and by the Extensors of the Fingers.

Effects and Uses. The muscle work is strong, often due to the tension of shortened opposing muscles, particularly Pectoralis Major and Minor and Latissimus Dorsi. Tension of the former expands the thorax and respiration (expiration) is difficult, and in the upright position the arterial circulation to the arms is impeded by gravity. The position is unsuitable for weak patients or those who suffer from respiratory conditions. It is strongly corrective for the position of the upper back and gives a feeling of stretching the spine. Elevation of the arms raises the centre of gravity of the body and affords additional leverage in many trunk exercises. Elevation to the oblique position (*obl. str. st.*) reduces the effect of the position. The hands may grasp some over-head support (*str. gr. st.*) or the fingers may be clasped (*str. clasp st.*). When one arm holds the position a lateral flexion of the thoracic spine to the opposite side maintains the equilibrium of the body ($\frac{1}{2}$ *str. st.*). This may be useful in the treatment of scoliosis.

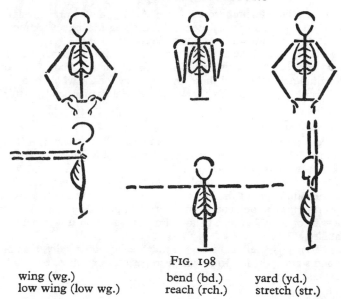

FIG. 198

wing (wg.)   bend (bd.)   yard (yd.)
low wing (low wg.)   reach (rch.)   stretch (str.)

POSITIONS USED TO FIX THE SHOULDER GIRDLE

The arms may be held to the sides while the hands grasp suitable apparatus (*low gr.*), they may be laterally rotated strongly (*A. rot. o.*) or folded across the chest (*A. folded. st.*). These positions are used during head exercises.

By Alteration of the Legs

These positions involve change in the shape or size of the base. Only the description and static muscle work which differs from, or is in addition to, that required for the fundamental position is given.

CLOSE STANDING (cl. st.)

The legs are rotated inwards at the hips so that the medial borders of the feet are adjacent.

Muscle Work. The Leg Muscles work more strongly than in the fundamental position.

Effects and Uses. The size of the base is reduced and balance is more difficult, it is therefore a progression on the *standing* position. Relaxation of the lateral rotators of the hip often results in a loss of the bracing effect on the whole leg including the longitudinal arches of the feet, which accompanies the contraction of these muscles when the foot is fixed.

TOE STANDING (Toe st.)

The heels are pressed together and raised from the floor.

Muscle Work. The Plantaflexors of the Ankle Joint work strongly against gravity to keep the heels elevated. All the Leg Muscles work more strongly than in the fundamental position to keep the balance.

Effects and Uses. The base is reduced and the centre of gravity raised, so this is used as a balance position. Strong work for the Foot Muscles braces the longitudinal arches and there is a tendency for the whole body to stretch, which is of value in the treatment of postural flat feet and posture training generally.

STRIDE STANDING (std. st.)

The legs are abducted so that the heels are two foot-lengths apart. The feet remain at the same angle as in the fundamental position and the weight is equally distributed between them.

Muscle Work. Because the width between the feet is greater than that of the pelvis the Adductors of the Hips may work to prevent the legs from sliding further apart if the position is taken on a slippery floor. On a matt surface, however, or if rubber-soled shoes are worn, friction is sufficient to maintain stability.

Effects and Uses. The effective base is much enlarged laterally, making this an easy and stable position from which to perform exercises, especially those in a frontal plane.

WALK STANDING (wlk. st.)

One leg is placed directly forwards so that the heels are two foot-lengths apart and are on the same line. The body weight is equally distributed between them.

Muscle Work. There is tension on the structures anterior to the hip and on the Calf Muscles of the posterior leg, therefore the Extensors of the Hip and Knee of this leg work strongly to maintain the position.

Effects and Uses. The base is much enlarged in the antero-posterior direction stabilising the body for exercises in a sagittal plane. Rotation of the pelvis towards the side of the forward leg is prevented by the position of the back leg, the position therefore may be used to localise rotation to the

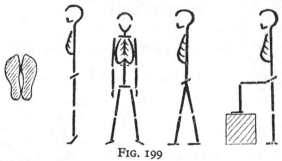

FIG. 199

Position of Feet   Toe standing   stride standing   walk standing   step standing
     in   (Toe st.)   (std. st.)   (wlk. st.)   (step st.)
close standing

spine. Tension on the Hamstrings of the forward leg likewise prevents forward tilting of the pelvis in trunk flexion exercises.

HALF STANDING ($\frac{1}{2}$ st.)

The whole weight of the body is supported on one leg, the other may be free or supported in a variety of positions.

Muscle Work

(*i*) The Abductors of the Hip of the standing leg work to maintain the centre of gravity over the base by a slight lateral tilting of the pelvis and—

(*ii*) The Lumbar Side Flexors of the opposite side work to bring the trunk into alignment.

(*iii*) All the muscles of the supporting leg work more strongly than in *standing* to support the additional weight and preserve balance.

Effects and Uses. The unsupporting leg is free for movement. Balance is more difficult as the size of the base is reduced.

The leg which is freed from body weight may rest in a variety of positions, e.g. on a stool with hip and knee bent (*step st.*); this relaxes the tension on the abdominal wall on this side and may be used after certain abdominal operations. The foot may be supported with the knee extended on apparatus of a convenient height (*F. sup. f. or o. st.*). Support of the foot in a forward direction results in tension on the Hamstrings and straightening of the lumbar spine, and support sideways increases the lateral tilt of the pelvis and the lumbar side flexion. Finally, the toes only may rest lightly on the floor (*Toe sup. st.*); this has the additional effect of bracing the arches of the foot and the leg may be supported in any direction (*f. o. b. or s.*).

By Alteration of the Trunk

LAX STOOP STANDING (lax. stp. st.)

The hips are flexed and the trunk, head and arms are relaxed so that they hang forwards and downwards. Balance is maintained by a slight planta-flexion at the ankle joints, causing a backward inclination of the leg (Fig. 178).

Muscle Work. Very little muscle work is required except in the region of the ankle joint, where the Dorsiflexors stabilise the position of the joint while the Intrinsic Foot Muscles grip the floor.

Effects and Uses. The amount of forward flexion is dictated by the tension which develops in the Hamstrings and Lumbar Muscles. The position may be used to train local relaxation of the upper body and to assist expiration. It is used prior to extension exercises of hips and spine, particularly those which occur progressively, as in uncurling to the upright position. The position is unsuitable for weak or elderly patients as the dependent position of the body causes an increased blood flow to the head which may be followed by depletion on raising to the upright position and consequent feeling of giddiness. When the knees are allowed to bend in the position (*lax stp. K. bd. st.*), tension on the Hamstrings and lumbar muscles is reduced, giving a feeling of relaxation right through the body.

STOOP STANDING (stp. st.)

The hip joints are flexed while the trunk, head and arms remain in alignment and are inclined forwards. The backward inclination of the legs is greater than in the previous position. The angle to which the trunk is inclined is usually about a right angle but depends on the tension of the Hamstrings which control the forward tilt of the pelvis when the knees are straight (Fig. 200).

Muscle Work

(*i*) The Muscles of the Feet work as in the previous position.

(*ii*) The Extensors of the Knees may work to counteract the tension of the Hamstrings.

(*iii*) The longitudinal and transverse Back Muscles and the Extensors of the Shoulders and Elbows maintain the position against the pull of gravity.

(*iv*) The posterior Neck Muscles, controlled by the Pre-vertebral Muscles, support the head.

Effects and Uses. The strong work for the Neck and Back Muscles with stretching of the spine, which occurs in the horizontal position, trains good posture of the upper back. Fixation in flexion of the lumbar spine localises movement to the joints above this level. It is a valuable but difficult position to hold correctly.

By Alteration of the Legs and Trunk

FALLOUT STANDING (fallout st.)

One leg is placed directly forwards to a distance of three foot-lengths and this knee is bent; the back leg remains straight and the body is inclined forwards in line with it.

Muscle Work

(*i*) The Extensors and the Foot Muscles of the forward leg work strongly to support most of weight, while the Extensors of the Back Leg

Fig. 200

| **lax stoop standing** **(lax stp. st.)** | **stoop standing** **(stp. st.)** | **fallout standing** **(fallout st.)** | **lunge sideways** **standing** **(lunge s. st.)** |

keep the trunk and leg straight. The Dorsiflexors of this foot work to keep the heel on the ground.

(*ii*) The Head and Trunk Muscles work as in *stoop standing*, but as there is a degree of rotation and lateral tilt of the pelvis away from the forward leg, balance is maintained by the action of the Trunk Rotators and the Lumbar Muscles on this side.

Effects and Uses. The muscle power and co-ordination required to hold the position is considerable, and it may be used in the treatment of spinal curvature.

When support is given to the arms or shoulders, it is an excellent position in which to utilise the body weight, either for giving pressure or resistance in the direction of the fallout.

The forward leg may be placed outwards (*fallout o. st.*) or sideways (*fallout s. st.*), or the toes of the straight leg may be stretched so that they only rest lightly on the floor (*toe fallout st.*).

Lunge positions are similar with regard to the placing of the legs, but the body always remains in a vertical position.

POSITIONS DERIVED FROM *KNEELING*

As in the case of the *standing* position, only the description and static muscle work to hold the position is given, that of the fundamental position is not repeated.

The positions of the arms are the same as in *standing* and may be added to the *kneeling* position as required.

HALF KNEELING ($\frac{1}{2}$ kn.)

One knee supports most of the body weight and the other leg is bent to a right angle at hip, knee and ankle so that the foot is supported on the ground in a forward direction (Fig. 201).

Muscle Work

(i) The Abductors of the Hip Joint of the supporting leg, and the Lumbar Side Flexors of the opposite side, work to balance the trunk (as in $\frac{1}{2}$ st.).

(ii) The Extensors of the Hip and Knee of the forward leg work slightly to assist balance.

Effects and Uses. This position is similar to *step standing* (see $\frac{1}{2}$ st. and may be modified by stretching the forward leg in a sideways direction (*L. str. $\frac{1}{2}$ kn.*). The pelvis is well fixed in the position for trunk side bending and rotation exercises when the trunk moves in a direction away from the supporting leg.

KNEEL SITTING (kn. sitt.)

The knees and hips are flexed so that the patient sits on his heels (Fig. 201). The position is sometimes used for small children, but most people find it very uncomfortable.

PRONE KNEELING (pr. kn.)

The trunk is horizontal, supported under the shoulders by the arms, and at the pelvis by the thighs, which must be held vertical. The head is held in line with the trunk (Fig. 201).

Muscle Work

(i) The muscles round the Shoulder and Hip Joints work to stabilise the supporting limbs at right angles to the trunk.

(*ii*) The Flexors of the Lumbar Spine prevent hollowing of the back.

(*iii*) The Extensors of the Neck and Head, controlled by the Pre-vertebral Neck Muscles, keep the head in alignment.

Effects and Uses. The position is stable and comfortable and suitable for many trunk and head exercises as the spine is relieved of the weight of the head and shoulders and therefore it tends to straighten and elongate. The pelvis is free for antero-posterior and lateral movement, but fixed for rotation. The body may be inclined forwards and downwards by abducting

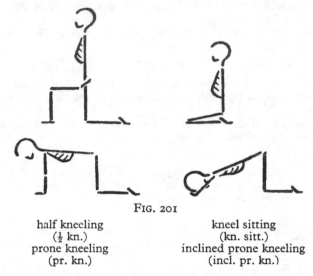

FIG. 201

half kneeling   kneel sitting
(½ kn.)   (kn. sitt.)
prone kneeling   inclined prone kneeling
(pr. kn.)   (incl. pr. kn.)

the shoulders and bending the elbows (*incl. pr. kn.*), this expands the thorax and localises lateral flexion to the thoracic region. Alternatively, the fore-arms may rest on the floor with the hands together and the head resting on them; in this way a weakened pelvic floor can be relieved of the weight of the viscera or the uterus may be assisted by gravity into the normal position.

POSITIONS DERIVED FROM *SITTING*

As in the case of the kneeling position, only the description and muscle work which differs from that of the fundamental position is given. The positions of the arms are the same as in standing.

Positions of the Legs

STRIDE SITTING (std. sitt.)

This is exactly similar to the fundamental position, except that the legs are abducted so that the feet are up to two foot-lengths apart. This increases the stability of the position, especially if the feet are pressed to the floor.

RIDE SITTING (ride sitt.)

The patient sits astride suitable apparatus, such as a gymnastic form, which may be gripped between the knees by the Adductor Muscles of the

Hips, making it a very steady position for head, arm and trunk exercises. When the position is taken on a high plinth (*high ride sitt.*), the thighs may be strapped to the plinth to afford additional fixation, in which case no muscle work is required in the legs.

CROOK SITTING (crk. sitt.)

When sitting on the floor, the knees are bent so that the feet are together and flat on the floor. The knees may be together or apart.

Muscle Work

(*i*) The Flexors of the Hip work strongly to prevent excessive flexion of the lumbar region and to support the thighs. The Flexors of the Knees

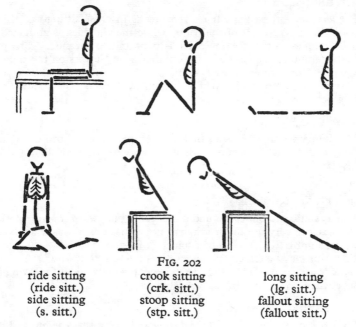

FIG. 202

ride sitting	crook sitting	long sitting
(ride sitt.)	(crk. sitt.)	(lg. sitt.)
side sitting	stoop sitting	fallout sitting
(s. sitt.)	(stp. sitt.)	(fallout sitt.)

and Plantaflexors of the Ankles may also work to afford additional fixation of the legs.

(*ii*) The longitudinal and transverse Back Muscles work strongly to maintain the upright position of the trunk.

Effects and Uses. The pelvis is fixed with a decreased tilt and the lumbar region is flexed so that movement can be localised to the upper trunk, as in the treatment of kypho-lordosis. Strong work for the Extensors of the Thoracic Spine to hold the position is of value in training their efficiency.

LONG SITTING (lg. sitt.)

This is similar to the previous position, but the knees are extended so that the whole leg is supported. The Extensors of the Knees work to counteract the increased tension of the Hamstring Muscles. When the legs are apart (*std. lg. sitt.*) this tension is somewhat reduced, but the position is difficult and unsuitable for most adults.

CROSS SITTING (X sitt.)

This is also similar to *crook sitting*, but the ankles are crossed and the hips strongly abducted and laterally rotated, so that the lateral aspect of the knees is pressed to the floor. Tension on the Hamstrings is reduced but the Adductors of the Hip are stretched. For this reason the position is uncomfortable for most adults, but suitable for children during head, arm and trunk exercises as the pelvis is fixed and stable.

SIDE SITTING (s. sitt.)

For left side sitting the left leg remains as in cross sitting and this hip supports the main weight of the trunk, while the right leg is abducted and medially rotated so that the lower leg is bent and to the side. The pelvis is tilted laterally to the left, and the Lumbar Side Flexors on the right side work to keep the trunk upright. The position is used to increase lateral mobility of the lumbar spine or for fixation in the *side bend* position when treating scoliosis (Fig. 202).

HIGH SITTING (high sitt.)

The fundamental sitting position is taken on a high plinth or table but the feet remain unsupported. This is convenient for some foot and knee exercises.

Positions of the Trunk

STOOP SITTING (stp. sitt.)

This is similar to but easier and more stable than *stoop standing* position, and is therefore very useful for arm and upper back exercises when hollowing of the lumbar region is to be avoided (Fig. 202).

The arms may be folded and supported on a table (*A. lean sitt.*) allowing the Back Muscles to relax. This arrangement is convenient for giving back massage when *prone lying* is impracticable.

FALLOUT SITTING (fallout sitt.)

The position is the same as *fallout standing* except that the hip and thigh of the forward leg are supported across a stool, balance is therefore easier and the patient is able to concentrate on movements which may be added (Fig. 201).

POSITIONS DERIVED FROM *LYING*

As in previous cases, only the description and muscle work which differs from the fundamental position is given.

Positions of the Arms

Those which are used are the same as in the standing position, the muscle work, however, is modified and usually reduced by the horizontal position of the body.

All the positions derived from *lying* (except Leg prone lying) can be used with the upper trunk supported on the forearms (Forearm support). The upper arm is vertical and pressure is taken along the whole of the forearm and the palm of the hand. Head and neck muscles are used to maintain its position, and the activity of scapular and shoulder muscles is stimulated. The elbow flexors and extensors and the wrist and finger flexors work to maintain stability.

Positions of the Legs

CROOK LYING (crk. ly.)

From *lying*, the hips and knees are bent so that the feet rest on the floor or plinth. Provided the feet are fixed by friction, very little muscle work is required apart from that of the Adductors and Medial Rotators of the Hips to prevent the knees from falling apart.

Effects and Uses. Tension is removed from the structures anterior to the hip joint so that the pelvis rolls backwards and the lumbar spine is relaxed on to the supporting surface. As the whole trunk is relaxed and

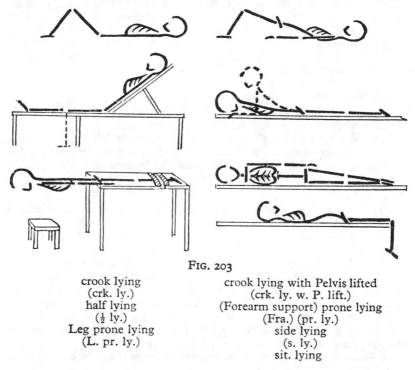

FIG. 203

crook lying	crook lying with Pelvis lifted
(crk. ly.)	(crk. ly. w. P. lift.)
half lying	(Forearm support) prone lying
(½ ly.)	(Fra.) (pr. ly.)
Leg prone lying	side lying
(L. pr. ly.)	(s. ly.)
	sit. lying

supported horizontally and fixed by its own weight it is an easy position and extensively used to train relaxation and posture.

CROOK LYING WITH PELVIS LIFTED (crk. ly. w. P. lift.)

From the previous position the pelvis is elevated so that the trunk rests on the shoulders and is brought into line with the thighs. A firm pillow may be used to support the buttocks, or the Extensors of the Hips may work to hold the position.

Effects and Uses. Pressure of the viscera on the pelvic floor is relieved by gravity as the weight of viscera is directed backwards and upwards towards the Diaphragm; because of this, breathing may be hampered slightly. The position is useful during re-education of the Muscles of the Pelvic floor, in such cases as visceroptosis or after childbirth.

HALF LYING ($\frac{1}{2}$ ly.)

The trunk is supported in the oblique position by inclination of the long end of the plinth, or by the arrangement of pillows, while the legs are supported horizontally. It is important to see that the trunk is in an alignment to avoid slumping and so impeding respiration (Fig. 203).

Effects and Uses. The body is relaxed and comfortable in this position and it is suitable for weak and elderly people because breathing is easier than in *lying*, the thorax being less fixed by the weight of the trunk. Movement of all parts of the body can be performed from *half lying*, and it is much used for ward exercises and in the treatment of many chest conditions.

The knees may be bent to increase relaxation of the abdominal wall (*crk.* $\frac{1}{2}$ *ly.*), or the lower leg may hang over the end of the plinth with the feet resting on the floor.

PRONE LYING (pr. ly.)

Lying face downwards, the body is fully supported anteriorly on the plinth or floor. The position may be active or relaxed.

The Active Position. When this is used as a static holding for posture training or prior to exercise, the head is slightly raised from the supporting surface and the shoulders are drawn down and backwards, the heels being held together and the toes stretched (Fig. 203).

Muscle Work

(*i*) The Pre- and Post-vertebral Neck Muscles work to maintain the position of the head.

(*ii*) The Retractors and Depressors of the Scapulae work to brace the upper back.

(*iii*) The Lateral Rotators of the Hips keep the heels together.

The Relaxed Position. No muscle work is required for the relaxed position (*lax pr. ly.*). In this case the head is usually turned to one side and rested on the hands for comfort and ease in breathing, while the heels roll apart. Tension may be still further reduced by placing a pillow under the abdomen and another under the lower leg, so that the hip and knee joints are slightly flexed and the feet rest free from pressure.

Effects and Uses. Breathing is somewhat restricted by the pressure of the weight of the body on the chest and abdomen, making the position unsuitable for those with heart or respiratory disease.

The active position gives a feeling of the correct alignment of the body which is required in upright positions and as the spine is relieved of weight it tends to elongate and straighten.

The relaxed version of the position is only comfortable for some people, usually the young and the slim.

LEG PRONE LYING (L. pr. ly.)

This is taken on a high plinth, the legs being supported from the anterior superior spines to the feet and stabilised by a strap. The body is held in line with the legs and is unsupported over the end of the plinth. A stool is in position under the trunk to afford support by the arms in the resting position (Fig. 202).

Muscle Work

(*i*) The Pre-vertebral and posterior Neck Muscles, the Extensors of the Hips, and the longitudinal and transverse Back Muscles work strongly to maintain the position of the trunk against gravity.

(*ii*) The Extensors of the Shoulders and Elbows hold the arms to the sides.

(*iii*) The Flexors of the Lumbar Spine control the lumbar region which tends to become hollowed.

Effects and Uses. The muscle work is strong and corrective for the position of the trunk, and strong arm, head and back exercises can be added to increase this effect.

For group exercises, the thighs only may be supported across a form, the feet being fixed between wall-bars or by living support. Care must be taken in this case to see that the fixation of the feet is firm and that it is maintained until the body is supported on the arms for the resting position.

SIDE LYING (s. ly.)

Details of this position vary considerably according to the purpose for which it is to be used.

(*i*) The patient rolls on to the side from *lying* or *prone lying*, using the under arm to support the head. It is an unsteady position used sometimes for strong trunk side bending exercises (Fig. 203).

(*ii*) Alternatively the shoulders may be stabilised by support from the upper arm resting on the ground or plinth in front, the legs being free for movement. When the under hip and knee are fully flexed the pelvis is relatively well-fixed, so that movements of flexion and extension can be localised to the hip joint of the uppermost leg. This is useful especially in sling exercises. Conversely, if the pelvis is stabilised by resting the uppermost knee on the plinth, shoulder exercises for this side of the body can be performed.

(*iii*) An ideal position for relaxation for many people is provided by adapting (*ii*). Three pillows are required, one for the head, one for the uppermost arm to support it and free the chest and so assist respiration, and a third to support the uppermost leg which is bent (Fig. 48).

SIT LYING (sit ly.)

The patient lies supine with the knees bent and the lower leg hanging vertically over the end of the plinth. There is a tendency for the lumbar region to extend owing to tension of the hip flexors.

POSITIONS DERIVED FROM *HANGING*

FALL HANGING (fall hg.)

The body is supported in the oblique position by the arms which grasp a horizontal bar, and by the feet which rest on the floor. The arms are vertical so that the shoulders fall directly below the hands, while the rest of the body is inclined and straight (Fig. 204).

Muscle Work

(*i*) The Flexors of the Fingers grasp the bar and the Wrist, Elbow and Shoulder Muscles work to reduce tension on these joints.

(*ii*) The Retractors of the Scapulae work strongly to draw the trunk upwards between the arms.

(*iii*) The Flexors of the Atlanto-occipital Joint and of the Cervical Spine prevent the head from falling backwards.

(*iv*) The longitudinal and transverse Back Muscles support the trunk.

(*v*) The Extensors of the Hips keep the trunk in alignment and the Plantaflexors press the feet to the floor.

Effects and Uses. The position requires very strong muscle work for the Back Muscles, especially the Scapulae Retractors, which work against gravity and the weight of the body.

OTHER POSITIONS, IN WHICH SOME OF THE WEIGHT IS TAKEN ON THE ARMS

CROUCH SITTING (crch. sitt.)

The hips and knees are fully bent while the trunk is straight and inclined forwards to allow the hands to rest on the floor. The weight is supported mainly on the toes, the heels being together and the knees pressed apart. Balance is maintained by the arms which are shoulder width apart and vertical.

Muscle Work

(*i*) The Intrinsic Muscles of the Feet grip the floor.

(*ii*) The longitudinal and transverse Back Muscles keep the back straight.

(*iii*) The Pre-vertebral and Posterior Neck Muscles support the head.

If additional weight is taken on the hands the Serratus Anterior Muscles work strongly to keep the scapulae against the chest wall, and the muscles round the shoulder joint and the Extensors of the Elbows brace the arms.

Effects and Uses. This is a useful starting position for strong leg extension exercises, as it is steady and the muscles concerned are stretched between their points of attachment. It is much used in training correct landing from high jumping.

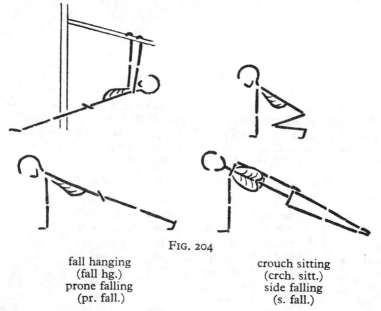

FIG. 204

fall hanging	crouch sitting
(fall hg.)	(crch. sitt.)
prone falling	side falling
(pr. fall.)	(s. fall.)

Children find it easy and comfortable and readily learn to take weight on their arms, as in the various forms of *crouch* or *'Bunny' jump.*

PRONE FALLING (pr. fall.)

The legs are extended in line with the trunk from the *crouch position* so that the body is supported on the arms, which are vertical, and on the toes.

Muscle Work

(*i*) The Extensors of the Elbows and all the muscles of the shoulder region work strongly to support the weight of the body, while Serratus Anterior holds the scapulae firmly against the chest wall.

(*ii*) The Neck Extensors, controlled by the Pre-vertebral Muscles, maintain the position of the head against the pull of gravity.

(*iii*) The Flexors of the Lumbar Spine prevent sagging of the trunk.

(*iv*) The Extensors of the Knees keep them straight.

(*v*) When the foot is fixed in dorsiflexion the long Flexors of the Toes work with excellent leverage to grip the floor.

Effects and Uses. Many muscles work strongly and the necessary co-ordination is difficult, the position is therefore only suitable for those whose arms are strong in relation to their body length and weight. The body may be taken through a quarter turn so that the weight is supported on the lateral border of one foot, and on one hand (*s. fall.*). In this case the muscles on the under side of the body work strongly and balance is difficult.

II

TERMINOLOGY

THERE are various methods of notating movement and in time another method may replace the following terminology. However, at present this is the easiest to learn and is acceptable for general use. Other methods give greater detail and can record performance of movement, but they are very time-consuming and their value needs to be proven.

ABBREVIATIONS OF TECHNICAL TERMS

1. *Parts of the Body*

These are denoted by a capital letter, indicating the plural, i.e. A = both arms. For a single or one the figure 1 is used, i.e. 1A = one arm.

Head	. .	H.	Pelvis . . .	P.	Fingers . . . Fing.
Forehead	. .	Frh.	Shoulder Blades	Sh. bl.	Legs . . . L.
Neck	. .	N.	Shoulders . .	Sh.	Knees . . . K.
Back	. .	B.	Arms . . .	A.	Heels . . . Hl.
Trunk	. .	T.	Elbows . . .	Elb.	Feet. . . . F.
Side.	. .	S.	Wrists . . .	Wr.	Ankles . . . Ank.
Abdomen	. .	Abd.	Hands . . .	Hnd.	Forearm . . Fra.

For parts not included in this list the whole word is written.

2. *Words denoting Position of Arms, Legs or Trunk*

standing	. . .	st.	kneeling	. .	kn.	sitting	. . .	sitt.
lying	. . .	ly.	hanging.	. .	hg.	position	. . .	pos.
wing	. . .	wg.	bend	. . .	bd.	reach	. . .	rch.
yard	. . .	yd.	rest	. . .	rst.	stretch	. . .	str.
grasp	. . .	gr.	close	. . .	cl.	stride	. . .	std.
walk	. . .	wlk.	relaxed	. .	lax.	stoop	. . .	stp.
prone.	. . .	pr.	crook	. .	crk.	long	. . .	lg.
cross	. . .	X.	crouch	. .	crch.			

When one limb only is involved, ½ is inserted before the name of the position, i.e. ½ yd = one arm sideways.

3. *Words denoting Movement*

For those ending in -ing, this suffix is omitted. e.g. bend = bending, and stretch = stretching. (Note that these differ from the abbreviations indicating *position*, where bend is bd. and stretch, str.)

Anatomical terms are shortened thus—

flexion	. . .	flex.	pronation	. .	pron.	rotation	. .	rot.
abduction	. .	abd.	extension	. .	ext.	eversion	. .	ev.
circumduction	.	⊙	adduction	. .	add.	supination	.	supin.
inversion.	. .	inv.						

296

4. *Words indicating Direction*

right	r.	horizontal	hor.	outwards	o.
forward	f.	inclined	incl.	towards	tow.
upward	u.	between	betw.	lateral	lat.
sideways	s.	left	l.	oblique	obl.
across	acr.	backward	b.	under	und.
medial	med.	downward	d.	behind	beh.

5. *Other Terms*

movement	movt.	jump	j.	wide	wd.
parallel	‖	spring	spr.	followed	foll.
support	sup.	assisted	ass.	reverse	rev.
together	tog.	passive	pass.	continuously	cont.
with	w.	stationary	stat.	rebound	reb.
alternate	alt.	opposite	opp.	repeat	rep.
rhythmically	rhythm.	with living		balance	bal.
pendulum	pend.	support	(.)	resisted	res.

METHOD OF DESCRIPTION

1. *The Order of Description*

a. When describing an exercise the starting position is put first and the movement follows.

 e.g. *yd. std. st.*; A. bend. and stretch.

b. When more than one part of the body participates in an exercise they are included in the following order:—Head, Arms, Trunk, Legs.

 e.g. ½ *yd. gr. st.*; 1A. swing. f. u. w. B. arch. and 1L. lift. b.

c. The part of the body to be moved precedes the description of the type of movement and the direction.

 e.g. *std. sitt.*; T. bend. s.

2. *Punctuation*

a. A semicolon concludes the description of the starting position. In addition, it is a good idea to underline the starting position to ensure that it is not omitted.

 e.g. ½ *ly.*; alt. Hip and K. flex. and ext.

b. A full stop is put after every abbreviation.

 e.g. *crk. sitt.*

c. A comma separates the parts of a series of movements.

 e.g. *st.*; 1L. swing. f. and b., K. bend. and stretch., std. j.

d. Brackets enclose figures indicating beat or count, apparatus used, or additional information.

 e.g. *ride sitt.* (form); T. rot. (1–4) (slowly), (5–8) (quickly).

BIBLIOGRAPHY

ADAMS, JOHN CRAWFORD, *Outline of Orthopaedics*, 8th edn, Churchill Livingstone, 1977

BRAIN, LORD, *Clinical Neurology*, 5th edn, ed. R. Bannister, Oxford University Press, 1978

CASH, JOAN E., *A Textbook of Medical Conditions for Physiotherapists*, 5th edn, Faber, 1977

CASH, JOAN E., *A Textbook of Chest, Heart and Vascular Disorders*, 2nd edn, ed. Downie, Faber, 1979

CASH, JOAN E., *Neurology for Physiotherapists*, 2nd edn, Faber, 1978

Clayton's Electrotherapy and Actinotherapy, 7th edn, by P. M. Scott, Baillière Tindall, 1975

CYRIAX, J., *Textbook of Orthopaedic Medicine*, Vol. II, 9th edn, Baillière Tindall, 1977

DELORME and WATKINS, *Progressive Resistance Exercises*, 1951

FRENKEL, *Treatment of Tabetic Ataxia*, Rebman, 1902

Gray's Anatomy, 35th edn, Churchill Livingstone, 1973

GRIEVE, G. P., *Mobilisation of the Spine*, 3rd edn, Churchill Livingstone, 1979

GUYTON, A. C., *Function of the Human Body*, 4th edn, W. B. Saunders, 1974

HOLLIS, M., *Practical Exercise Therapy*, Blackwell, 1976

KABAT, H., 'Studies on Neuromuscular Disfunction', in *Archives of Physical Medicine*, Sept. 1952

KALTENBORN, F., *Manual Therapy for the Extremity Joints*, Olaf Norlis Bokhandel, Oslo, 1974

KEELE, C. A. and NEIL, E., *Samson Wright's Applied Physiology*, 12th edn, Oxford University Press, 1971

KNOTT, MARGARET and VOSS, DOROTHY, E., *Proprioceptive Neuromuscular Facilitation, Patterns and Techniques*, 2nd edn, Cassell, 1968

LAWTON, E. B., *Activities of Daily Living for Physical Rehabilitation*, McGraw-Hill, 1963

LOCKHART, R. D., *et al.*, *Anatomy of the Human Body*, 2nd edn, Faber, 1965

MCKENZIE, A. E., *Physics*, 4th edn, Cambridge University Press, 1971

MAITLAND, G. D., *Vertebral Manipulation*, 4th edn, Butterworth, 1977

MENNELL, J. M., *Joint Pain*, Little Brown & Co., Boston, 1964

MERCER, WALTER, *Orthopaedic Surgery*, 8th edn, Edward Arnold, 1979

MITCHELL, LAURA, *Simple Relaxation*, 2nd edn, John Murray, 1980

MOCK, 'Principles and Practice of Physiotherapy', in *Extracts from Progressive Relaxation by Jacobson*, 1938

ROAF, R., *Posture*, Academic Press, 1977

WALSHE, F. M. R., *Diseases of the Nervous System*, 11th edn, Churchill Livingstone, 1970

WATSON JONES, R., *Fractures and Joint Injuries*, 5th edn, ed. Wilson, Churchill Livingstone, 1976

WELLS, K. F., *Kinesiology*, 6th edn, W. B. Saunders, 1976

Aids to the Investigation of Peripheral Nerve Injuries, Medical Research Council, 1943

Handling the Handicapped by the Chartered Society of Physiotherapy, 4th impression, 1978

INDEX